The Allergy Self-Help Book

Sharon Faelten

The Allergy Self-Help Book

A step-by-step guide to drug-free relief of asthma, hay fever, headaches, fatigue, digestive problems and over fifty other allergy-related health problems

Foreword by Dr Richard Mackarness
Author of *Not All In The Mind* and *Chemical Victims*

Pan Books
London and Sydney

First published in the United States of America 1983 by Rodale Press, Inc., Emmaus, Pennsylvania
First published in Great Britain 1987 by Pan Books Ltd, Cavaye Place, London SW10 9PG
9 8 7 6 5 4 3 2

ISBN 0 330 29912 3

Phototypeset by Input Typesetting Ltd, London
Printed and bound in Great Britain by
Richard Clay Ltd, Bungay, Suffolk

NOTE

While self-help is vital to effective relief of allergies, many readers will also need medical guidance. In infants and children, for instance, food allergy may be hard to distinguish from a serious infection without medical help.

The information in this book can help you to control your allergies; however, it is not meant to replace medical diagnosis or treatment. If you are under the care of a doctor for your allergies, be sure to inform him or her of any major changes you make in your diet or environment. In some cases, your medication may need to be adjusted.

To Alycia

CONTENTS

LIST OF TABLES, CHARTS AND BOXES

FOREWORD

Ten years ago, in 1977, when food allergy was not widely recognised as a common cause of symptoms, this book would have been regarded as cranky and unnecessary.

Today, with more and more people coming to appreciate the importance of food allergy as a diagnostic option, this guide to self-help enables food allergy victims to pin-point their allergies and assume more responsibility for their own treatment, saving their doctors' time.

Food allergy is not a new phenomenon, Hippocrates described it it 400 BC, and there is no doubt that it now afflicts more people in developed countries than it ever did 100 or even 50 years ago. The reason for this is the increasingly artificial nature of modern, mass-produced food and the enormous number of chemical additives – chemicals which never existed in the old days – which are required in order to prolong the shelf-life and enhance the taste and look of food processed in factories and sold in supermarkets. Since it is possible to become allergic to anything if you eat it often enough and allergy runs in your family, you need to be aware of the risk of developing food allergy so that you can guard yourself against it and help yourself recover if you succumb. This book tells you how.

When I was a medical student at the beginning of World War II, it used to be taught that the more symptoms a patient complained of, the more likely they were to be neurotic or psychosomatic. Nowadays, I suspect that multiple symtoms *and* neurosis are both in many cases caused by allergy to foods and chemicals affecting the brain.

The word 'allergy' bothers some people because over the years since 1906 when it was invented, its meaning has changed. Originally, it meant any unusual reactin on contact with a physical substance – which included inhaling, swallowing or just having the substance land on your skin.

Today, most doctors and scientists restrict the word to a special sort of reaction involving the combination of antigen with antibody. All other types of adverse reaction are called idiosyncracy or hypersensitivity and deemed 'not allergic'. This book goes back firmly to the original, wide definition of allergy as *any altered or unusual reaction to a substance* no matter what the internal mechanics of its production may be. Such a definition is simple and understandable, requiring no specialised knowledge at all.

Historically, this divergence of views on the meaning of allergy took place in the 1920s, along with the growth of the infant subject of immunology. Immunologists study what is going on inside you when you are trying to defend yourself against any harmful agent: bacteria, viruses and the things which can cause allergy, by fractionating the body into smaller and smaller parts. The food-allergic person who will benefit from reading this book, does not need to know any immunology, only how to spot the foods and chemicals which are causing symptoms and how to construct a healthy diet and environment which excludes the troublemakers. This book explains how this can be done.

The last section: Allergic Reactions from A to V, is for people who have health problems which remain unsolved. Look up your own complaint under the appropriate heading and you will find a lot of useful information which could give you a fresh point of view and guide you towards better health.

Richard Mackarness MB, BS, DPM
Consultant Psychiatrist
Alcohol, Drug and Forensic Branch
Mental Health Division
Department of Health, Victoria, Australia
Author of *Not All In The Mind* and *Chemical Victims*
(Pan Books)

ACKNOWLEDGEMENTS

I wish to thank several allergy doctors and medical professionals who took considerable time from their busy schedules to share their expertise with me as I researched this book: Iris R. Bell, M.D., Ph.D., San Francisco, California; Robert W. Boxer, M.D., Skokie, Illinois; Lyn Dart, R.D., Carrolton, Texas; Constantine J. Falliers, M.D., Denver, Colorado; the late Benjamin F. Feingold, M.D., San Francisco, California; Kendall Gerdes, M.D., Denver, Colorado; Sue Herbig, R.N., Carrolton, Texas; Joseph J. McGovern, Jr., M.D., Oakland, California; Theron Randolph, M.D., Chicago, Illinois; William J. Rea, M.D., Dallas, Texas; Phyllis Saifer, M.D., Berkeley, California; Del Stigler, M.D., Denver, Colorado; and Wellington S. Tichenor, M.D., New York, New York.

In addition, I would like to thank Doris J. Rapp, M.D., for her helpful suggestions, Meyer B. Marks, M.D., for providing the photographs in Chapter 2 and James C. Breneman, M.D., for use of dietary guidelines from his book *Basics of Food Allergy* (Charles C. Thomas, 1978).

Special thanks, too, to my editor, William Gottlieb, and to my research associate, Christy Kohler, who took great pains to doublecheck the accuracy of the text, and to her research assistants, Lee Anne Gaspari and Christine Tatarian.

Finally, I thank the countless allergic individuals who, by sharing their experiences with me, helped me to understand better what being allergic means.

PART I

Understanding Allergy

CHAPTER 1

WHAT IS AN ALLERGY?

Half the people in the world have allergies. Millions suffer the runny nose, watery eyes and sneezing fits of hay fever. Or the itchy blotches of hives. Or the rash of eczema. Or the wheezing and shortness of breath of asthma.

Life with an allergy becomes an obstacle course of triggers to avoid. Pollen counts are followed like the FT Share Index. The cat is farmed out. The house is purged of all dust, with the bedroom stripped of curtains and carpets. Favourite foods are shunned. Arms are turned into pin-cushions by dozens of skin tests. 'Injections' are wincingly endured.

And yet for many, the misery remains.

But now there's hope, thanks to the pioneering work of a small but growing number of doctors who treat allergy in a new and different way. Their approach – sometimes known as clinical ecology – is an offshoot of traditional allergy treatment, yet at the same time challenges some widely accepted concepts about allergy. They've even questioned the definition of what an allergy is.

Breaking the allergy stereotype

In plain English, an allergy is an out-of-the-ordinary sensitivity to substances that don't bother most people. Most people, for instance, can tolerate normal amounts of dust around the house. For others, however, a day's accumulation guarantees a stuffy nose and a tough time breathing. Likewise, most people can eat tomatoes with no problem. A small number, however, immediately break out in a rash. Yet the allergy stereotype of the wheezy kid who can't have a dog or the young woman whose skin breaks out whenever she goes near a tomato is only part of the story. Dust, pollen, moulds, fur and foods such as tomatoes, strawberries or seafood are only a few of the everyday items to which people can be allergic. Dyes, soaps, detergents, cleaning supplies, pesticides, cosmetics, plastics, drugs and pollutants are also potential troublemakers. (Many substances that are toxic in moderate or large doses, such as pesticides or food additives, tend to cause allergy in much smaller, so-called safe doses.) *In short, anyone can be allergic to anything under the sun.* (And sometimes even sunlight itself!) So even if fur, dust, tomatoes or some other common allergy trigger is identified as the major cause of your troubles, you and your doctor may be overlooking other, less common but important contributing causes. And unless *all* potential allergy triggers are considered, your symptoms may stubbornly persist.

Moreover, there's much more to allergic reactions than wheezing, sneezing and itching. Unsuspected allergies can masquerade as any one of dozens of problems – anxiety, headaches, fatigue, depression, backaches, arthritis, colitis, gallbladder problems, hyperactivity, ulcers, even high blood pressure and compulsive eating or drinking. (And that list is far from complete.) In other words, while the skin, nose and lungs are the most common targets for allergy, any part of the body – muscles, brain, joints and so on – can and does react.

The following problems are just a few of the ways in which allergy can disguise itself as other illness, but they give you a pretty good idea of the scope of allergy-related conditions. (A more complete inventory appears in Part IV, Building up your Defences.)

- Alcoholism may actually result from sensitivity to the grains and fruit from which spirits, beer and wine are made.
- Arthritis in some people may simply be an allergic reaction in the joints to common foods such as beef or wheat.
- Bedwetting may be caused by spasms of a bladder irritated by allergy to milk or citrus fruit.
- Criminal behaviour may result when people become depressed or hostile after eating sugary foods to which they are allergically addicted. [More about allergic 'addiction' in Chapter 3, Finding your no-allergy diet.)
- Headaches – especially migraines – in many cases seem

to be a direct result of sensitivity to certain foods or household chemicals.

• Heart problems such as chest pains or irregular heartbeats (and even some forms of heart disease) may be triggered by chemicals and air pollution.

• Hyperactivity, learning disabilities and autism in many children may be caused by a problem in the diet or environment, not a problem child.

• Menopause troubles, such as hot flushes, can be exaggerated by allergy to foods or chemicals.

• Vaginitis may actually be an allergy to such diverse items as nylon stockings, milk or pollen.

Writing as co-author of the landmark text, *Food Allergy* (Charles C. Thomas, 1972), Dr Albert Rowe summed up the situation: 'Allergy cannot be ruled out because there is no history of hay fever, asthma or eczema.'

Furthermore, age is no defence. Young and old alike can and do have allergies. The belief that an allergic child will 'grow out of it' is largely a myth. That may hold true in some cases, but in the majority, the child hasn't so much grown out of it as the allergy has instead gone underground, so to speak, only to manifest itself in less obvious ways. Allergic children tend to grow into allergic adults – unless the allergy is properly diagnosed and dealt with. And many adults are surprised to discover that they're suddenly allergic to something they've previously tolerated all through life.

Some experts estimate that 60 per cent of the people in doctors' surgeries have symptoms that are either caused or complicated by allergies. Sometimes the problems have been a part of life for so long that they're easily overlooked or ignored. Other symptoms are written off with the throwaway diagnosis of 'stress' or 'emotional tension'. Or even attributed to imagination and hypochondria. Many allergic reactions, in fact, are exactly the kinds of problems that send so many people from one doctor to another, only to hear 'There's nothing wrong with you' or 'Learn to live with it'. Unless you're wheezing to beat the band or your skin looks like it's been attacked by Brazilian fire ants, your doctor is not apt to suspect allergy.

So if you're tired of feeling miserable for no discernible reason, it might be time to consider factors in your diet, home or workplace – especially if you've been diagnosed as allergic but go through periods when nothing seems to help. (More about your doctor's role later in this chapter and in Part III, What Your Doctor Can Do for You.) Formaldehyde fumes seeping from the woodwork or carpets in your newly renovated office may be at the root of your annoying and persistent headaches and itchy eyes. Gas fumes from the pilot light on your stove or home heating system may be causing your out-of-character moodiness and irritability at home. Perfectly healthy and nutritious foods like wheat or corn. – safe, it seems, for everyone else – may be causing that sour stomach or abdominal bloating.

After you begin to look at allergies outside of the allergy stereotypes, you can learn to walk away from needless suffering. Once the culprit or culprits are properly identified – and then eliminated – you'll be well on your way to relief.

But what is allergy, anyway?

When the immune system acts on the wrong cue

Why can some people eat wheat with confidence while others suffer? Or, for that matter, why does one individual feel sick after breathing, touching or swallowing something that doesn't seem to bother the rest of us?

The explanation seems to lie in the intricate workings of the immune system, our bodies' defence against outside invaders. Although not yet fully understood, immunity is basically our cells' ability to recognize and destroy anything perceived to be foreign and harmful: bacteria, viruses, fungi and poisons (collectively called antigens). Understanding immunity helps you to understand both the causes and the treatment of allergy.

Think of immunity as a series of defensive actions by your body. 'Search and destroy' missions are controlled by two special kinds of white blood cells called B-lymphocytes (or B-cells) and T-lymphocytes (or T-cells, which hail from the thymus gland). Together, B-cells and T-cells wage war against all invading antigens.

B-cells set up camp in the lymph nodes and bone marrow, launching large numbers of special antigen-fighting proteins called antibodies into circulation at the first sign of an invasion. T-cells, meanwhile, pitch in by 'pretreating' the invading antigens, changing them into a form easily neutralized or destroyed by antibodies.

It's a remarkably sophisticated battle plan. The antibodies (called immune bodies or immunoglobulins by scientists) are of five general types: IgA (shorthand for Immunoglobulin A) and, similarly, IgD, IgE, IgG and IgM. Within each group, molecules link up in such an infinite variety of patterns that a specific antibody is produced for just about every possible antigen in the world. Luckily for us, that ability to produce an unlimited variety of customized antibodies develops *without prior exposure to the antigen*, be it a virus, bacteria or something else. In other words, antibodies are able to recognize the enemy, sight unseen.

The immune response rolls into action as soon as any substance perceived as foreign enters the body, whether it's inhaled, swallowed, touched or injected. As a system for fighting off infections and disease, the antigen-antibody reaction works quite well. And like any good military system, it has a reserve plan. Once the activated B-cells have done their initial duty, some continue to reside as 'memory' cells in the body's lymph glands. There they stand ready for future encounters should the antigens they fought once again trespass into body territory. Those very same memory cells, in fact, provide continued immunity after our first exposure to certain diseases, such as a childhood bout with the mumps or this season's strain of the flu.

However, a popular saying states that if anything can go wrong, it will – and the immune system provides no exception. In many allergic people, lymphocytes mistake a perfectly normal and harmless substance like wheat or dust or pollen for an enemy antigen. Inappropriately, the lymphocytes jump into action to initiate plasma production of antibodies – usually the IgE type – against what they seem to regard as the enemy. Antibodies, in turn, latch on to either of two types of cells within the body; basophils, a type of white blood cell; or mast cells, found in the respiratory tract (nose, throat and lungs), gastrointestinal tract (stomach and intestines) and skin. The IgE-loaded cells grow sensitive to that allergen, as the mistaken antigen (be it wheat, dust or whatever) is known.

Figure 1: Some allergic reactions and their triggers

IgE-Mediated Allergy **Non-IgE-Mediated Allergy**

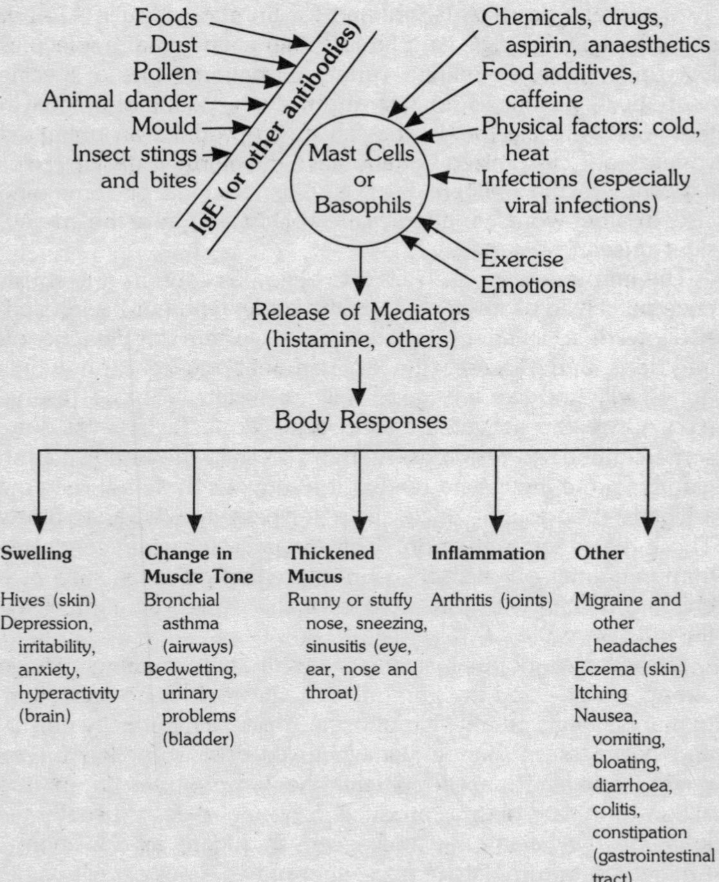

This diagram demonstrates how a variety of factors in the diet or environment can trigger allergy and produce discomfort in many parts of the body.

SOURCE: *Adapted from 'Diagnostic Methods to Demonstrate IgE Antibodies: Skin Testing Techniques' by W. T. Kniker, et al.,* Bulletin of the New York Academy of Medicine, *September 1981.*

Whenever the allergen is encountered, sensitized cells release a flood of natural body substances – mainly histamine, plus other histaminelike substances called allergy-mediators. Normal amounts of those substances do us no harm, but too much tends to expand blood vessels, causing inflammation and discomfort. If the cells in the nose, eyes and sinuses are affected by histamine or other allergy-mediators, the allergic person sneezes, has a runny nose and itchy eyes – the symptoms known as hay fever to you and allergic rhinitis to your doctor. If the skin is affected, hives (or urticaria) appear. If the digestive tract is affected, you suffer with nausea, vomiting or diarrhoea. In the lungs, an allergic response can lead to tightened and clogged airways – the hallmarks of asthma.

An allergic reaction can begin immediately – within seconds or minutes – or be delayed for a day or two. If severe enough, any allergic reaction can land you in hospital for medical help. The worst reaction by far is what's called anaphylactic shock: the throat swells shut and the lungs fill with fluid. It's like trying to breathe with a plastic bag pulled over your head. Fortunately, anaphylactic shock is relatively rare, especially with good allergy management.

In some people, an allergy may not become obvious until late in life when, after repeated contact with the allergen, a person suddenly develops a sensitivity. What happens is that after the first few uneventful encounters, a certain threshold of resistance is surpassed. You might unexpectedly break out one day after eating tomatoes – having eaten them freely all your life. (For more about why some people become allergic and others don't, see Chapter 2, Are you allergic?)

How one allergy can lead to another

You can start out with an allergy to, say, wheat and eventually develop allergies to other, related foods like barley, rye or rice, all members of the cereal family. Apparently, antibodies become less choosy and may begin to react with related allergens once the allergic response is established. Some immunologists believe that cross-reactions that were too weak to be noticed at first later surface as antibodies develop greater and greater affinity for that particular kind of antigen.

Furthermore, one allergy may exacerbate another, even if they're not necessarily related. A person with both milk and pollen allergies, for example, may react to milk only during the pollen season, when his or her system is overloaded. Interrelated allergies (co-allergies) underlie the importance of considering all possible allergens.

Controversy in allergy

Not all unpleasant reactions to everyday substances are accompanied by a jump in IgE or other antibodies in the blood. You can develop a stomach upset, a headache, heart palpitations or anxiety from drinking coffee, yet your antibodies don't budge an inch. Tartrazine (E102), a widely used food colouring, produces hives or asthmatic attacks in sensitive people – with no apparent rise in antibodies.

The fact that some reactions are not accompanied by measurable levels of antibodies doesn't prevent them from being called allergies by some doctors. There are, after all, other mechanisms in the immune response besides the antigen-antibody reaction – some only recently discovered, some no doubt awaiting discovery. Some doctors believe, for instance, that chemicals and drugs that cause allergic-like reactions work directly on the basophils and mast cells with no antibody intervention whatsoever.

Out of that school of thought has evolved the concept that anything in our environment – including the food we eat, the air we breathe, the water we drink and the places where we work and play – can trigger unpleasant reactions in certain people. That concept harks back to the original definition of allergy; *any* unusual adverse reaction. So this view, while revolutionary when compared to the modern understanding of allergy, at the same time makes simple, old-fashioned common sense.

Many doctors who espouse the new approach call themselves clinical ecologists. Some are allergists; others are ear, nose and throat specialists, doctors of internal medicine, psychiatrists or primary care physicians. These doctors take up where traditional allergists leave off. Environmental factors have more of an impact on health and well-being than has been previously acknowledged, they say. So in addition to considering well-known allergies to dust, mould, pollens, fur and a handful of foods, doctors taking this tack give special attention to individual susceptibility to factors usually overlooked by traditional allergists – pesticides, herbicides, food additives and other chemicals infused into the food, water, air and homes of the twentieth century.

That in itself is the subject of considerable debate. Because reactions to environmental additives don't always trigger a rise in immune complexes like IgE, they are not always regarded as a bona fide allergy by doctors in the mainstream of medical practice. Sensitivity, yes, agree traditional allergists. But allergy? No. And that difference of opinion as to what is and isn't allergy has also led to differences in the methods of treatment.

Why injections don't always work

A thorough examination of your medical history is the first step in any approach to allergy. Sooner or later, though, the subject comes around to tests and treatment.

There's scarcely an asthma or hay fever sufferer alive who hasn't been pinched, punctured and impaled by skin tests or allergy injections – or both. Most traditional allergists use skin tests to identify the responsible allergens. (More about other, less widely used tests in Chapter 9, Allergy tests: what they can and cannot tell.) Minute quantities of purified extracts of suspected allergens – dust, pollens, moulds and so on – are applied to or injected into the skin on the lower arm (or, less frequently, the back). If a red welt or bump (what doctors call a 'weal') flares up at the site of the test, it's assumed that the person is allergic to the extract. No welt, no allergy.

And so it goes for twenty or thirty items. Traditional allergists usually concentrate on inhalants – particles of dust, pollen, mould and animal dander (fur or feather residue) – all items that provoke an IgE response. Many allergists say they cannot use conventional skin tests alone for food allergies; they just aren't reliable enough. Instead, many prefer to use skin tests along with elimination diets. Foods are avoided and then reintroduced one by one to determine which ones can be tolerated and which cannot. Or elimination diets alone may be used. Either way, the most common food allergens – milk, wheat, corn, eggs and a few others – are the key suspects.

Avoiding what bothers you has always been the stock advice for people with allergies. That makes sense. If you start to sneeze and itch when a dog or cat enters the room, you don't take in stray animals. If you go through truckloads of tissues when the pollen season gets underway, you don't take long drives in the country. If strawberries make you break out in hives, you eat raspberries instead.

Many times, though, people become so sensitive that the smallest amounts of pollen, dust or whatever make them ill. Or they're allergic to things that are impossible to avoid. Traditionally, allergists have attempted to build up an allergic person's tolerance of such items with standard doses of the allergen. The idea is to stimulate immunity without causing an out-and-out reaction. Basically, immunotherapy (sometimes called hyposensitization or desensitization) seems to work on the same principle as vaccination against smallpox, cholera, diphtheria, tetanus and so on.

Standard immunotherapy against allergy takes about six months to build up to a protective dose, beginning with a very weak, standard dose that is gradually increased every week until protection is achieved. Injections are then given either on a regular basis or whenever a reaction is anticipated, such as at the start of the pollen season.

Yet many people go through standard allergy diagnosis and immunotherapy and still suffer. Why?

Traditional allergists are often the first to admit that skin tests aren't always what they're cracked up to be.

'Some authorities claim that a good history and careful skin testing are reliable 95 per cent of the time in allergy diagnosis,' write Dr William T. Kniker and colleagues from the Division of Immunology-Allergy, Department of Pediatrics, University of Texas Health Science Center in San Antonio. 'In many instances it is clear that results are not that good because *too many patients are incorrectly diagnosed* as sensitized to various allergens and inappropriately given immunotherapy. . . . Because skin testing . . . uses unstandardized antigens, testing techniques and scoring systems, it is to be expected that *misinformation commonly is obtained.*' (Italics ours.) The doctors add, 'Skin testing in the diagnosis of allergic disease is, in reality, not a uniform technique comparably practised by all.' (*Bulletin of the New York Academy of Medicine*, September 1981.)

Obviously, any treatment based on a shaky diagnosis will be doomed from the start.

'Undoubtedly, thousands of persons are receiving "allergy shots" on the basis of skin tests that were incorrectly performed or erroneously interpreted, or both,' stated *Postgraduate Medicine* (March 1980).

Incidentally, immunotherapy is only available for a few select allergies and doesn't always bestow complete protection. So, many allergy patients are routinely prescribed drugs like antihistamines and steroids to relieve their symptoms. However, drugs do not cure allergy either and they all have unpleasant side effects. Chapter 10 discusses the drawbacks of allergy medication and offers some drug-free alternatives.

A better approach to allergy

Doctors employing the new approach to allergy take a complete medical history before they do anything else. In fact, they'll probably ask more questions about your diet and environment than anyone else ever has. If necessary, they'll also take tests and use immunotherapy. But most use different methods of diagnosis and treatment from those of traditional allergists. (These are detailed in Chapter 9, Allergy tests: what they can and cannot tell, and Chapter 11, Immunotherapy – a matter of choice.) Above all, though, doctors taking the more comprehensive approach emphasize that you – the allergic person – must help to identify your allergens and then avoid them whenever you can. In this way, your sensitivities will tend to get better instead of worse.

Part of the success of this person-centred approach to allergy lies in the fact that it can help to uncover allergies that other doctors may not consider. After all, if you have five stones in your shoe and you remove only one, walking will still be painful.

But don't rush to your regular allergy doctor with the good news that factors he or she hasn't considered may be your problem. As we've already mentioned, these new developments in allergy constitute one of the most controversial areas in medicine today. (See Chapters 9 and 11 for more details on just how these two approaches differ.) Doctors advocating the broad approach, however, feel that it's just a matter of time before the newer view is incorporated into conventional allergy practice.

As it stands now, many people who finally seek out a clinical ecologist have been to as many as twenty or thirty traditional doctors without finding satisfactory relief. The extended approach to allergy has come to the rescue of thousands of allergy sufferers who've tearfully parted ways with the family pet, cleaned the house from attic to basement and sworn off their favourite foods, only to feel miserable because non-traditional triggers were not considered. The approach has also helped – and proved right – many people whose complaints were previously written off as 'nerves' or hypochondria.

This new approach has also helped many clinical ecologists and other doctors who often have allergy problems themselves or have a family member with chemical sensitivities. In many cases, that's what hooked them into the approach in the first place, explained Dr Wellington S. Tichenor, a doctor of internal medicine in New York City, who incorporates the broader approach to allergy in his practice. Dr Tichenor described clinical ecologists as 'people who are observant enough to realize that when they eat beef, they become bloated . . . or when they eat chicken, they get diarrhoea . . . or when they eat honeydew melon, they get a sore throat. And their own experience may make them more sympathetic and supportive than other doctors.

'If what the clinical ecologists are saying is true, it's going to have a very significant impact on medicine in general and allergy in particular,' Dr Tichenor continued. Scientific documentation, he told us, has only recently started to accumulate. But it's going to have a significant impact on society, since the potential benefits in terms of health expenditures and economic costs are immense. Society and businesses will save money because allergic people will be on the job and functioning at their best. Tracking the cause of your fatigue or chronic discomfort to the office copy machine or commuter bus exhaust means fewer days missed from work due to illness – and doing a better job overall. In very sensitive people, it can mean the difference between earning a living or going on disability benefit.

Where to begin

By now you may suspect that you have allergies you never considered. What's your next move?

'The first thing that a person can do,' Dr Tichenor told us, 'is pay very close attention to his or her body for a period of time – a week or a month or whatever. Try to see if there's any health problem that can be related to certain foods or anything else in [his or her] daily life.'

'Start by learning to be your own detective,' says Doris J. Rapp, a pediatrician and allergist in Buffalo, New York. 'If you feel fine only when you're away from home, and worse within several hours after you return, chances are that something in your house is causing the problem. On the other hand, if you feel fine at home but ill at work, at school or when travelling, that's a sign that you're sensitive to something outside the home. If allergic symptoms are unrelated to where you are and never disappear with change of location, you may have a food allergy. That is particularly true if you've had the allergy since infancy.'

Food allergy, in fact, is a number one suspect for most people with allergy problems, according to Albert Rowe, Jr, a California doctor who practised with his late father and has treated allergy patients for over thirty years. Dr Rowe feels strongly that food allergy is far more prevalent than allergies to chemicals and inhalants.

'One way to approach an unknown food allergy is to eliminate a suspected food for a period of several days and then reintroduce it in large amounts for a day and see what happens,' Dr Tichenor told us. Chances are if you have a severe, immediate reaction to eggs or seafood, you don't need to test your sensitivity. (See Chapter 3, Finding your no-allergy diet, for details on elimination diets.) 'Those with allergies outside the home usually experience a worsening of symptoms during the warm months of the year, indicating a sensitivity to pollen or mould,' says Dr Rapp. 'Also, if you smell chemicals before others and either detest or crave the odour, it may indicate a chemical sensitivity.'

That kind of detective work – an investigation of your water, your home, your workplace, your prescription drugs, your clothing – is what this book is all about.

'Allergies sometimes can be relieved entirely or in part within one to two weeks by making changes in a person's home or by altering what's eaten,' wrote Dr Rapp in her book, *Allergies and Your Family* (Sterling Publishing, 1980).

Highly sensitive people or those who are allergic to many, many things will probably have to make more and larger adjustments than less sensitive people. No doubt some people will realize that their allergies are complex enough that they need to see a doctor to help them with their avoidance programme. If you want to make an appointment with a clinical ecologist, write to the Society for Clinical Ecology for the addresses of doctors in your area who can try to help you. The address for the Society appears in the Appendix at the end of this book.

A couple of final points. If you are currently being treated for asthma or other allergic problems, it's important that you continue taking your present medication or injections unless otherwise advised by your doctor. And if you have medical problems unrelated to allergy, they should be treated. In the event that you go to an eye doctor, a gynaecologist, a primary care doctor or any medical professional for other matters, he or she will have to know about your allergies and how they're being handled. It's a good idea to take along a list of what you're allergic to. If your second doctor doesn't believe in your sensitivities, or dismisses them as unimportant, don't hesitate to ask your allergy doctor to refer you to someone who is more receptive. There's no sense in going to a doctor who's going to disregard factors that you know are harmful to you.

One last word of encouragement. Allergies are a special challenge. But as you'll discover as we go along, they *can* be licked. No one promises that it will be easy. But chances are it will be worth it.

CHAPTER 2

ARE YOU ALLERGIC?

Plenty of people are sneezing, wheezing and itching without the foggiest notion why. Others endure nameless aches and pains without so much as an inkling that their problems may be allergy based. Yet it's often easy to recognize the characteristic habits, complaints or physical signs of an allergy – *if you know what to look for.*

This chapter will tell you *exactly* what to look for. It will help you figure out whether or not you (or any of your family) are allergic. And if you are, it will also help you focus on whether the cause is your diet, your environment – or both. As a first step, take the following quiz.

Allergy self-quiz

Do you have watery, itchy red eyes?
Do you habitually rub your eyes, nose or ears?
Do you have a stuffy, runny nose?
Do you get coughing spells followed by wheezing?
Do you breathe through your mouth?
Do you speak in a nasal tone?
Do you have a high-pitched, squeaky voice?
Do you constantly clear your throat?

At this point, you may be saying to yourself, 'This sounds more like a cold than an allergy'. Well, some eye, ear, nose and throat allergies – like hay fever – *can* easily be taken for a hard-to-shake cold, especially in children and adults who frequently get colds. The difference? Colds usually last only a few days, then disappear. If the sniffing and stuffiness linger, or if the 'colds' occur more than six times a year, you're probably dealing with an allergy.

Here are some other telltale signs that could mean you have an allergy:

Allergic shiners are dark circles or bags under the eyes – a discoloration caused by swelling of tissues around the nose (see Photo 1). Occasionally, shiners will be accompanied by an annoying spasm of the eyelid.

Long, silky eyelashes – inexplicably – often coincide with allergy.

Gelatinelike discharge from the corner of the eye is often part of hay fever.

Frequent sties, cysts (chalazia) or tiny white scales along the lower edge of the upper eyelids can be marks of allergy.

Facial grimaces – like nose twitching and mouth wrinkling – are common to people with nasal allergy. 'Rabbit' or 'bunny nose' contortions momentarily relieve itching (see Photo 2).

A nose crease is a horizontal line across the lower third of the nose, where the soft, bulblike portion meets the more rigid bridge (see Photo 3). Either an allergic salute or habitual rubbing produces this wrinkle.

The allergic salute – in which a person pushes the nose upward with the palm or heel of the hand (see Photo 4) – is almost a dead giveaway of a nasal allergy. The 'salute' is basically a reflex attempt to relieve an itchy nose or to free sticky nasal accumulations and let more air into the nostrils.

Although many of those signs are accepted hallmarks of an inhalant allergy (such as that to pollen, moulds or pets), people who suffer from other types of allergies can have them, too. And there are also a number of other symptoms that can bother allergy sufferers of all kinds. For instance:

Are you bothered by itching of the roof of your mouth or throat?

Do you have ringing in your ears, perhaps accompanied by dizziness?

Is your hearing good at times, but poor at others?

Do you ears frequently 'pop'?

Do you often experience a feeling of fullness in your head?

Do you get headaches?

Is your face very pale?

Do your cheeks bloom in round, red patches, like blotches of rouge?
Do you have pimples around your mouth and chin?
Do you get rashes on your face, neck, inner elbows, inner wrists, hands or knees?
Do you get hives?
Do you have any other skin problems?
Are your lips swollen and puffy?
Do you have exquisitely tender spots, which tend to bother you off and on?
Are your hands and feet cold?
Are your fingers stiff and swollen, especially in the morning?
Do you have unusual body, hair or foot odour that persists no matter how often you wash?

If you answered yes to any of the above, it's quite possible you suffer a hard-to-pin-down allergy. Until now, you may not have even associated your difficulties with allergy.

'People have symptoms of allergy that they don't think of as symptoms at all,' said Phyllis Saifer, a pediatrician and allergist in Berkeley, California. 'For instance, I hear patients say, "I thought everybody got diarrhoea after they drank milk." Or they say, "I always loosen my belt after I eat. Doesn't everybody?" '

Is it something in your diet . . .

The two symptoms Dr Saifer was talking about are found mainly in people who have a food allergy. But they aren't the only two signs of food allergy. If you answer yes to any of the following questions, your problems may be food related:

Did you have colic as an infant?
Do you have frequent attacks of indigestion, nausea, vomiting, diarrhoea or gas?
Are there foods that you can eat freely in one season (winter, for example), yet they bother you during other times of the year?
Do you feel tired after you eat?
Do you feel better if you skip a meal?
Do you have to loosen your belt after meals?
Are there any specific foods that you particularly dislike?
Are there any foods that you crave or eat frequently?

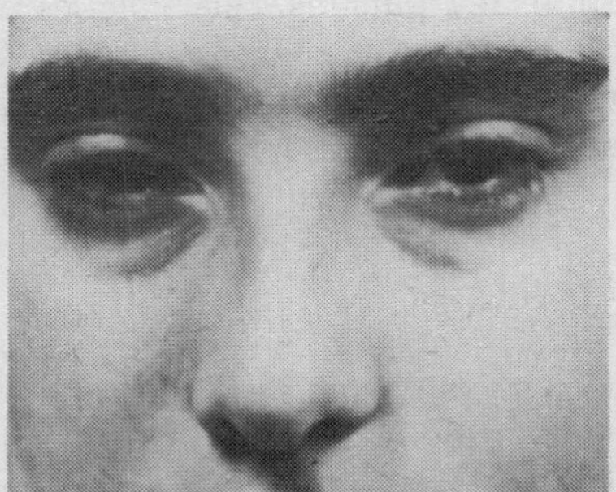

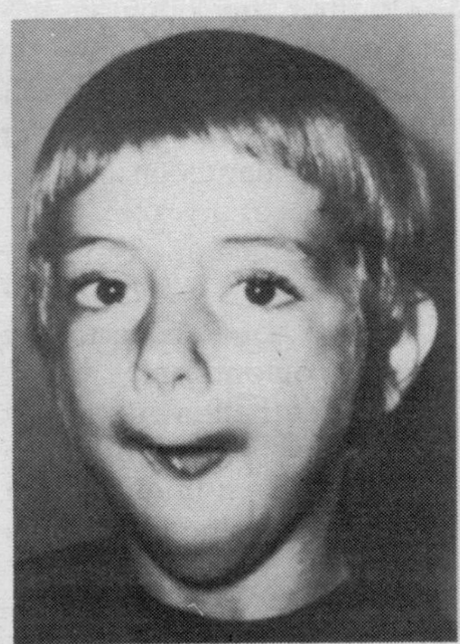

Photo 1: Allergic shiners (*above*) are caused by swelling of tissues around the nose, due to longstanding allergic reactions.
Photo 2: Facial grimaces like nose wrinkling (*shown here on right*) momentarily relieve itching for those with nasal allergies.

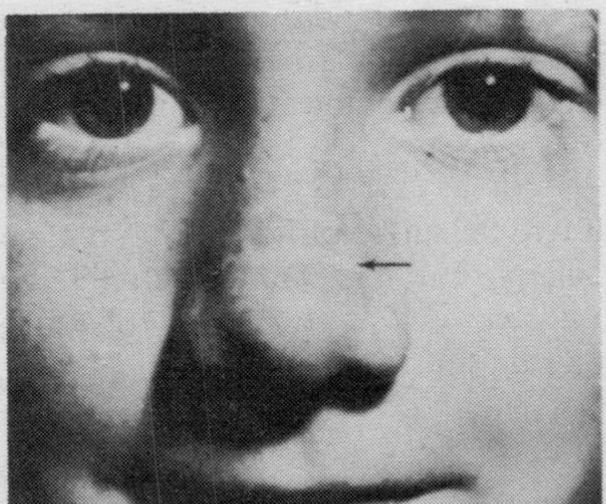

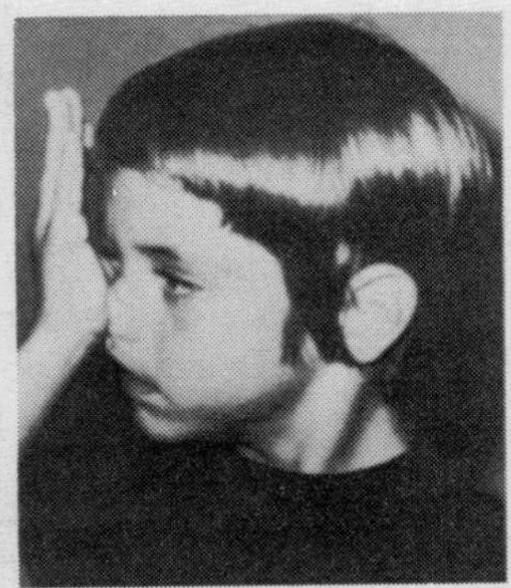

Photos courtesy of Meyer B. Marks, M.D.

Photos 3 and 4: A nasal crease (*left*) forms after two years or more of pushing the nose upward and backward to relieve itching and free a clogged nose. This gesture is known as the allergic salute (*right*).

Another sign often associated with (but not limited to) food allergy is a patchy tongue. Little round or oval smooth patches appear on the back, edges and tips of the tongue. They tend to come and go. (We'll be telling you in Chapter 3, Finding your no-allergy diet, how to figure out exactly *which* foods you're allergic to.)

. . . Or is it something in the air?

Chemical allergy is another problem that can sneak up on you. Billions of pounds of chemicals are produced each year, to say nothing of the fumes given off by cars, industry and even home appliances. Ultimately, chemicals and fumes end up in our bodies. And invariably, some people can't tolerate them. Maybe you, too, are chemically sensitive – but don't know it.

'You may have a gas stove, yet never suspect you're allergic to gas when you're home every day,' says Dr Theron Randolph, a well-known allergist in Chicago, Illinois. 'Yet when you take a vacation – say, up to the mountains where the air is good – you may come home only to become sick within minutes after walking through the door. But when you were living with the same stove every day, you never suspected it.'

Petroleum-derived chemicals, by virtue of their infinitesimal size, find their way into the most sensitive parts of the body – like the brain. In fact, since petrochemicals are fat-soluble and have a special affinity for the nervous system, they tend to affect sight, hearing, personality, memory and reasoning.

The following questions will help you evaluate whether or not you're sensitive to chemicals.

Are you more aware of smells and odours than other people seem to be?

Do the odours of perfumes, marking pens, correction fluid, freshly printed newspaper, car exhaust, fresh paint or new car interiors make you ill?

Do you (or your child) do well in school one day and poorly the next?

Is your behaviour unpredictable, turning from Dr Jekyll to Mr Hyde (and back again) at the drop of a hat?

Are you cranky, listless, impatient and ill-tempered more often than not?

Did any health problems begin shortly after exposure to a

chemical – after refinishing furniture, cleaning a carpet, mopping up spilled petrol or doing pool maintenance?

'There are an awful lot of folks who could be helped if it occurred to them that they may have an allergy,' said Dr Saifer. She added that once they realize they have an allergy, their aim should be to reduce their overall exposure to allergens by using 'avoidance tactics' – specific methods to keep the allergens with which they come in contact to a minimum.

Reducing exposure not only eases existing allergies, but may also prevent allergy from surfacing in the first place.

Who gets allergies – and why

If neither of your parents have allergies, you have only one chance in ten of being allergic yourself. If one of your parents is allergic, your chances are fifty-fifty. If both your parents are allergic, your chances of being allergic rise to 75 per cent.

That's not because we inherit allergies. We do, however, inherit genes that make us more likely to be allergic. Scientists call this 'genetic predisposition', and what it means is that heredity sets the stage, but nothing happens unless you encounter an allergen (or several). Then – bingo! – you've got a reaction.

Beyond that, doctors and medical researchers know little about why some people and their families develop allergies and others get off scot-free. What they do know is that delaying our initial encounters with common food allergens such as milk, wheat, eggs, corn and food additives in infancy seems to go a long way towards preventing food allergies from taking hold. Chalk up another one for breastfeeding. And when foods are eventually introduced, doctors say the best game plan is to introduce them singly, and even then for only a few days at a time. That enables parents to recognize a food allergy right from the start, before the connection between allergen and allergy is muddled by exposure to a whole gamut of foods. Food additives, of course, can be withheld indefinitely with no nutritional loss. (We'll be talking more about preventing food allergies in the next chapter, Finding your no-allergy diet.)

Children are also far less likely to develop allergies *of any kind* if the people around them – especially parents – don't smoke. Following this principle of 'early avoidance' with *all* highly allergenic materials – such as dust, pollen, pets, moulds and toxic chemicals – may prevent allergies even in highly allergy-prone families.

Scientific research bears that statement out. In one experiment, for instance, doctors focused on the health of fifty newborns who, based on family history and blood levels of IgE, were bound to become allergic. A few simple preventive steps were taken with twenty-five of these children: they were breastfed for at least six months and ate no other food except hypoallergenic milk substitutes; their bedrooms were kept as free as possible of dust and moulds; and no pets were allowed in their homes. By the time the toddlers were two years old, only six had any sign of allergy, even though all twenty-five were allergy prone. In contrast, no preventive steps were taken to safeguard the other twenty-five infants. Consequently, sixteen of the unprotected children – *nearly three times as many* as the protected group – developed allergy within the first two years (*Journal of Allergy and Clinical Immunology*, October 1975).

That doesn't, however, imply that opportunities for allergy control cease at age two. Many allergies don't show up until early school age – or even adulthood. If anything, the need for avoidance tactics increases throughout life. Infections, exposure to industrial pollution, degenerative diseases (such as diabetes and atherosclerosis) and the ageing process all play a role in heightening an inherited tendency towards allergy.

Above all, though, exposure stokes the fires. Fortunately, there are hundreds of avoidance tactics, major and minor, at your disposal. You may need to make just a few simple changes in your routine to get your allergies under control. Highly sensitive people may need to make more or bigger adjustments. Regardless of your degree of sensitivity, though, the sooner you begin your natural allergy relief programme, the better. Chapters 3 to 8 will show you how.

PART II

Discovering Unsuspected Causes of Allergy

CHAPTER 3

FINDING YOUR NO-ALLERGY DIET

Eating is one of life's greatest pleasures, no doubt about it. Yet 60 per cent of the population may be allergic to one or more foods. That wouldn't be a problem if those allergies were limited to foods such as prawns, chocolate or peanuts – foods we could probably give up without cramping our lifestyles too much. But reactions to such seldom eaten, easily incriminated foods as prawns account for only 5 to 10 per cent of all food allergies. Rarer still is a dramatic, life-threatening reaction to these once-in-a-while foods. The vast majority of food allergies are nagging symptoms produced by foods (and food ingredients) that most people eat *every day* – milk, wheat, eggs, corn, citrus fruits and yeast. (See Table 1.)

Think about it. It's not just corn on the cob that you may be allergic to – it's corn syrup, corn starch, corn oil. It's not just those poached eggs – it's the eggs that are used in almost every baked good on the market. We don't want to kid you: pinpointing a food allergy and keeping the offender out of your diet can be tough. But it can be done – thousands of *formerly* ill people attest to that. Yes, it will take some patience. And some Dick Tracy-type detective work. And a bit of re-education about how food works in your system. But it's worth it in the long run – and there's an added bonus.

If you have a food allergy, it's likely you also have a problem with at least one type of airborne substance – be it dust, mould, animal dander or chemicals. Well, managing food allergy goes a long way towards increasing your tolerance of airborne allergens. So overcoming food allergy can make a *big* difference in

TABLE 1

Common and Uncommon Causes of Food Allergy

While anyone can become allergic to any food, some foods are more apt to cause allergies than others.

Most Commonly Cause Allergies	Often Cause Allergies	Sometimes Cause Allergies	Seldom Cause Allergies
Corn	Alcohol (in adults)	Bananas	Apples
Eggs*	Berries	Beef	Apricots and their juice
Fish*	Buckwheat	Celery	Barley
Milk	Cane sugar	Cheese	Beets
Nuts*	Chocolate	Cherries	Carrots
Wheat*	Coconut	Chicken (in females)	Chicken (in males)
	Coffee (in adults)	Colouring agents	Cranberries and their juice
	Mustard	Cottonseed	Grapes and their juice
	Oranges or other citrus	Flavouring agents	Honey
	Peanut butter	Garlic	Kiwi Fruit
	Peas	Green beans	Lamb
	Pork	Melons	Lettuce
	Potatoes*	Mushrooms	Lobster
	Soya (in adults)	Onions	Marrow
	Tomatoes*	Plums	Oats
	Yeast	Prunes	Peaches and their juice
		Spices	Pineapples and their juice
		Spinach	Raisins
		Vitamins	Rice
		Water: tap, chlorinated and softened	Rye
			Salmon
			Salt
			Soya (in children)
			Sweet potatoes
			Tapioca
			Vanilla extract
			Vinegar (apple cider)

SOURCE: *Adapted from* Basics of Food Allergy, *by James C. Breneman (Springfield, Ill.: Charles C. Thomas, 1978).*

**Odours of these foods can cause symptoms.*

how well you feel and how much you enjoy life. Ready to get well? Then read on, and remember we're right there with you.

Anatomy of a food allergy

Food allergies are a lot harder to pin down than allergies to airborne substances, cosmetics or drugs. Skin tests are little help – doctors say they're far less reliable for food than for inhalants such as dust or pollen. And symptoms don't usually fall into simple, easily observed patterns because of the complex (and not fully understood) way that foods trigger allergy, and because of the motley makeup of our modern diet.

A few people can feel their lips, mouth and throat begin to swell or itch even before the food in question reaches their stomach. More often than not, however, trouble erupts farther along, as food is processed by the digestive system – resulting in anything from nausea and queasiness to gas and diarrhoea, plus various difficulties in between. As food allergens wend their way to the rest of the body, symptoms are no different from those of inhalant allergy – wheezing, or skin rashes, or dizziness, or joint pains and so on. These symptoms can take time to develop – a few hours, maybe, or a day or so. Because of that time lag, you may have difficulty linking what you ate to how you feel. Granted, some people – about one out of twenty – are so sensitive that the smallest nibble of an offending food can spark an immediate, recognizable reaction. If you break out in hives each time you eat prawns, you've got an open-and-shut case of prawns allergy. But it's seldom that simple. Since food takes about four or five days to journey from entrance to exit, most people react later. So you might blame your symptoms on the cheese you ate at lunch, when the real cause is the eggs you ate for breakfast. Or the melon you ate yesterday.

Here's another variable: do you seem to tolerate a food sometimes, but not others? You still can be allergic to a food even if you don't react every time you eat it. The problem food may very well be eaten for quite a while, with no symptoms. Then, as antibodies accumulate to a certain threshold, the attack occurs. One doctor compares this 'allergic threshold' to water filling a rain barrel. All's well until the water level reaches the brim. Then a tiny drop causes an overflow. By rotating foods, or eating troublesome food only at widely spaced intervals, you can keep most food allergies from reaching that critical point. (We'll tell you about the 'Rotary Diet' later in this chapter.)

How close you come to going over the edge also depends on how much you eat, and when. Perhaps you're only mildly allergic – you may be able to get away with one or two strawberries, but eating a whole punnet is a full-scale disaster. Or, since cooking breaks down food to a degree, you may discover, for instance, that you can eat celery cooked, but not raw. Or your symptoms may appear only if two or more allergenic foods are eaten at the same meal – in effect, overwhelming the system. That's particularly true for closely related foods like beef and milk, or mushrooms and yeast. (We'll talk more about 'food families' later in this chapter.)

By the same token, you may react to a food only during the pollen season or when suffering from other airborne particles. Or when you have a cold. Or when drinking alcohol. Or if eaten on an empty stomach.

Another interesting twist is that allergic reactions are not always uncomfortable. In fact, you may feel *better* after eating allergenic food. Doctors call that reaction 'allergic addiction', and compare it to the temporary lift one gets from smoking cigarettes. And just as a craving for cigarettes is a sure sign of a confirmed smoker, a food craving may very well point to a food to which you are actually allergic. The leading proponent of this theory is Dr Theron Randolph, a Chicago allergist, who told us that if you continue to eat foods to which you are allergically addicted, they will eventually make you chronically ill, even if they now give you temporary lifts.

To completely unravel a food allergy problem, you'll have to sort out not only your symptoms but also exactly what's in your diet. Food labels, unfortunately, do not spell out every last ingredient. 'Spices', for example, can include any of several unnamed ingredients, natural and synthetic. 'Vegetable oil' can mean corn, soybean, peanut, sunflower, coconut, olive, cottonseed or other oils. Sometimes labels are completely misleading. 'Non-dairy' creamers and other dairy substitutes may contain whey, lactose or casein – all milk products.

All that isn't to discourage you, but to sharpen your awareness. (We'll show you how to decipher even the most cryptic food label later in this chapter.)

Dining out? Restaurant meals are a potpourri of several ingredients. Even a simple meatball sandwich may contain up to two dozen ingredients, including beef, soya, pork, onion, oil, butter, milk, egg, black pepper, wheat, rye, yeast, sugar, caramel and others. Add a dash or two or ketchup, and you add tomatoes, vinegar, corn sweetener, onion powder, assorted spices and flavourings.

No wonder food allergy can be a hard case to crack! To help you sort it all out, your doctor will probably ask you to be your own – or your child's – detective. And the first step in solving this 'crime' against your health is gathering the clues. (If you already know what foods you're allergic to, you can skip ahead to the sections on Elimination diets and the Rotary diet further on in this chapter.)

Step 1: Keeping a food diary

A record of what you eat, how much you eat and how you feel afterwards can signal what you're allergic to – especially if your symptoms come and go unpredictably (as symptoms are wont to do). The accompanying sample diary shows you how to correctly record entries. Your diary will be most helpful if you keep a few basic rules in mind.

1. List all ingredients of mixed dishes and combination foods. If you eat a ham sandwich, for instance, note the kind of bread and dressing.

2. Don't rely on your memory. Fill in the information just before or after you eat. Carry the diary with you in your handbag, pocket or attaché case to record meals eaten away from home. Or jot down some notes and add them later.

3. Rate your symptoms on a scale of one to four to distinguish between mild and severe reactions. For example, a mildly unpleasant or slightly noticeable symptom would get a one; an extremely unpleasant or very marked reaction would rate a four.

4. Weigh yourself every morning after going to the bathroom. A sudden weight gain plus increased thirst, decreased urine output, tighter shoes or tight rings are all signs of oedema, or fluid retention – a common food reaction.

5. Note any foods you crave.

Sample Food Diary

This format will help you organize your diary of food-related symptoms. All entries are hypothetical. Foods mentioned are simply examples, not necessarily a suggested menu.

Monday, October 26		**Tuesday, October 27**	
Time	**Food, drink, medications**	**Time**	**Symptoms**
8.15 a.m.	orange juice wheat flakes, sugar and milk toast and butter, marmalade coffee, sugar and cream		
		9.30 a.m.	runny nose sneezing
		10.00 a.m.	no symptoms
12.30 p.m.	vegetable soup ham sandwich (wholewheat bread, butter and mustard) chocolate sponge cake coffee		
		1.00 p.m.	felt faint (lasted 10 minutes)
7.15 p.m.	tomato juice fried chicken (corn oil) peas, mashed potatoes and butter salad (lettuce, tomato, carrots, pepper, salad cream) vanilla ice cream and chocolate sauce		

SOURCE: *Patient information from Robert Giller, M.D.*

Symptoms to look for

James C. Breneman, chairman of the Food Allergy Committee of the American College of Allergists, has noticed that food allergy symptoms often fall into certain patterns:

– Hives, runny nose, asthma, heartburn, sleepiness or drowsiness can occur within one hour;
– abdominal cramps, gas pains or headaches may occur within two to four hours;

– delayed hives may appear six to twelve hours later;
– a weight gain or water retention can occur within twelve to fifteen hours;
– confusion, forgetfulness, depression, inability to concentrate or other mental symptoms may appear within twelve to twenty-four hours; and
– canker (cold) sores, aching joints, muscles or back can occur after three to five days.

Other symptoms to note include rashes, itching or burning skin, cramps, nausea, diarrhoea, constipation or bloating; weeping or itchy eyes, visual problems, sneezing, sinusitis; ringing in the ears or earaches; sore throat, hoarseness or cough; inexplicable fatigue; nervousness, tension or anxiety; a floating feeling; insomnia, dark, puffy circles under the eyes – or any of the signs of allergy described in Chapter 2, Are you allergic?

It goes without saying that there can be other medical reasons for all of those complaints. But if you've already seen a doctor, and he or she cannot explain why you are ill, food allergy should be considered. As a matter of fact, people with food allergy often have a long history of undiagnosed health problems – backed up by a slew of X-rays and gastrointestinal tests that don't explain their problems.

Note: Chronic infection in infants and young children can mimic gastrointestinal problems associated with milk and wheat allergies. In the case of a child who is vomiting or choking, or who has diarrhoea or difficulty in swallowing, consult a doctor without delay.

After you've kept a diary for a week or two, you can use it to help recognize problem foods. Doris J. Rapp, a pediatrician and allergist in Buffalo, New York, suggests that you make a list of all foods eaten on a day you felt well. Compare that list to a list of foods eaten on a day you felt terrible. Cross out all foods which appear on both lists. The foods left on the second list are your prime suspects. Then you eliminate them.

Step 2: Elimination diets

Basically, an elimination diet is simply a self-test. You avoid a prime suspect such as milk or wheat, *in all forms*, for up to three weeks, and see how you feel. Then you eat the food again – preferably in generous portions at several meals. Meanwhile, continue to observe your symptoms.

Obviously, you only need to test the food or foods you're unsure of. If you go into anaphylactic shock, get giant hives or suffer a splitting headache each time you eat shellfish, eggs or any other food, there's certainly no need to test them. Just avoid them. Elimination diets are designed to help people (or their doctors) confirm suspicions about a particular food. And they provide a starting point for those individuals who experience symptoms every day but don't have the foggiest notion which foods are to blame. Elimination diets are especially useful for diagnosing people who may have many, many food allergies.

If you're one of those people, begin by testing common food allergens – milk, eggs, wheat, corn, yeast, beef and so on – continuing with the less common ones until you've identified all the culprits. Tailor the plan to your individual problem, though. If you have a hunch about wheat, by all means start with wheat. The same goes for eggs, corn and so on.

Allergy doctors sometimes ask hard-to-diagnose people to fast – to go without any food at all – for three days or so before starting an elimination diet. This makes it somewhat easier to pinpoint the allergen. However, going without food can be extremely stressful (and hazardous in some cases), so we don't recommend that you fast without close medical supervision.

Even if you don't fast, the first four or five days on an elimination diet can be pretty rough – if you're on the right track. For one thing, foods like milk, wheat and eggs – so often the glue and mortar of baked goods and other dietary staples – aren't easy to avoid. And even if you eliminate every trace, you may at first feel worse instead of better: withdrawal symptoms, more or less. Don't let all that discourage you, though. By the fifth day or so, you'll feel much better.

'If food allergy is the problem, the patient is virtually well on the fifth or sixth day,' wrote Dr Breneman in an article on elimination diets, published in the *New York State Journal of Medicine* (December 1979).

After two or three weeks on an elimination diet for, say, milk or wheat, try the excluded food. Choose a day on which you feel free of symptoms until lunchtime. Then eat the food in various forms for three consecutive meals. To test milk, for example, you could have a big cheese sandwich at lunch, a generous scoop of cottage cheese with dinner, and milk and cereal for breakfast the next morning. If the food provokes symptoms, stop eating it. Proceed to the next prime suspect. Dr Rapp emphasizes that it's important to test only on a day when you've felt well all morning. And for good reason. If you wake up with a headache, for example, and your headache gets worse after you've tested the food, you won't be sure if the food made you worse or if your headache was due to something else and would have got worse anyway.

Like all good detective work, food diaries and elimination diets take some time and careful observation. There may be a false lead or two along the way. If you get to the point where you feel you really need the guidance of an allergy doctor, by all means take along your diary and other records. They'll be an enormous help in fine tuning the diagnosis.

Milk-free diet

Cow's milk is probably the most common item in the UK diet. It's no wonder that allergists tell us that milk is also the number one cause of food allergy, especially for children. Common milk reactions include wheezing, runny nose and congestion, ear infection, rashes, vomiting and bloody diarrhoea. Those symptoms don't show up immediately, though; there's usually a time lag between drinking milk and feeling ill.

What makes good old milk so troublesome? Allergic people react to one or more of three milk components: protein, fats and carbohydrates.

'Certain milk proteins are absorbed unchanged in allergic people,' explains Del Stigler, a pediatrician and allergist in Denver, Colorado. 'Beta-lactoglobulin, for instance, is a relatively large protein molecule which the normal intestine will strain out. But the intestine of an allergic person is abnormal, and larger molecules like lactoglobulins penetrate into the bloodstream unchanged, triggering reactions.' Casein is another troublesome milk protein. But *heating* milk, says Dr Stigler, breaks down both.

'Some people who are allergic to milk can tolerate milk that's been heated. For instance, we don't see as much allergy to formula or evaporated milk, which have been processed at a high temperature of 260 to 280 degrees. That breaks down the protein. People who are allergic to raw milk,' Dr Stigler adds, 'can often tolerate well-cooked milk.' On the other hand, Dr Stigler told us that some people can drink raw milk, but *not* the heated, homogenized-pasteurized type.

He also says that whole milk (and butter and cheese) is sometimes better tolerated than skim or low-fat. Fat, it seems, slows the time that the stomach takes to empty food into the intestines, allowing more time for milk to be absorbed and fewer problems to develop.

Milk allergy or lactase deficiency?

Still others cannot digest lactose, the main carbohydrate (or sugar) in milk. Normally, fingerlike projections along the intestinal wall, called villi, secrete lactase, an enzyme specifically designed to digest lactose. But lactose-intolerant people produce little or no lactase. So the milk passes through undigested, producing one heck of a belly-ache: abdominal discomfort, bloating, gas pains and often diarrhoea.

Lactase activity is generally highest at birth and slows down as we grow into adults. Many of the world's peoples – including blacks, Mexicans, Indians, Asians and those of Mediterranean descent – lose lactase in childhood. Others, particularly whites from northern or western Europe and their descendants, lose lactase later. Also, a bout with the flu or another virus can shut down anyone's lactase activity for several days. When the intestines are inflamed the tips of the villi are broken off and produce little or no lactase. That's why a milk-loving child may spurn the drink – or get a tummyache from it – after a stomach virus.

Many lactase-deficient people find they can tolerate milk if they simply cut down on milk and milk products, or consume small amounts throughout the day. Others can drink milk that's been treated with *Lactobacillus acidophilus*, a special (and perfectly safe) bacteria that breaks down the lactose, doing the work their intestines can't.

Lactobacillus, incidentally, is the same bacteria that turns milk into yoghurt. In Mediterranean, Asian and African countries, where people are frequently lactase deficient, yoghurt is the most widely used milk product.

Some cheeses, such as Cheddar and Cheshire, are very low in

lactose, while aged Gouda and Edam are lactose-free. Cottage cheese has 86 per cent less lactose than milk.

You can also try adding Lact-Aid powder, a lactose-digesting enzyme product, to milk. (All these products, incidentally, are available in most health food stores and many supermarkets.)

Until recently, milk allergy and lactose intolerance were regarded as totally separate problems. If you had both, it was considered a coincidence. Now, some doctors are convinced that, in many people, lactase deficiency actually develops as the result of an allergic reaction to either milk or some other food. That's because food allergy usually causes intestinal inflammation, which mows down the villi and creates lactose intolerance. Doctors who advance this theory believe that 95 per cent of the people who experience stomach distress after drinking milk have lactose intolerance secondary to an allergy of some kind. Of course, you can be allergic to milk without developing lactose intolerance.

In any case, many people with food allergies – children and adults alike – will have to eliminate milk in all forms if they're ever going to feel better. 'If a child comes in with a stomach ache, leg aches and a stuffy or runny nose, and they're also drinking a lot of milk, we take them off milk,' Dr Stigler told us.

For parents who are concerned that growing children will miss out on much-needed calcium without milk in their diet, Dr Stigler has some reassuring words. 'Many of us working in the field of allergy feel that allergic people don't absorb a lot of the calcium in milk. If you're sensitive to milk, the intestines reject it. So allergic kids aren't necessarily using the calcium in milk anyway.' (For dietary sources of calcium other than milk, refer to Chapter 12, Nutrition for allergy control.)

Take away the milk, says Dr Stigler, and as with most people who give up a food to which they are allergic, a child will probably feel worse for the first couple of days.

'But their symptoms will start to clear up after the first three or four days,' Dr Stigler predicts. 'In a week's time, if milk was the cause of the stomach aches and the leg aches and the runny nose or whatever, it will all go away.'

Dr Stigler also told us that, when milk is eliminated, children may eat ravenously for three or four days, whereas before they were just picking at their food. 'Take away the quart and a half or two quarts of milk a day – the average amount an allergic kid will drink – and they'll then make up for milk calories with other food. They'll eat extra of something else to make up the difference.'

Milk allergy, like simple lactose intolerance, may be dose related, Dr Stigler adds, especially when it causes digestive or respiratory upset. 'It may take half a pint or more to cause the stomach ache. But if you have a child who has eczema – a skin rash often caused by milk allergy – very often as little as a teaspoon of milk will cause the reaction.'

Table 2 provides guidelines for following a totally milk-free diet. Avoiding milk may sound easy at first, but you have to stay on your guard against hidden sources.

'You think you're staying away from milk. But if you eat a hot dog or spaghetti, they may contain milk,' pointed out Constantine J. Falliers, an allergist and asthma specialist in Denver, Colorado.

So you'll need to read labels carefully – advice that applies to *any* allergy elimination plan. Look for the code words 'caseinate', 'lactose' or 'whey' – all are milk additives. As we mentioned before, most 'non-dairy' creamers contain just such milk additives. (Non-dairy creamers also contain ingredients from other foods – corn, soya, animal and vegetable fats; flavour additives; and petroleum-based chemicals – which may trigger allergy on their own.)

You can confidently buy bread, margarine and other foods marked pareve or parve – those are made without a trace of milk to conform to kosher food laws. And if you're anywhere in the neighbourhood of an ethnic bakery, drop in and stock up. Kosher bread (challah) is free of milk, as are some French, Italian and Syrian breads.

If you're allergic to penicillin, check to find out if your dairy supplier uses penicillin before you reintroduce milk to your diet.

To cook without milk, experiment by substituting water, soya milk or fruit juice in your family's favourite recipes.

By the way, a small number of people with milk allergy are also allergic to soya, so switching to soya milk may not clear up their symptoms. Some people can tolerate goat's milk as a substitute; others cannot. Only trial and error will tell.

TABLE 2
Milk-free diet

Food Category	Foods You Can Eat, unless Allergic	Foods to Avoid
Meat, poultry and fish	Beef, veal, lamb, pork, chicken, turkey, guinea fowl, fish,* seafood, nuts, nut butters	Be careful of gravies and breadings, which may contain milk
Dairy products	Soya milk (if tolerated)†, margarine marked 'pareve' and other margarine not containing milk products	Whole, dry or evaporated milk‡; butter cream, cheese§, yoghurt and margarine containing milk products; ice cream and sorbet; cream substitutes with whey, lactose or casein
Eggs	Hard or soft cooked, fried, poached, scrambled	Milk, cream or butter in cooking
Grain products	Cereals served with fruit juice	Cereals served with milk or cream
	Homemade bread without milk, water bagels, crackers made without milk (read labels carefully)	Any bread made with milk, waffles and other baked goods made with milk
Soups	Soups made without cream, milk or cheese	Soups with cream, milk or cheese
Vegetables	Fresh or frozen vegetables are recommended, although canned are allowed*	All creamed vegetables; mashed potatoes, unless milk-free
Fruit	Fresh, frozen or dried fruit is preferred, but canned is allowed*	
Fats and oils	Vegetable oil	
Desserts	All that do not contain milk or milk products	Puddings and other desserts containing milk or milk products
Beverages	Fruit juice, carbonated water	
Miscellaneous	All foods labelled 'pareve' or 'parve'	

SOURCE: *Adapted from* Basics of Food Allergy, *by James C. Breneman (Springfield, Ill.: Charles C. Thomas, 1978).* The Elimination Diets, *by Albert Rowe, Jr, Colin E. Sinclair, and Peter H. Rowe (Oakland, Calif.:* Holmes Book Co., 1976*).*

* *See also sections on sulphur additives and sugar, later in this chapter.*
† *Ten to twenty per cent of people with milk allergy are also allergic to soya.*
‡ *People with lactose intolerance may tolerate Lact-Aid brand milk or milk treated with Lact-Aid brand commercial enzymes.*
§ *Lactose-intolerant people can usually digest Camembert, Cheddar, Edam, provolone, Swiss and pasteurized processed cheese, which are lactose-free.*

The cheese stands alone

You may find you can tolerate every other milk product except cheese, not even lactose-free varieties. The trouble may stem from the mould-type fermentation that turns milk into cheese. Cottage cheese is mould-free. Dr Breneman told us that some cheese-sensitive people can tolerate farmer's cheese and home-made cheese, which are often mould-free.

If moulds aren't your problem, but cheese still makes you miserable, you may be sensitive to tyramine, a natural substance in cheese and other foods – notably chocolate, yoghurt, beer, red wine, gin, bourbon and vodka – that tends to trigger migraine headaches. If that's the case, you may be able to eat only a tiny sliver of cheese, as long as you don't eat any other tyramine-containing food or drink along with it.

Egg-free diet

We tend to forget that a *lot* of foods contain eggs. They show up in all kinds of goodies. Puddings, cakes, pancakes and waffles all contain eggs. And eggs are the stuff noodles, custards and mayonnaise are made of. Eggs show up in ice cream and marshmallows. Occasionally, eggs are even used to make root beer foam.

Like those allergic to milk, people allergic to eggs may be sensitive to only a part of the food: in this case, either the white or the yolk. (Whites are usually the problem.) The method of cooking also makes a difference. Some people can tolerate hard-boiled eggs, but not soft-boiled. Others can cook their eggs until they're tough as golf balls and still be allergic. Very rarely, a person is so sensitive to eggs that he or she can't tolerate chicken either. Another egg-related product – vaccines grown on egg cultures – should also be approached cautiously if you're allergic to eggs. (Ask your doctor about a vaccine's base if you are allergic to eggs.)

So what can you eat, if not eggs? Plenty. Practically all meats and vegetables. Potatoes. Rice. Fruit. (Table 3 gives a complete egg-free diet.) Watch out for code words for eggs on food labels: vitellin, ovotellin, livetin, ovomucin and albumin.

A word about egg substitutes: so many of these products contain other highly allergic substances and additives – notably yellow food dye – that we can't recommend them. You may end up trading one allergy for another.

TABLE 3

Egg-free diet

Food Category	Foods You Can Eat, unless Allergic	Foods to Avoid
Meat, poultry and fish	Beef, veal, lamb, pork, chicken, turkey, guinea fowl, fish,* seafood, nuts, nut butters	Any meat mixtures containing eggs (croquettes, hamburgers, meatballs, meat loaves, timbales)
Dairy products	Milk, all cheeses	Any cheese mixtures containing eggs; ice cream and sorbet
Eggs		Eggs (yolk or white) in any form; powdered eggs
Grain products	All cereals Most breads and rolls; French bread, unless glazed with egg white (read labels)	Any bread containing eggs or glazed with egg white; pancakes, muffins (unless egg-free), waffles; pretzels Breaded foods or foods coated with batter Noodles, pasta
Soups	All soups not containing egg as a thickener or cleared with egg	Bouillon, consommé, egg drop soup, noodle soup
Vegetables	Fresh or frozen vegetables are recommended, although canned are allowed*	Vegetable soufflés
Fruit	Fresh, frozen or dried fruit is preferred, but canned is allowed*	
Fats and oils	All	
Desserts	All that do not contain eggs (read labels)	Cakes, biscuits, ices, icings, doughnuts, pudding powder, custards, macaroons, meringues, cream pies; sauces, puddings or gelatine desserts made with egg
Beverages	Most (fruit juice, most carbonated beverages)	Eggnog; wine or coffee clarified with egg whites; Ovaltine
Condiments and seasonings	Herbs, spices	Mayonnaise, hollandaise sauce, tartare sauce, boiled dressing
Miscellaneous	Wheat-free, corn-free baking powder (see recipe in box, Cooking without wheat, in this chapter)	Commercial baking powder

SOURCE: *Adapted from* Basics of Food Allergy, *by James C. Breneman (Springfield, Ill.: Charles C. Thomas, 1978).*

* *See also sections on sulphur additives and sugar, later in this chapter.*

Wheat-free diet

Bread was so basic to the Roman diet that the word was synonymous with food. Most of us today still eat bread or a similar grain food at least two or three times a day. Cereal or toast for breakfast. A sandwich for lunch. Noodles, pasta or breaded fish or chicken for dinner. Plus crackers, biscuits and cakes. And a flaky-crusted pie or quiche now and then.

Wheat is by far the most popular grain in the West, where people put a premium on light, springy baked goods and pasta. However, gluten – the elastic protein in wheat that makes baked goods springy and light – is a prime cause of wheat allergy. Some people are sensitive not only to wheat but to grains low in gluten like barley, rye and oats. Symptoms commonly caused by wheat or gluten allergy are: eczema; abdominal problems like indigestion, cramps, colitis, bloating, gas and diarrhoea; and respiratory problems like asthma and hay fever. Wheat and gluten sensitivity is now being recognized as a possible cause of headaches, depression and even symptoms resembling neurosis and schizophrenia. (Coeliac disease, a food-related illness that responds to the elimination of grain from the diet, is not an allergy.)

Table 4 shows foods you can eat freely on a wheat-free diet. As you can see, much of the problem can be solved by cooking foods yourself rather than buying prepared foods. To sidestep wheat or gluten completely, however, you have to know a few tricks. Commercial bread and baked goods labelled 'wheat-free' or 'gluten-free' don't always hold to their word. Getting bread to rise without gluten is like trying to make a fluffy soufflé with too few egg whites. So some bakeries add just a little wheat anyway. Other bakers and food manufacturers may list wheat in a disguised form. Look out for products that list not only the obvious – flour, wheat flour, wheat starch, gluten flour or cracked wheat – but also monosodium glutamate, hydrolyzed vegetable protein or durum flour.

Malt is derived from barley or other grains and is a hidden source of gluten. Most dry breakfast cereals and baked goods contain malt in some form.

Start a wheat-free diet by eliminating just wheat. If you still experience symptoms, eliminate wheat plus barley, oats and rye.

TABLE 4
Wheat-free diet

Many foods must be avoided because they are unsuspected sources of hidden wheat.

Food Category	Foods You Can Eat, unless Allergic	Foods to Avoid
Meat, poultry, fish and vegetable protein	Beef, veal, lamb, pork, chicken, turkey, fish,* shellfish, liver, dried beans and peas, nuts, nut butters	Any commercially prepared products containing cereals; luncheon meat, frankfurters, meat loaf, sausage, meat or fish patties, and gravies usually contain one or more grains and should be avoided unless made from pure meat Beware of casseroles made with grain flour, and canned or frozen foods with thickened sauces
Dairy products	Milk, butter, margarine, cheese	Milk drinks mixed with malt, cheese spreads with cereal fillers
Eggs	Hard- or soft-boiled, fried, poached, scrambled	Eggs in grain-thickened sauces
Grain products	Barley, corn, oat, rice and rye cereals, if tolerated	Check labels for cereal grains not tolerated; avoid wheat, wheat gluten, wheat flakes, wheat germ, shredded wheat and bulgur (cracked wheat)
	Wheat-free breads made from rice, potato starch, potato flour, lima bean flour and gluten-free wheat starch; breads made from barley flour, cornmeal, oat flour, 100% rye flour and soyabean flour, if tolerated	Wheat flour bread; dumplings; commercially prepared biscuits, pancakes, doughnuts, waffles, pastries, cakes, pies, crackers or pretzels made from wheat flour, wheat gluten or grains not tolerated; communion wafers†; melba toast; bread crumbs and

SOURCES: *Adapted from* Basics of Food Allergy, *by James C. Breneman (Springfield, Ill.: Charles C. Thomas, 1978).* The Elimination Diets, *by Albert Rowe, Jr, Colin E. Sinclair and Peter H. Rowe (Oakland, Calif.: Holmes Book Co., 1976).*

* *See also sections on sulphur additives and sugar, later in this chapter.*
† *Ask about ingredients.*

TABLE 4 – *Continued*

Food Category	**Foods You Can Eat, unless Allergic**	**Foods to Avoid**
Grain products – *Continued*		croûtons, unless from tolerated grain
	Gluten-free pasta	Noodles, pasta
Soups	Broth; homemade soups made from foods allowed; creamed soup with potato thickener, but not flour	Bouillon cubes, commercially prepared soups thickened with grain
Vegetables	Fresh or frozen vegetables are recommended, although canned are allowed*	Vegetables cooked with grain-thickened sauces; casseroles or puddings containing flour, bread or crumbs as ingredients
Fruit	Fresh, frozen or dried fruit is preferred, but canned is allowed*	Check labels for grain-based thickening agents
Desserts	Gelatine desserts, tapioca pudding, homemade ice cream	Commercial ice cream
Sweets/ sweeteners		Chocolate candy, candy bars; cane sugar, molasses
Beverages	Fruit juice, herbal tea (except lemongrass tea)	Coffee substitutes made with grains; instant mixed beverages with malt or cereal added; beer, ale, whisky, vodka, gin‡; lemongrass tea
Condiments	Salad dressing without grains	Commercial salad dressing thickened with grain, soy sauce
Miscellaneous	Apple cider vinegar; wheat-free, corn-free baking powder (see recipe in box, Cooking without Wheat, on page 46)	White vinegar, baking powder, chewing gum (read labels)

‡ *See also section on alcohol, later in this chapter.*

If you have the time to bake your own bread and baked goods, avoiding wheat and gluten is less of a guessing game. The box, Cooking without wheat, tells you how to substitute low-gluten or gluten-free starches like rice and rye in baked goods and offers some basic recipes to help you get started.

Corn-free diet

Corn may be a gift from the Aztecs. But if you have corn allergy, it's a nuisance. Perhaps it's easy enough to avoid corn meal, corn-starch, corn flour, corn syrup and maybe even corn oil. But a glance at Table 5 shows how easily corn can creep into practically every meal, obvious or disguised, unless you plan your diet carefully. As with milk-free and wheat-free diets, you have to learn the tricks of the food trade when it comes to hidden sources of corn. Oil added to peanut butter, for instance, isn't peanut oil at all, but corn oil.

Sometimes the corn problem is in the container. 'You think you're avoiding corn, but then you drink from a paper cup, and that may be coated with cornstarch,' says Dr Falliers. 'Or your milk carton may have cornstarch. I know people who get their milk in glass containers for that reason.'

The less processed and sugar laden your diet, the easier it will be to avoid corn in its many guises. In addition, follow these general rules.

1. Read labels carefully. Avoid any food listing not only corn, cornflour, corn oil and corn syrup, but the sugars: glucose, dextrose, dextrin, dextrimaltose and fructose. Corn is also a major source of sugar. Any sugar not specifically marked 'cane sugar' or 'beat sugar' may contain corn.

2. Cough syrups, cough drops, lozenges, pills, tablets and suppositories often contain corn. 'If your allergy pills contain cornstarch.' Dr Falliers told us, 'they may actually make you sicker.' If you must take medication, ask your pharmacist for a corn-free product. Consult your doctor before changing or stopping any medication.

3. Vitamin and mineral supplements may also be corn based. See the Appendix for a list of corn-free nutritional supplements.

4. Arrowroot or tapioca may be substituted in recipes calling for cornflour as a thickener.

If you're puzzled because you can eat corn on the cob but not commercial canned or frozen corn, you may be allergic to the sulphur dioxide used in corn processing rather than the corn itself. (We'll discuss allergy to food additives later in this chapter.)

COOKING WITHOUT WHEAT

If you're sensitive to wheat but no other gluten grains, you can use any of the substitute flours mentioned below. If you are sensitive to all glutens, stick to potato, rice, soya or tapioca flours.

Baked goods made with these substitutes will tend to be heavier and more crumbly than those made with wheat flour. Potato flour and soya flour are best used in combination with other flours, such as rice or tapioca. Rice flour gives a certain graininess to baked goods. Rye flour has a more distinct flavour.

Flour	**Amount to replace 8 oz/225 g of wheat flour**
Barley	10 oz/275 g
Oat	10½ oz/290 g
Potato*	6 oz/175 g
Rice	6 oz/175 g
Rye	10½ oz/290 g
Soya	10½ oz/290 g
Tapioca‡	8 oz/225 g

SOURCE: *Adapted from* Baking for People with Food Allergies, *Home and Garden Bulletin No. 147, by Lois Fulton and Carole Davis (Washington, D.C.: Agricultural Research Service, US Department of Agriculture, 1975).*
NOTE: *Some doctors say that although buckwheat is not related to wheat, it tends to cause allergies, too. Other doctors, however, say virtually the opposite – that buckwheat is a safe alternative for their wheat-allergic patients. You'll have to try it yourself to know where you stand.*

* *Potato flour is made from cooked potatoes. Potato starch is made from raw potatoes. They are not necessarily interchangeable.*
‡ *Tapioca is starch from the root of the cassava or manioc plant.*

VEGETABLE PASTA

2 medium courgettes
½ pint/300 ml tomato sauce

Shred the courgettes and steam briefly to cook through. Serve with the heated tomato sauce.
Serves: 1
Variations: substitute steamed finely shredded cabbage or blanched mung beans for the courgettes.

WHEAT-FREE, CORN-FREE BAKING POWDER

Baking powder is a general term for certain leavening agents consisting of a carbonate, an acid and some kind of starch or flour. Wheat-sensitive and corn-sensitive people must avoid wheat-based or corn-based baking powder. Dr Albert Rowe, Jr, an allergy doctor in San Francisco, suggests the following grain-free baking powder.

6 oz/175 g cream of tartar
9 tablespoons bicarbonate of soda
6 tablespoons potato starch

Sift three times, mixing well each time. Store in an airtight jar.

SOURCE: *Reprinted by permission of the publisher from* The Elimination Diets, *by Albert Rowe, Jr, Colin E. Sinclair and Peter H. Rowe (Oakland, Calif.: Holmes Book Co., 1976).*

WHEAT-FREE WAFFLES

12 oz/350 g cooked short-grain brown rice
4–5 tablespoons butter
2 fl oz/50 ml honey
6 fl oz/160 ml milk
2 eggs, separated
12 oz/320 ml brown-rice flour
2 teaspoons wheat-free, corn-free baking powder (see above)
¾ teaspoon cinnamon
¼ teaspoon nutmeg

In a 4-quart saucepan, heat rice, 3 tablespoons butter, honey and milk together until butter melts. With a wire whisk, beat the egg yolks until frothy and add to rice mixture. Remove from heat.

In a small bowl, mix flour, baking powder, cinnamon and nutmeg and add to the rice mixture. Let stand while beating egg whites until stiff. Fold in egg whites. Melt a small amount of the remaining butter on a heated waffle iron.

Spread an eighth of batter on waffle iron. (Batter will be thick.) Cook waffles approximately 10 minutes. Use a small amount of butter to coat iron before making each waffle. Keep waffles warm and serve with maple syrup.

Yield: Five 8-inch waffles

NOTE: Because these waffles take a little longer to cook than conventional wheat waffles, we suggest you put them in a warm oven as they come off the iron, keeping them hot until all the waffles are done.

TABLE 5

Potential Sources of Hidden Corn

Corn-sensitive people may have to be extra vigilant in order to eliminate all traces of corn. Processed foods often contain corn sugar (dextrose). Read labels carefully to locate corn-free items in each category.

adhesives: envelopes, stamps, stickers, tapes
ale
aspirin
bacon
baking mixes e.g. cheese cake mixes, bun and cake mixes
baking powders
batters for frying
beans, canned
beers
beverages, carbonated
bleached white flours
bourbon and other whiskies
breads and pastries
biscuits
cakes
cream cheese and other processed cheeses
chili
chop suey
coffee, instant
cornflakes
corn sugar: glucose and dextrose
cough syrup
cups, paper
dates, confectioners'
deep fat frying mixtures
excipients of diluents in capsules, lozenges, ointments, suppositories, tablets, vitamins
flour, bleached
French dressing
fruits, canned
fruit juices, sweetened
frying fats
gelatine capsules
gelatine dessert
glucose products
grape juice, sweetened
gums, chewing
gin
hams, cured, tenderized
ice creams
icing sugar
inhalants: bath powders, body powders, cooking fumes of fresh popcorn, starch, starch while ironing, starched clothing, talcums
jams
jellies: dessert jellies and jelly sweets
leavening agents: baking powder, yeasts
liquors: ale, beer, gin, whisky – malt and malted preparations
meats: bacon, bolognese, meat gravies, luncheon meats, sausages, frankfurters
milk in paper cartons
monosodium glutamate
paper containers: boxes, cups, plates
pastries: cakes, tarts
peanut butter
peas, canned
plastic food wrappers (the inner surface may be coated with cornflour)
preserves
puddings: blancmange, custards, lemon pie
rice pudding
salad dressings
sandwich spreads
sauces for sundaes, meats, fish, vegetables
sorbets
soups, creamed, thickened
soya bean milks
string beans, canned
sugar
syrups
teas, instant
toothpaste
tortillas
vanillin
vegetables, canned
vinegar, distilled

Yeast-free diet

Yeasts are wondrous little one-celled plants that turn dough into bread and cider into vinegar. Like moulds, yeasts are a fungus – and just as apt to cause allergies in people sensitive to fungus. To avoid yeast (and mould) in your diet, you'll need to steer clear of not only the obvious foods – mushrooms, bread and vinegar – but also certain cheeses, condiments, drugs and nutritional supplements. Table 6 spells out exactly how to go about eliminating yeast and yeast-related foods. As you've discovered from our guidelines for other elimination diets, it's a lot easier to eliminate a food ingredient of any kind if you avoid commercial packaged foods and stick to whole, unprocessed food.

Testing additional foods

If you've tried the basic elimination diets outlined so far and still aren't satisfied that all of your food allergies have been identified, continue to test individual foods in the approximate order (most often to seldom) they fall in Table 1 at the beginning of this chapter. For instance, to test beef, eliminate beef in all forms for three weeks. Then eat generous portions of beef for three consecutive meals. If allergic symptoms develop, stop eating beef. If allergic symptoms do not develop, you can probably assume that beef is acceptable. Continue to eat beef while you test the next food in the same manner.

If all goes according to plan, elimination diets will leave you with a list of foods responsible for your allergies. Those foods, of course, should be avoided for several months.

Notice we didn't say 'avoided *forever*'. Allergies change. After a year or more, you may lose your sensitivity to a food to which you are now allergic. After not eating the food for several months, test it once more. If symptoms reappear, you will have to continue to avoid it indefinitely. If nothing happens, however, you can add that food to your diet at intervals of four days or longer. (We'll cover four-day food rotations at length later in this chapter, under the heading 'Rotary diets'.)

If you've tested every food in your diet and still have symptoms, the next step is to eliminate food additives or pesticides – or both.

TABLE 6

Yeast-Free Diet

Many foods contain yeast, either naturally or because of the way they are prepared. To avoid yeast, follow these guidelines. As you can see, making foods 'from scratch' can help to avoid unsuspected sources of yeast.

Food Category	Foods You Can Eat, unless Allergic	Foods to Avoid
Meat, poultry, fish and vegetable protein	Beef, veal, lamb, pork, chicken, turkey, fish,* seafood, dried beans and peas, nuts, nut butters	Cold cuts, croquettes, luncheon ham, sausage, commercial fish and meat patties or loaves, hamburger, mince unless 100% beef, meats breaded in batter
Dairy products	Milk, butter, margarine, cottage cheese, cream cheese, farmer cheese, homemade cheese	Milk fortified with vitamins (see 'Vitamin and mineral supplements', below), buttermilk, malt-flavoured milk drinks, yoghurt, sour cream, most cheeses
Eggs	Hard- or soft-boiled, fried, poached, scrambled	
Grain products	Corn and rice products	Cereals containing malt, cereals fortified with vitamins, farina Breads made with wheat or rye; crackers; dumplings; matzos Noodles, pasta
Soups	Bouillon, homemade stock or broth, soups made with permitted foods, creamed soups thickened with milk	Soups thickened with wheat flour, chili

SOURCE: *Adapted from* Basics of Food Allergy, *by James C. Breneman (Springfield, Ill.: Charles C. Thomas, 1978).*

* *See also sections on sulphur additives and sugar, later in this chapter.*

Food Category	Foods You Can Eat, unless Allergic	Foods to Avoid
Vegetables	Fresh or frozen vegetables are recommended, although canned are allowed*	Chili pepper, mushroomns, truffles, sauerkraut, tomato sauce
Fruit	Fresh or frozen fruit is preferred, but canned is allowed*	Dried fruit, mince pie, frozen or canned citrus juice (only fresh-squeezed citrus juice is yeast-free)
Fats and oils	Vegetable oil	
Sweets/ sweeteners	Honey, homemade jams and jellies (be sure they are free of any trace of mould)	Sweets made with malt
Beverages	Carbonated water, herbal tea	Root beer, ginger ale, alcoholic beverages, black tea (leaves are fermented)
Condiments and seasonings	Mayonnaise and salad dressing not thickened with wheat flour or containing vinegar; mustard, garlic, herbs, spices	Ketchup, horseradish, meat sauce, soy sauce, pickles
Miscellaneous		Vinegar, brewer's yeast, baker's yeast, torula yeast, yeast extract
Vitamin and mineral supplements	Most	B vitamins made from yeast; multiple-vitamin supplements containing B vitamins made from yeast; selenium and chromium (trace minerals) derived from yeast
Drugs†		Antibiotics made from mould cultures; tetracyclines; penicillin; mycin drugs; Chloromycetin; Lincocin

† *Be sure to check with your doctor before discontinuing any medication.*

The additive-free diet

If you're not allergic to a food itself, you may be allergic to a food additive: a colouring, flavouring, stabilizer, emulsifier or preservative. While considerably fewer people are allergic to additives than to food, additives are still a significant cause of adverse reactions.

One doctor tells of a member of her family who experienced sudden weakness, extreme fatigue and a swollen throat whenever eating cornflakes or instant potatoes. The problem was neither corn nor potatoes, however, but BHA and BHT (E320 and E321), two common preservatives.

Needless to say, a food such as cornflakes is apt to contain not one but *several* additives, any or all of which can cause the problem, Dr Bernard J. Freedman, of King's College Hospital in London, found that 30 out of 272 of his asthmatic patients reacted to orange drinks, even though they weren't allergic to oranges. As it turned out, most of those people were actually reacting to a triad of additives commonly found in yellow-hued, acidic beverages: tartrazine (E102), sodium benzoate (E211) and sulphur dioxide (E220) (*Clinical Allergy*, September 1977).

A lot of people are in the same predicament. The late Dr Benjamin Feingold, author of *Why Your Child Is Hyperactive* and *The Feingold Cookbook for Hyperactive Children*, believed that additives are the most common cause of *all* adverse reactions, affecting not just childhood behaviour but every system in the body. 'Any problem can result from exposure to additives,' Dr Feingold told us. 'Hives are common. Nail problems. Asthma. Rashes of all kinds.

'Food chemicals are no different from drugs,' Dr Feingold said. 'If a youngster takes a drug and reacts, no one is surprised. But if he or she eats a food chemical and reacts, why be surprised? What's the difference?'

As a matter of fact, food-additive allergy is often linked to drug allergy. Eggs dipped in penicillin, to retard spoilage, can be a problem for people who are highly allergic to penicillin. And people who are allergic to aspirin also tend to react to tartrazine, one of the most common artificial food colourings. Tartrazine is present in thousands of foods, beverages, cosmetics and drugs. Distressing reactions to tartrazine commonly include

WHAT YOUR PULSE CAN TELL YOU ABOUT ALLERGY

In some people, eating troublesome food will speed up their pulse. First noticed by Arthur F. Coca, an allergist and immunologist, that phenomenon was described at length in his book, *The Pulse Test* (Lyle Stuart, 1967). According to Dr Coca, taking your pulse after meals helps to identify allergy-causing foods.

Say you have a hunch you're allergic to wheat. Take your pulse when you first get up in the morning. Lightly press two or three fingers of one hand over the artery just inside the wrist of the opposite hand, below the thumb. (Don't try to feel your pulse with the thumb – it's got a pulse of its own.) Count the beats felt in exactly one minute and write it down. (The average is about 60 to 80 per minute.)

Take your pulse again just before eating a single serving of the wheat alone (or any other suspected food). Then take it again 30 minutes and 60 minutes after the test serving. An abnormal increase in pulse – unrelated to infection, exercise or stress, that is – presumably indicates an allergy.

Sounds pretty remarkable. But William J. Rea, a cardiovascular (heart) doctor in Dallas, told us that the pulse test doesn't work for everyone. 'In about one-third of the people, the pulse *will* go up,' he says. 'In another third, it will go down. And in another third, it stays the same. And some people will experience any one of those changes at different times, depending on what they eat.

'So it's only good if there's a definite, consistent change in the individual,' he continued. 'For example, I have one secretary who, anytime she has a food reaction, also has a ten-point or higher elevation in pulse. Every time. No question about it. So for her, it works.

'We do use the pulse test routinely,' Dr Rea told us, 'because it's one objective measure. But we don't rely on the pulse test alone. After all, no test is 100 per cent reliable.'

In other words, the pulse test is a tool that may be helpful if used *along with* a food diary and elimination-and-challenge diets.

asthma, coughing fits and difficulty in breathing, facial swelling and purpura (broken capillaries beneath the skin, such as bleeding gums and bruises). But you don't necessarily have to be allergic to aspirin to react to tartrazine.

To alert fellow doctors that the yellow dye causes many problems among allergic people, two physicians from the Milton S. Hershey Medical Center in Pennsylvania reported the case of a young man who landed in a hospital emergency room every time he swallowed anything containing yellow dye. It all started when the twenty-five-year-old medical student – who had a life history of allergy and asthma – ate some cauliflower with yellow cheese sauce at dinner. He hadn't even finished his meal when he became short of breath and felt his throat tighten up. Before he knew it, he broke out in hives and couldn't swallow at all. His wife, a registered nurse, gave him a shot of adrenaline, to no avail. In the hospital, doctors brought him around with more adrenalin, oxygen and emergency medication.

Five weeks later, the young man ate three yellow jelly beans. A little while later, during his regular hospital rounds, he felt lightheaded, his scalp itched and his throat began to close up. Again, hives appeared and his blood pressure dropped severely. Adrenalin and medication once again put things right. Two days later – while still hospitalized – he reacted once more, to a drug containing yellow dye.

Now, of course, he knows better and stays away from anything he suspects of containing yellow dye. Robert E. Desmond and Joseph J. Trautlein, the two physicians reporting the story, wrap up the article by alerting other doctors to the ubiquitous nature of yellow dye and its potential for both life-threatening and milder reactions, especially in allergy-prone people (*Annals of Allergy*. February 1981).

Tartrazine may be the most notorious food dye, but it's only one of several additives with allergy-provoking potential. Any of the food dyes listed in Table 8 can trigger an allergy. That's because many artificial colours (like so many other food additives) are made from coal tar, a substance with a special knack for making people ill. But additives not made from coal tar aren't any better; they're made from petroleum. Bananas, apples, pears, oranges and tomatoes, for instance, are usually picked before they're ripe and gassed with ethylene, a petroleum-based chemical that hastens ripening. Now, you might expect to encounter coal tar and petroleum in car exhaust, printer's ink, dry-cleaning solvents, carpeting, clothing dye and even perfume – explaining any reactions to fumes from those items. But as food ingredients, the same chemicals can catch you offguard. And if you're allergic to petroleum in the air – any kind of air pollution for that matter – you're also apt to react to the chemicals you swallow.

Sulphur additives are a case in point. Sulphur dioxide, a main component of air pollution, is a major threat to anyone with asthma. In the form of metabisulphite and other compounds used to preserve foods, beverages and drugs, sulphur is equally liable to trigger asthma, flushing or even shock in allergic people.

Some foods are treated with sulphur as a matter of course. Unless otherwise specified, for instance, all dried fruits are automatically treated with sulphur dioxide. So is molasses. Look for fruits and molasses that are clearly labelled 'unsulphured'.

Many wines are laced with sulphites. Unfortunately, wine and other alcoholic beverages are not required to have their ingredients listed on their labels.

TABLE 7

Additives in Wine

Most wines made in the conventional manner contain additives, particularly sulphur dioxide and other sulphites which are used as preservatives. These do not have to be listed on the label. EEC regulations govern which substances are permitted to be added to wine, or used in the wine-making processes. They also lay down maximum permitted levels of sulphur dioxide in wine made in member countries. A report in Which? *magazine (May 1986) however described how their laboratories tested a range of wines widely available in the UK and found some that came close to or exceeded these maximum limits.*

Some growers in France, Italy, Germany and Britain are now producing wine organically – without using chemicals in the vineyards, nor in the wine-making process. The addresses of some suppliers of these can be found in the appendix.

Monosodium glutamate (MSG) is perhaps the most famous instigator of 'restaurant allergies'. Have you ever gone out to eat Chinese food only to come home feeling headachy and nauseated? Or flushed, warm and numb throughout your arms

TABLE 8

Common Food Sources of Artificial Colouring

Listed here are the types of food most likely to contain artificial food colouring, in descending order of prevalence. Not all foods within each category will contain the colouring in question. To avoid artificial colourings, read labels and look for foods marked 'no artificial colourings'. See also the Appendix for suppliers of colour-free food.

Colouring	Use in Foods
E102 Tartrazine	packet convenience foods, rind of cheese, smoked fish, chewing gum, tinned fruit pie filling, canned processed peas and other vegetables, salad cream, cakes, biscuits, marzipan, piccalilli, brown sauce, maple flavoured syrup, gelatines, puddings, custards, sweets, lime and lemon squash, orange squash, seafood dressing, mint sauce and jelly, packet dessert topping, fizzy drinks, shells of capsules, some tablets, canned fruit and some fruit juice drinks, breakfast cereals, soup and soup mixes, some alcoholic beverages, milk foods, snack foods
E122 Carmoisine	packet soup mix, blancmange, packet breadcrumbs, jellies, sweets, cheesecake mixes, brown sauce, savoury convenience food mixes, swiss roll, sponge puddings, marzipan, chocolate mousse, jams, milk shake mixes, some alcoholic beverages.
E110 Sunset Yellow	hot chocolate mix, packet soups, sweets, puddings – trifle and sorbet mixes, Swiss roll, apricot jam, lemon curd, fruit sauce, fruit cake, ice cream, jam tarts, yoghurt whips, cheese sauce mix, orange squash, marzipan, coffee whiteners, dessert toppings, fish fingers, milk shake syrup, pork pies, jams, table jelly
E124 Ponceau Red 4R	packet puddings – trifle and cheesecake mix, cake mixes, packet soups, condiments – seafood dressings, dessert topping, canned fruit – strawberries and raspberries, canned fruit pie fillings – cherry, redcurrant

Colouring	Use in Foods
E124 Ponceau Red 4R – *Continued*	and raspberry, jelly mixes, fruit sauces, cheese sauce mix, chicken dishes, custard, fish fingers, jam and lemon curd, milk shake syrups, pork pies and sausages, table jellies, savoury rice
E132 Indigo Carmine	canned vegetables, sweets, baked goods, gelatines, blancmange and other packet pudding mixes, chewing gum, frosting, some alcoholic beverages, biscuits
E131 Patent Blue	Scotch eggs, mint sauce, tinned peas, puddings, chewing gum, sweets

and chest – maybe with a pain in your chest or stomach? Chances are you had a brush with 'Chinese Restaurant Syndrome'. The root of the problem is actually MSG, a flavour enhancer used not only in Chinese but also in Japanese and South Asian cuisine, and in many packaged foods as well. In fact, MSG is sold on supermarket spice racks right next to the marjoram and mustard seed.

For years, MSG reactions were dismissed by doctors as merely imaginary, or at most a slight irritation of the oesophagus. Then reports began to appear in medical journals telling of people who developed more than just annoying numbness – some experienced asthma and serious breathing difficulties after eating anything containing MSG. Finally, two doctors in England discovered that a fellow physician had a bona fide allergy to MSG: he lost all feeling in his hands and feet – once for three years straight. He discovered, though, that if he stayed away from certain foods, especially those containing MSG, he could prevent the problem entirely. His two doctor friends ran him through a battery of food challenges and lab tests. Nerve tests showed that, for one thing, the numbness was quite real. And blood tests showed that every time he ate MSG and felt numb, his blood IgA levels rose – often regarded as a sign of allergy (*Annals of Allergy*, February 1982).

There are few reliable tests for food allergy; there are *none* for additive allergy. The only way to test for allergy to an additive is to eliminate it just as you eliminate milk or wheat. To avoid additives, though, your label reading skills have to be doubly sharp.

TABLE 9

Common Food Sources of Flavour Additives

To eliminate flavour additives, choose a diet from the last group of foods.

Highest Amounts of Flavour Additives

Baked goods and baking mixes	Hard sweets and cough drops
Beverages, alcoholic and nonalcoholic	Herbs, spices, seasonings, blends, extracts and flavourings
Chewing gum	Meat products (such as sausage)
Condiments and relishes	Reconstituted vegetable proteins
Confections and frostings	Snack foods
Frozen dairy desserts and mixes	Soft sweets
Fruit and water ices	Soup and soup mixes
Gelatines, puddings and fillings	Sweet sauces, toppings and syrups
Gravies and sauces	

Lesser Amounts of Flavour Additives

Breakfast cereals	Nuts and nut products (such as
Coffee drinks and exotic teas	Poultry products (such as chicken croquettes
Fats and oils	Processed fruit and fruit juices
Fish products (such as fish sticks)	Processed vegetables and vegetable juices
Imitation dairy products (such as non-dairy creamer)	
Milk products (such as ice cream)	

No Flavour Additives

Cheeses	Fresh poultry
Fresh eggs	Fresh vegetables and potatoes
Fresh fish	Grain products and pastas
Fresh fruit and fruit juices	Jams and jellies, homemade
Fresh meats	Milk, whole and skim

SOURCE: *Reprinted by permission of the publisher from 'The Role of Flavours', by Richard L. Hall and Earl J. Merwin,* Food Technology, *June 1981, p. 51.*

Label reading for allergy relief

Food labels are far less complete than allergy sufferers and doctors would like. The law says that all ingredients must appear on the label, in descending order by weight. Additives such as preservatives must be specified by name and/or E number. So far, so good. *But flavourings – one of the most common causes of allergic reactions – do not have to be individually identified.* As a rule, the more processed the food, the more flavourings it has (see Table 9), and as many as 125 chemical flavours can be used in a single processed food (40 is about average). Yet a manufacturer can list them all under the umbrella term 'artificial flavouring' without specifying the exact substances used.

Incidentally, it's not unheard of for people to be allergic to *natural* flavourings – like cinnamon, vanillin or peppermint – as well as artificial flavourings. And that holds true for other natural additives. Papain, an enzyme derived from papayas and used to tenderize meat, has been known to trigger asthma in sensitive people. Sesame flour – widely used in cakes, breads and as a binder in meat products – may be made not only from sesame seeds but pulverized orange peel, so if you're allergic to citrus you could react to it. Citric acid, a natural preservative, may come from corn or beet molasses, lemons or pineapple. Modified food starch may be made from wheat, corn, sorghum, arrowroot, tapioca or potatoes.

'Food processors who do not label their products adequately place an unacceptable health burden on a rapidly growing segment of the public,' says Joseph B. Miller, clinical associate professor at the University of Alabama Medical Center and a member of the food committee of the American College of Allergists (*Annals of Allergy*, August 1978).

Your job will be much easier if you avoid packaged, processed food as much as possible, carefully selecting only those items which you and your family are sure to tolerate.

One last note: some people are so sensitive to plastic and the chemicals it imparts to food that they cannot tolerate food and packaged in plastic wrap or tubs. If you suspect plastic-wrapped food may give you trouble, find a butcher who sells meat in cellophane paper. Buy other foods in bulk or loose and store them in glass jars at home.

The pesticide-free diet

Allergy to pesticides (which may be petroleum-based chemicals) is related to allergy to food additives, and can make the task of

TABLE 10

Contents of Some Common Foods

The information here will help you to distinguish between allergy to a basic food and allergy to one or more of the additives it may contain.

Food Category	Food	*Ingredients which may or may not appear on the label* Must Contain	May Also Contain
Meat, fish and vegetable protein	minced beef and onions	beef, onions and salt	sugar, modified starch, beef fat, E460 cellulose, E150 caramel, MSG, E450 sodium polyphosphates, stabilizer, emulsifying agent
	sausages, e.g. pork	pork	cereal, MSG, E450, E223, E307, E304 modified starch, guar gum E128
	cooked ham	ham	sugar, salt, various emulsifying agents e.g. E450, E250, E301, MSG
	nuts		various antioxidants e.g. E307
	fish fingers	fish, breadcrumbs	sugar, salt, modified starch E450, MSG, E110, E102

Food Category	Food	Ingredients which may or may not appear on the label: Must Contain	May Also Contain
Dairy products	margarine	animal or vegetable fat	milk, whey, various vegetable oils, salt, added vitamin D, emulsifiers, lecithin colouring e.g. E160
	yoghurt	milk	sugar, colours, citric acid stabilizer, guar gum, thickener
	skimmed milk	milk	emulsifiers, stabilizers, silica, lecithin, antioxidants e.g. E320, E160
Grain products	bread rolls	wheat flour	unspecified shortening, milk, eggs, sugar, yeast, cornflour, soya flour, iodine, emulsifiers E472, E481, preservative E472 and E282
	macaroni	wheat flour	egg, salt, milk, carageenan
	rice	rice	talcum and glucose
	wheat flour	wheat	barley flour, ascorbic acid, hypochlorite and other bleaching agents

TABLE 10—*Continued*

Food Category	Food	Ingredients which may or may not appear on the label: Must Contain	May Also Contain
Vegetables, canned		specified vegetables	unspecified natural flavour, salt, sugar, colourings e.g. E142, E102, E133
	tomato products	tomatoes	salt, unspecified sweetener, colourings, spices, onions, garlic
	tomato paste	tomatoes	salt, baking soda, flavouring
Fruit, canned		specified fruit, fruit juice	sugar, apple juice, vinegar, ascorbic acid, unspecified natural or artificial flavourings
	fruit pie filling	fruit, sugar, salt, modified starch	antioxidants e.g. E331, E330, citric acid, E401, stabilizer, thickener, preservatives e.g. E202
Beverages	orange squash	oranges, sugar	flavouring, preservative e.g. E223, E330, colours e.g. E110 and E102
	soda water	carbonated water	unspecified artificial or natural flavours and colours, caffeine

Food Category	Food	*Ingredients which may or may not appear on the label* Must Contain	May Also Contain
Sweeteners	fruit jam	specified fruit or fruits	E440 pectin, E330 citric acid, E163 anthocyanis, E124 Ponceau red 4R
Condiments	salad cream	eggs, vinegar, vegetable oil, sugar, lemon juice	E410 locust bean gum, E260 acetic acid, E102, E415 corn sugar gum
	brown sauce	vegetables, sugar	modified starch, E150, E202 preservative, guar gum, E102, E122, E151 colours

Colours

E102 tartrazine, E150 caramel, E151 black PN, E122 carmoisine red, E110 sunset yellow FCF, E124 Ponceau red 4R, E128 red 2G, E142 acid brilliant green, E133 brilliant blue, E160 alpha-carotene, beta-carotene, gamma-carotene, yellow orange colour.

Preservatives

E202 potassium sorbate, E223 sodium metabisulphite, E260 acetic acid, E250 sodium nitrite, E282 calcium propionate.

Antioxidants, emulsifiers and stabilizers

E301 sodium L ascorbate, E304 Palmitoyl L ascorbic acid, E307 synthetic alpha tocopherol, E320 butylated hyroxyanisole, E330 citric acid, E331 sodium citrate, E401 sodium alginate, E460 alpha cellulose, E450 sodium polyphosphates, E440 pectin, E410 locust bean gum, E415 corn sugar gum, E474 acetic acid esters of mono and di glycerides of fatty acids, E481 sodium stearoyl -2- lactylate

MSG monosodium glutamate

isolating exactly what a person is allergic to even more difficult, especially when that person is very sensitive.

'A person may eat some grapes today and they don't bother him. But three days later, he may eat grapes that were sprayed with chemicals, and those grapes bother him,' said Dr Falliers.

Dr Theron Randolph tested patients who swore they were allergic to peaches. After eating peaches from the supermarket, one patient developed a rash and welts, another had an attack of asthma, and a third a headache. When they ate peaches picked from an abandoned orchard where the fruit wasn't sprayed, all three felt perfectly fine.

'One good effect of this discovery,' writes Dr Randolph, 'was that patients who had long stopped eating fruit, from the belief that they were made sick by it, were able to start again, provided they ate only organically grown, uncontaminated fruits.' (*An Alternative Approach to Allergies*, Lippincott & Crowell, 1979.)

Tree fruits – such as peaches, apples and cherries – are sprayed with more chemicals, more often, than almost any other crop. But virtually no commercial produce escapes the blizzard of pesticides (insect and rodent killers), herbicides (weed killers) and fungicides (mould inhibitors). And once food has been sprayed, no amount of washing will get rid of it. Paring does no good, either. Chemicals penetrate the skin of the growing fruit or vegetable and infiltrate the pulp itself. So if you are chemically sensitive (a problem we cover in Chapter 4, Clearing the air) and you suspect allergy to chemical food sprays, eating only organically grown produce may be the only way to achieve total relief. Shop around for a local supplier or track down the nearest co-op.

Avoiding pesticides is one of many good reasons to plant a home vegetable garden – plus a couple of fast-growing dwarf fruit trees, even if you have just a few square yards of available space. Canning, freezing or drying your harvest gives you a year-round supply of nonallergenic fruits and vegetables at the right price: *low*.

Other special food problems

If you've ruled out everything we've mentioned so far and still suspect that your problems are caused by diet, think about the following.

Ragweed Relatives. Sunflower seeds and chamomile tea are members of the same plant family as ragweed and chrysanthemums. If you're allergic to ragweed, you could very well develop an allergy to those foods.

Iodine. As a nutrient, iodine is an essential mineral that prevents goitre. But 1 to 3 per cent of the population happens to be allergic to high levels of iodine in the diet over a period of time. Iodine itself isn't an allergen in the strict sense. Rather, iodine molecules are 'haptens' – a chemical that attaches itself to a protein which then triggers the reaction.

For a small number of people, eating a lot of iodine-rich foods – such as kelp, sea fish or iodized salt – can trigger or aggravate acne, eczema and other skin reactions. Iodine-sensitive people may also have to avoid other, unsuspected sources of iodine: certain drugs and food additives, dairy foods processed with equipment cleaned with iodine solutions and commercial breads baked with iodine-containing dough conditioners.

Alcohol. If you get a hangover from wine but not vodka, you could be allergic to grapes, but not grain. If you're allergic to grains such as wheat and corn, a few sips of whisky may make you feel positively dreadful. And since alcoholic beverages are fermented with yeast, all liquor spells trouble if you're allergic to yeast.

In other words, if you're allergic to a food, don't drink alcoholic beverages made from it. (Table 11 shows the food origin of most alcoholic beverages.)

Aside from its origin, though, alcohol of any kind tends to be a problem for people with allergies. Alcohol worsens food allergies of any kind by dilating blood vessels and by speeding up the absorption of foods into the bloodstream. One physician told us about a woman who usually tolerated prawns quite well – unless she had a cocktail or wine with dinner, in which case she suffered from hives, facial swelling and diarrhoea.

Sugar. If you are allergic to grains and grasses, cane sugar may trigger allergy. If you're allergic to corn, you could also be allergic to corn sugar. The same goes for cane and corn molasses. (Other people are allergic to beet sugar.) The problem is that food labels don't always tell you what sort of sugar or molasses you're getting.

'Sugar labelling is notoriously inadequate,' commented Dr Theron Randolph. 'And processed foods tend to contain all

TABLE 11

Food Content of Alcoholic Beverages

	Grains							Fruits				
Alcohol	Corn	Barley	Rye	Wheat	Oats	Rice	Milo (a grass)	Grape	Plum	Citrus	Apple	Pear
Cane												
Fruit	○							●	●	●	●	●
Grain	●	●	●	●	○	○	●					
Brandy												
Applejack	○										●	
Apricot	○											
Blackberry	○											
Cherry	○											
Cognac								●				
Fruit	○							●	●	●	●	●
Grape	○							●				
Juniper												
Neutral	○							●	●	●	●	●
Peach	○											
Plum	○								●			
Raisin	○							●				
Cordials and Liqueurs	●	●	●	●	●	○	○	●	●	●	●	●

SOURCE: *Reprinted by permission of the publisher from* Clinical Ecology, *by Lawrence Dickey (Springfield; Ill.: Charles C. Thomas, 1976), pp. 326 and 329.*

Key:

- ● More commonly used source materials
- ○ Sources used in smaller amounts or less frequently

Fruits				**Miscellaneous**										**Sugar, Yeast, Water**				
Apricot	Peach	Cherry	Berries	Carob	Hops	Juniper	Coconut	Cinnamon	Chocolate	Mint	Misc. Herbs	Cactus	Potato	Honey	Beet	Cane	Yeast	Water
																	●	●
●	●	●	●														●	●
																●	●	●
															○	○	●	●
●															○	○	●	●
			●												○	○	●	●
		●													○	○	●	●
															○	○	●	●
●	●	●	●												○	○	●	●
															○	○	●	●
						●											●	●
●	●	●	●												○	○	●	●
	●														○	○	●	●
															○	○	●	●
															○	○	●	●
●	●	●	●				●	●	●	●	●		○	○	●	●	●	●

TABLE 11—Continued

	Grains							Fruits				
	Corn	Barley	Rye	Wheat	Oats	Rice	Milo (a grass)	Grape	Plum	Citrus	Apple	Pear
Gin												
Cane												
Grain spirits	●	●	●	○	○	○	●			●		
Malt Beverages												
Ale	●	●	○	○	○	●	○					
Beer	●	●	○	○	○	●	○					
Flavoured beer	●	●	○	○	○	●	○	●		●		
Miscellaneous												
Aquavit				●						○		
Tequila												
Rum												
Domestic	●							●				
Jamaican												
Vodka												
Domestic	●	●	●	●								
Some imported	○			●								
Whisky												
Straight												

Key:

- ● More commonly used source materials
- ○ Sources used in smaller amounts or less frequently

	Fruits				Miscellaneous										Sugar, Yeast, Water				
	Apricot	Peach	Cherry	Berries	Carob	Hops	Juniper	Coconut	Cinnamon	Chocolate	Mint	Misc. Herbs	Cactus	Potato	Honey	Beet	Cane	Yeast	Water
							●		●		●	●					●	●	●
							●		○		○	●				○	○	●	●
						●												●	●
						●												●	●
						●												●	●
														●				●	●
													●				●	●	●
												○					●	●	●
																	●	●	●
														○		○	○	●	●
														○		●		●	●

TABLE 11—Continued

	Grains							**Fruits**				
	Corn	Barley	Rye	Wheat	Oats	Rice	Milo (a grass)	Grape	Plum	Citrus	Apple	Pear
Bourbon	●	●	●	○	○	○	○					
Corn	●	●	●	○	○	○	○					
Malt	●	●	●	○	○	○	○					
Rye	●	●	●	○	○	○	○					
Wheat	●	●	○	●	○	○	○					
Blended Straight												
Bourbon	●	●	●	○	●	●	○					
Corn	●	●	●	○	●	●	○					
Malt	●	●	●	○	●	●	○					
Rye	●	●	●	○	●	●	○					
Rye-malt	●	●	●	○	●	●	○					
Wheat	●	●	●	●	●	●	●					
Blended	●	●	●	●	○	○	○	○	○	○	○	○
Light	●	●	●	○	○	○	○	○	○	○	○	○
Spirit	●	●	●	○	○	○	○	○	○	○		
Canadian (blended)	●	●	●	●				●	●	○		
Unblended Scotch (all malt)	○	●										
Blended Scotch	●	●										
Irish		●	●	●	●							
Blended Irish		●	●	●	●	●		●	●	○		

Key:

- ● More commonly used source materials
- ○ Sources used in smaller amounts or less frequently

Fruits				**Miscellaneous**										**Sugar, Yeast, Water**				
Apricot	Peach	Cherry	Berries	Carob	Hops	Juniper	Coconut	Cinnamon	Chocolate	Mint	Misc. Herbs	Cactus	Potato	Honey	Beet	Cane	Yeast	Water
																	●	●
																	●	●
																	●	●
																	●	●
																	●	●
																	●	●
																	●	●
																	●	●
																	●	●
																	●	●
																	●	●
○	○	○	○	○									○		●	●	●	●
○	○	○	○	○									○				●	●
													○		●	●	●	●
															○	●	●	●
															○	○	●	●
															○	○	●	●
																○	●	●
															○	○	●	●

TABLE 11—Continued

Wine	Grains							Fruits				
	Corn	Barley	Rye	Wheat	Oats	Rice	Milo (a grass)	Grape	Plum	Citrus	Apple	Pear
Apricot	●											
Blackberry	●											
Champagne								●				
Cherry	●											
Cider (apple wine)	●										●	
Citrus	●									●		
Flavoured	●							●	●	●	●	●
Fruit	●							●	●	●	●	●
Grape	●							●				
Honey	●											
Peach	●											
Perry (pear wine)	●											●
Plum	●								●			
Prune	●								●			
Raisin	●							●				
Raspberry	●											
Sherry	●							●				
Vermouth	○	○	○	○	○	○		●				

Key:

- ● More commonly used source materials
- ○ Sources used in smaller amounts or less frequently

Fruits				**Miscellaneous**										**Sugar, Yeast, Water**				
Apricot	Peach	Cherry	Berries	Carob	Hops	Juniper	Coconut	Cinnamon	Chocolate	Mint	Misc. Herbs	Cactus	Potato	Honey	Beet	Cane	Yeast	Water
●															●	●	●	●
			●												●	●	●	●
															●		●	●
		●													●	●	●	●
															●	●	●	●
															●	●	●	●
●	●	●	●								●				●	●	●	●
●	●	●	●												●	●	●	●
															●	●	●	●
														●	●	●	●	●
	●														●	●	●	●
															●	●	●	●
															●	●	●	●
															●	●	●	●
															●	●	●	●
			●												●	●	●	●
															●	●	●	●
											●				●	●	●	●

three types – cane, corn and beet – in a liquid blend.' To avoid a sugar allergy problem. Dr Randolph continued, 'prepare desserts at home so you know what you're getting.'

From the standpoint of allergy, honey is a relatively safe substitute for sugar since few people are allergic to it.* Once in a blue moon, buckwheat honey may be a problem for those sensitive to buckwheat, or orange blossom honey for those sensitive to citrus. Pure maple syrup is also safe. Saccharin, however, is out. Not only is it strongly suspected of causing cancer, but as a coal tar product saccharin has been known to cause allergy.

Coffee. Doctors such as Theron Randolph feel that coffee should be eliminated entirely if an allergic person is to find any relief at all from food allergies. The caffeine alone will make your heart race, your blood pressure climb, your nerves jangle and your kidneys and adrenal glands work overtime – allergies or no.

Switching to a decaffeinated brew may not help. Some doctors report that certain people are allergic to the chemicals used to remove caffeine from coffee beans. Which just goes to show that coffee, like any processed food, has its share of additives and pesticide residues. To add fuel to the fire, most coffee beans are roasted with gas heat – a growing source of allergy problems (which we discuss in Chapter 4, Clearing the air). And coffee drinkers tend to take their brew several times a day, every day – a sure sign of allergic addiction. Add it all up, and it comes as no surprise that coffee wreaks havoc with so many allergy diets.

Cola drinks and other soft drinks, which also contain caffeine, can aggravate allergy. So can chocolate. Your wisest step is to wean yourself not only from coffee, but its cousins, too.

Chocolate. Just what is it about chocolate that puts it on so many allergists' blacklists? For one thing, chocolate sweets, sauces, icings, puddings and cakes are full of sugar, which may cause problems on its own, as we've just mentioned. But there's more to chocolate's bad reputation than sugar. One doctor in particular – Joseph H. Fries, affiliated with Methodist Hospital in Brooklyn, New York – feels that the many additives that

* The American Academy of Pediatrics says that children under six months, however, shouldn't eat honey because it's been blamed for some cases of infant botulism, a severe form of food poisoning.

embellish chocolate are the real culprits (*Annals of Allergy*, October 1978).

Even 'pure' chocolate is a highly complex product. Like coffee, it contains methylxanthines and other druglike substances. Plus it's loaded with phenylethylamine, a substance that produces a giddy response comparable to an amphetamine high.

If you are truly allergic to chocolate, you'll also have to be careful to avoid its close relatives – not only cocoa, but cola and karaya gum (often listed as 'vegetable gum'). Luckily, nature has given us carob – a dark, sweet powder that can be substituted for chocolate. Carob powder and carob snacks can easily be found in all health food stores and many supermarkets.

Could it be your water?

If you've tried everything and still can't pin down the cause of your problems, give some thought to the water you're drinking – and cooking with, and brushing your teeth with. Tap water is likely to contain chemicals that are deliberately added (chlorine or fluoride), plus industrial wastes and agricultural chemicals (like formaldehyde) that inevitably seep into local water supplies. And that goes for wells, springs, rivers or reservoirs, too.

(Incidentally, if you find you are allergic to fluoride – only a few people are – you'll also have to avoid fluoride in toothpaste, vitamin supplements and dental treatments.)

As a vehicle for so many substances – even in amounts well below so-called toxic levels – tap water has been known to aggravate allergy in highly sensitive people.

William J. Rea, a cardiovascular (heart) doctor in Dallas, Texas, specializing in environmentally triggered reactions, has seen a whole slew of symptoms squarely attributed to something in the water – everything from hay fever, post-nasal drip, bronchitis and asthma to mouth pain, mouth ulcers, nausea, diarrhoea, bloating and urinary problems, among others.

We hope you aren't that sensitive. But water is certainly something to take into account when trying to solve unexplained problems.

The ideal method of testing for water allergy is to fast for two days in a controlled setting – a hospital unit free of airborne contamination – and then sample various waters such as tap water, bottled water and so on to determine which do and which don't cause problems. For home testing, you can start by substituting bottled spring water for tap water for four or five days and see if your symptoms subside. Be sure to buy bottled water in glass containers, not plastic, which leaches chemicals into the water. Even that precaution may be in vain, however. 'Bottled spring water is transported in plastic-lined trucks and stored in plastic vats, *then* bottled in glass,' says Dr Rea. So if symptoms persist, switch to another brand until you find one you can tolerate.

'We try to encourage people to drink the least expensive water they can tolerate, because they have to not only drink it, but cook their food in it and wash in it,' says Sue Herbig, R.N., assistant to Dr Rea and general manager of the Ecology Unit at Carrolton Community Hospital in Carrolton, Texas, a small community near Dallas.

Of course, anything you can do to purify your tap water is likely to be cheaper in the long run than going through stockpiles of bottled water daily. For some people, ousting allergenic substances from their tap water is as easy as boiling it for thirty minutes or storing it in an uncovered glass pitcher in the refrigerator overnight to allow the volatile chemicals to escape. Others will have to look into home water-treatment equipment.

Running your tap water through ordinary charcoal filters won't do the job unless the charcoal is combined with some other purification material, such as activated carbon. In fact, you might as well skip the charcoal and just use the carbon. Activated carbon is charcoal that's been specially treated with heat and steam in the absence of oxygen so that particles cling to it like a pollution magnet; water that passes through it is as clean as mountain dew. Studies show that activated carbon filters effectively remove chlorine, industrial chemicals and some pesticides, as well as bad taste and odours. Of course, a carbon filter must be replaced every three weeks or twenty gallons of water (whichever comes first) to avoid recontamination.

The best activated carbon filters come in double canisters that are installed below the sink and then attached to a separate tap that bypasses the existing water line. They're more expensive than the small filters that hook up to your tap. But if you have a water problem, they're worth it. (See the Appendix for addresses of suppliers.)

Dr Rea says that some water-sensitive people do equally well on distilled water. Distilled water is heated until it turns to steam, and then recondensed into water. Presumably, the chemicals and other debris are left behind. In truth, only 'fractional' water distillers actually get rid of all objectionable particles. (Addresses of suppliers of fractional water distillers also appear in the Appendix.)

Water distillers have several drawbacks. They require a lot of water and they're hard to keep clean. If you decide you want a water distiller anyway, look for one that's easy to maintain.

Once your tap water has been filtered or distilled, store it in clean, glass containers in the refrigerator. Or you can buy bottled distilled water – just make sure it's been 'fractionally' distilled.

If you are indeed allergic to something in your water, the most practical arrangement of all probably would be to purify your tap water and drink bottled water away from home.

Rotary diets (or: If it's Tuesday, this must be chicken)

If you're allergic to a food that you eat several times a week, your body is never free of that food and you'll never feel completely well. Taking it from there, Dr Herbert J. Rinkel, a pioneer in allergy treatment, proposed that some people can build up their tolerance to foods – and prevent new food allergies from developing – by following a four-day 'Rotary Diet'. First, you avoid the problem food or foods completely for up to six months, to give your body an allergy rest period. Then you reintroduce the food to your diet – but no more often than once every four days. This four-day rotation allows antibody levels to subside before you once again encounter the food in question. If you eat beef on Monday, for instance, you don't eat beef in any form until Friday or later. Instead, you eat chicken, then fish, then lamb (or other meats from those food families, in whatever order you prefer). Eventually, rotation increases your tolerance to beef – or any other rotated food – simply by exposing you to it less often. Best of all, perhaps, a

Rotary Diet allows you to eat at least some of the foods you really love without suffering for it.

'The key to overcoming food allergy is rotation,' emphasized Dr Boxer, one of the small but growing number of allergists in America who now prescribe the Rotary Diet.

In fact, following a Rotary Diet is all some people need to do to control their food allergies, Dr Boxer told us. 'If you took all the people who are allergic to foods and did nothing more than rotate their foods, you would probably diminish their symptoms by 80 per cent,' he said. 'That's because the average allergic person is eating something he or she is allergic to every day, day in and day out.

'But you can often increase your ability to tolerate that food just by eating it less often,' he continued. 'Let's say I'm very allergic to eggs but I've been eating them every day, because I didn't know it. I've been having all kinds of symptoms and all of a sudden somebody tells me to eat them only every fourth day, and I do that. Over four, five or six months, or one or two years, I will probably gradually get better and have less trouble, I might be a little sick every fourth day, then less and less unless I have a 'fixed' food allergy (in which case avoidance will *not* alter subsequent responses), which is considerably less common than cyclic food allergy which does tend to respond to rotation. And I'll still be better on the other days. So you really will find that the patient will improve. It's a very effective technique.

'Some people come in here and I don't even test them,' he added. 'They say, "I can't afford testing" or "I don't have the time" or "I hate needles. Is there something you could suggest?" I put them on a Rotary Diet.

'And it's something people could try on their own, even before they go to a doctor. You may feel so well on a Rotary Diet that you really don't need any professional help.' If you're severely allergic, you will need more help, Dr Boxer added. But he said it still couldn't hurt to rotate foods.

All you need to start your own Rotary Diet is a list of foods to which you are not allergic, plus others to which you are only mildly allergic.

'Completely avoid all those foods to which you have immediate, severe reactions,' says Dr Randolph, a leading advocate of the Rotary Diet. 'Then allow yourself foods to which you have no allergy or only mild allergies, once every four days.'

A sample Rotary Diet is shown here. But your diet may be completely different. No two people are allergic to the same identical list of foods. Nor do they have the same likes and dislikes. Plan your diet to manage individual allergies. To help you, Table 12 lists commonly eaten members of each major food family. On your day for melon, for example (assuming you can tolerate melon), you can choose from any of the foods in that family – cucumbers, watermelon, cantaloupe – provided you don't eat any food in that family again for the next three days. And so on. Dr Boxer emphasizes that some people may need to rotate foods every seven or fourteen days. Four days is the *minimum* interval recommended.

The immediate advantage of a Rotary Diet is that it prevents the gradual buildup of troublemaking antibodies, thus enabling you to continue to enjoy foods to which you were moderately allergic. Dr Marshall Mandell, author of and contributor to two books on allergy, says that a Rotary Diet will, in time, enable an allergic person to eat 50 to 70 per cent of the foods he or she was previously allergic to – that is, all but those foods that cause severe symptoms every time they're eaten.

The long-term advantage of a Rotary Diet is that it prevents you from developing allergies to yet more foods. And it's worth repeating that Rotary Diets also increase your tolerance of airborne allergy offenders – pollens, dust, mould, animal dander and chemicals.

What people miss most on a Rotary Diet is not so much their favourite foods but the spontaneity of eating what they want, whenever they want. A therapeutic diet of any kind takes at least some organization and planning. If you are in the habit of not deciding what to serve for dinner until you're driving home from work at 5.15, a Rotary Diet will require some self-discipline. But the minor inconveniences are better than feeling miserable all the time. Feeling better, in fact, will reinforce your determination to stick with it and enjoy what you *can* eat all the more.

Doctors who treat food allergies with the Rotary Diet say people will have better luck if they follow a few basic rules.

1. For the first few weeks, try your best to avoid all foods to which you know you are even moderately allergic – giving

Sample Rotary Diet

	Sunday	**Monday**	**Tuesday**
Breakfast	fresh melon natural yoghurt (cow's) rosehip tea	poached or boiled eggs fresh apple lemon verbena tea	grilled kipper fresh orange basil tea
Lunch	grilled lamb chops, peas, green beans, mint	cashew nuts, aubergine, tomato and garlic fried in sesame seed oil or olive oil	goat's cheese, raw celery
	apricots or peaches	blackcurrants with honey or apple	raspberries, strawberries or blackberries
Dinner	salmon, boiled rice, spinach	grilled steak, potatoes, steamed broccoli	roast chicken, carrots, parsley
Snack	walnuts	currants	hazelnuts

yourself an allergic 'rest period'. If you wish, you can start a Rotary Diet without that initial rest period. However, you'll probably experience some symptoms for the first few cycles.

2. Learn about food families. Nature is full of surprises, and learning about relationships between foods can be fun. White potatoes and sweet potatoes are not related, for instance. Neither are tuna and prawns. Or raisins and prunes. Peanuts are not really nuts, but legumes. Ginger, clove and cinnamon are three totally different plants. So there is no such thing as an allergy to all spices. Or all nuts, for that matter. Or all fish. Chances are you can find suitable and appetizing alternatives to your favourite foods by choosing members of unrelated families.

Surprises work the other way, too. Asparagus is related to onions and garlic. Cucumbers are related to melons. Carrots

Wednesday	Thursday	Friday	Saturday
oatmeal porridge prunes pineapple juice or nettle tea	sago crispbread and banana	rye bread or crispbread	grapefruit, buckwheat, cooked with honey
	peppermint tea	fresh grapes dandelion coffee or chamomile tea	grapefruit juice or raspberry leaf tea
sardines with lettuce and cucumber fresh pineapple	cauliflower with cow's milk cheese fresh pear	plain omelette (olive oil for frying), grilled tomato plums or nectarines	tuna fish with avocado pear and lemon juice gooseberries and honey
grilled pork chops, braised onions with red and green peppers	grilled plaice, artichoke, boiled beetroot	veal steak, courgettes	turkey, asparagus, turnip
peanuts	brazil nuts	almonds	dates

are related to celery. Working out a Rotary Diet teaches you to think about foods in a new way.

3. Diversify your foods. By working in members of food families that are new and different for you, you make your menus more interesting and find it easier to stick to the diet. Within familiar food families, eat a variety of foods. Diversification also helps to prevent future allergies.

4. Stick to primary foods – fish, meat, poultry, fruits and vegetables – as close to their natural state as possible. Avoid secondary or combination foods – mixes, sauces, blends or packaged foods.

5. Similarly, rotate only wholesome, nutrition-packed food, not cupcakes, soda and the like. 'I tell my patients to rotate *and* stay off junk food,' said Dr Boxer. And stay away from alcohol,

coffee and tobacco. (We'll tell you more about the importance of a wholesome diet in Chapter 12, Nutrition for allergy control.)

6. Select a minimum number of foods for each meal and fill up on them, rather than choose a potpourri of multiple foods. For instance, an eight-ounce portion of broiled fish, half a plateful of steamed broccoli and a large potato would comprise a typical Rotary Diet meal.

7. Whenever possible, avoid eating the same food more than once a day.

8. Grow as much organic, additive-free food as you can. Or buy organic food when you're *absolutely* sure it's the real thing and not a fake-labelled, high-cost ripoff.

9. Don't forget to rotate spices, cooking oils and beverages. Soyabean, safflower and sunflower oils, for instance, are derived from different families. Among herb teas, lemongrass, mint, sassafras, verbena, hibiscus and rosehips are unrelated to each other.

10. Write down everything you eat. Otherwise, it's practically impossible to keep foods straight.

TABLE 12

Food Families

Allergy to one member of a family of foods often means sensitivity to other members. This chart of commonly eaten foods will help you to plan an enjoyable, varied diet and avoid food allergies at the same time.

Family	Plant Foods
Apple	Apple, crab apple, pear, quince
Banana	Banana and plantain
Beech	Beechnut and chestnut
Berries	Blackberry, boysenberry, loganberry, raspberry, rose hips, strawberry
Birch	Filbert, hazelnut, oil of birch (wintergreen)
Buckwheat	Buckwheat, garden sorrel, rhubarb
Cashew	Cashew, mango, pistachio
Chocolate	Chocolate (cocoa), cola, gum karaya

Family	Plant Foods
Citrus	Citron, grapefruit, kumquat, lemon, lime, orange, tangerine
Composite	Artichoke, chamomile, chicory, dandelion, endive, escarole, lettuce, safflower, sunflower seeds, tarragon
Conifer	Juniper berry (gin) and pine nuts
Fungus	Certain cheeses, mushroom, truffle, yeast. (Antibiotics and the moulds that cause inhalant allergy belong to this family.)
Ginger	Cardamom, ginger, turmeric
Gooseberry	Currant and gooseberry
Goosefoot or Beet	Beet, chard, lamb's lettuce, spinach, sugar beet
Grain (cereal or grass)	Bamboo shoots, barley, corn, lemongrass, millet, oats, rice, rye, sorghum, sugar cane, wheat, wild rice
Heath	Blueberry, cranberry, huckleberry
Laurel	Avocado, bay leaf, cinnamon, sassafras
Legume	Alfalfa, bean (kidney, lentil, lima, mung, navy, pinto, soya, string), carob, guar gum, gum acacia, kudzu, liquorice, pea (black-eyed, chick-pea, green), peanut
Lily	Asparagus, chive, garlic, leek, onion, sarsaparilla, shallot
Mallow	Cottonseed, hibiscus, okra
Melon or Gourd	Cantaloupe, cucumber, gherkin, honeydew, muskmelon, pumpkin, squash, watermelon
Mint	Basil, catnip, horehound, lemon balm (melissa), marjoram, mint, oregano, peppermint, rosemary, sage, savory, spearmint, thyme
Morning-Glory	Jicama and sweet potato
Mulberry	Breadfruit, fig, mulberry
Mustard	Horseradish, mustard, radish, swede, turnip, watercress and varieties of cabbage: broccoli, brussels sprouts, cauliflower, Chinese cabbage, collards, kale, kohlrabi
Myrtle	Allspice, clove, guava

TABLE 12 – *Continued*

Family	Plant Foods
Nightshade or Potato	Aubergine, potato, tobacco, tomato. This family includes all foods called 'pepper' (except black and white pepper), such as cayenne, chili pepper, green pepper, hot pepper sauce, paprika, pimiento, red pepper
Palm	Coconut, date, sago starch
Parsley	Carrot, celeriac, celery, lovage, parsley, parsnip. Also these spices: angelica, anise, caraway, celery seed, coriander, cumin, dill, fennel
Plum	Almond, apricot, cherry, nectarine, peach, plum, prune, wild cherry
Walnut	Black walnut, butternut, English walnut, hickory nut, pecan
Yam	Chinese potato and yam

Family	Birds
Dove	Dove and pigeon
Duck	Duck, goose and their eggs
Grouse	Ruffed grouse (partridge)
Pheasant	Chicken, guinea fowl, peafowl, pheasant, quail and their eggs
Turkey	Turkey and their eggs

Family	Fish
Bass	White perch and yellow bass
Codfish	Cod, haddock, hake, pollack, whiting
Flounder	Dab, flounder, halibut, plaice, sole, turbot
Mackerel	Albacore, bonito, mackerel, skipjack, tuna
Perch	Sauger, walleye, yellow perch
Salmon	All salmon species and all trout species

Family	Mammals
Bovine	Beef cattle (including veal), buffalo, goat, sheep (lamb and mutton) and their milk and milk products
Deer	Caribou, deer (venison), elk, moose, reindeer

Family	Shellfish
Clam	Clam and quahog
Lobster	Crayfish, langoustine, lobster
Shrimp	Prawn and shrimp

Foods without Relatives

The following foods are the only members of their biological family which are commonly used as foods in most parts of the world.

Arrowroot
Brazil nut
Caper
Catfish
Chicle (chief ingredient of chewing gum)
Coffee
Crab
Elderberry
Flaxseed
Grape
Hog (pork)
Honey
Kiwi fruit
Macadamia nut
Maple sugar
Nutmeg (mace)
Olive
Oyster
Papaya
Persimmon
Pineapple
Poppy seed
Rabbit
Saffron
Scallop
Sesame seed
Squirrel
Swordfish
Tapioca
Tea
Vanilla
Whitefish

SOURCE: Adapted from *Clinical Ecology*, by Lawrence Dickey (Springfield, Ill.: Charles C. Thomas, 1976).

An Alternative Approach to Allergies, by Theron Randolph and Ralph Moss (New York: Harper and Row, 1980).

If you go off the diet

Sooner or later, you're going to eat something you shouldn't – largely because eating is not only a nutritional duty but a social and aesthetic experience. Dinners are shared in other people's homes. Birthdays and anniversaries are celebrated in restaurants. So are business lunches, even family get-togethers. (We won't even *mention* holidays!) Few people have 100 per cent control over their diet all the time. Besides, nobody likes to be a killjoy. So you eat the cheese dip or chicken croquettes and hope for the best. Thankfully, there are a few emergency measures you can use to undo your errors. An ice pack will take the sting out of the hot and pounding lip discomfort of a food reaction. For more generalized symptoms, you can force yourself to vomit recently eaten food by sticking your fingers down your throat. Sounds unpleasant, we know. But quick and lasting relief is worth a few seconds of discomfort, and several doctors we interviewed suggest the technique. If you prefer, you can take a cathartic like plain milk of magnesia instead, to help nudge food through the intestines more rapidly.

Doctors also tell us that a solution of mineral salts – such as plain old baking soda diluted in plenty of water – seems to help neutralize the effects of an allergic food, nipping an adverse reaction in the bud. For people watching their sodium intake, potassium bicarbonate alone is a better alternative. It's available at most chemists.

Mineral salts are all right in a pinch – before a dinner party or other occasion where what you eat is beyond your control, or as an after-dinner bromide. Don't make a daily habit of mineral salts or cathartics, though – they're strictly emergency outs, to help you cope with inadvertent violations. Avoidance is still the name of the game.

Allergy doctors who prescribe the Rotary Diet encourage people with food allergies to follow the four-day plan for life, speaking well of its ability both to relieve existing food allergies and prevent future problems. (Not to mention the fact that allergy injections have a poor track record for removing problems.) Invariably, compliance comes down to two things: how allergic you are, and how essential is the offending food to your diet. If you get giant hives or splitting headaches from wheat, you'll need little encouragement to avoid it completely. But if you feel only slight fatigue or a little depressed, you'll probably be inclined to risk minor discomforts for the convenience of eating wheat. You really owe it to yourself to rotate, though – or to encourage your child to rotate.

We're not so naive as to suggest that sticking to a Rotary Diet is always easy. Few people, after all, have the patience and perseverance to deal with a rigid schedule of permitted and forbidden foods with no let-up for months on end. Doctors know that, too. Kendall Gerdes, an allergist in Denver, Colorado, told us that some people are able to return to their customary eating habits as long as they periodically return to a Rotary Diet long enough to build up their resistance to troublesome foods. 'Three months down the line,' says Dr Gerdes, 'I want them to go back on a Rotary Diet for three cycles to reestablish their tolerance.'

Leniency of that sort helps enormously when you're trying to get your allergic child to stick to a Rotary Diet – although Dr Boxer told us that he found some kids are often surprisingly co-operative about food rotation. 'We've got a lot of kids who are great about it,' he told us. 'They'll say, "No, thanks, this isn't my day to eat that food." ' In some ways, children may find a Rotary Diet easier to follow than adults, since it all seems like a game. And they don't have twenty or thirty years of entrenched eating habits to change.

But childhood is dotted with enough important social events like birthday parties and school festivities to tempt even the most self-disciplined child. On special occasions, it's probably wiser to allow children to eat forbidden food an to have them feel they are different or less healthy than their friends – unless they're going to get severely ill.

Preventing food allergies in children

Speaking of children, youngsters tend to have more food allergies than adults. It's never too early to take steps to prevent those food allergies. Even what women eat during pregnancy can head off eventual sensitivities.

'If you do the right thing early enough, allergies can be controlled,' Dr Falliers told us. 'I have so many examples. I've seen some of the worst asthmatics have three or four very healthy children.'

Food allergies may be passed on to the developing foetus by way of the placenta. Expectant mothers should avoid highly allergic foods or foods to which they know they're allergic.

And of course, doing the 'right thing' after childbirth includes breastfeeding, if at all possible.

'I've found time and time again that children who are nursed for at least the first year or fifteen months of life develop substantially fewer allergies,' says Dr Stigler. 'Starting with the infant, the only milk I want children to have is breast milk.'

The longer an infant stays away from cow's milk, the less apt he or she is to become allergic to milk – or anything else, for that matter. As we mentioned in Chapter 1, What is an allergy?, withholding cow's milk from babies' diets may even prevent nonfood allergies – such as dust and pollen sensitivities – later in their lives.

An editorial in the medical journal, *Lancet*, points out that there's something about cow's milk that encourages sensitivity to environmental allergens of all kinds. Perhaps, suggest the authors, it's because of milk's effect on the intestine. In any case, they encourage breast-feeding in no uncertain terms: '. . . children born to allergic parents would be better off without the acquaintance of cow's milk and dairy products in the first six months. We must be sure that simple practical advice about this now reaches the many parents whose children will be genetically predisposed to allergy.' (*Lancet*, February 12 1977.)

'There's nothing as good as breast milk,' Dr Falliers told us, adding, 'I could talk for the next hour about the reasons for breast-feeding – not simply to avoid allergy to cow's milk, but to provide antibodies that help the white cells resist disease.'

'Twenty years ago, I was batting about 50 to 60 per cent in getting mothers to breastfeed,' said Dr Stigler. 'Now, I think I have only two mothers in my practice who are not breastfeeding. So, it's up to 95 per cent or better at this point. It's not 100 per cent because there's the uncommon person who doesn't want to. And there's the rare person who can't.'

Suppose the nursing mother has allergies herself?

'If the mother has food allergies, she must avoid allergic food to avoid transmitting her allergies to her baby,' Dr Stigler told us. Nursing babies may not inherit the same identical allergies. Mum may be allergic to corn and the baby may be allergic to something else. Even if Mum doesn't have food allergies, though, what she eats can affect her breastfed baby. 'Wheat comes out in breast milk. Soy comes out in breast milk. Cow's milk comes out in breast milk,' says Dr Stigler. 'For example, the colicky breastfed infant is most often allergic to milk – not the mother's milk but the cow's milk the mother is drinking. Take the mother off cow's milk, and the baby is well in two or three days.'

Either way, nursing mothers, like pregnant women, should avoid foods to which they know they are allergic or to which their baby is likely to become allergic – especially cow's milk. To compensate for that source of calcium, Dr Stigler asks nursing mothers to continue to take the calcium-containing supplements routinely prescribed during pregnancy, and to eat other dietary sources of calcium. (See Chapter 12, Nutrition for allergy control, for more on calcium supplements.)

When the time comes to introduce solid foods into a baby's diet, don't blitz the child with several foods at once. Single foods should be added one at a time to check for tolerance before adding subsequent foods. A Rotary Diet, in fact, is an excellent way to head off food allergies in children born to allergy-prone parents.

'The best answer is for mothers to breastfeed their babies for a full year,' Dr Randolph told us. 'Then hold back on the speed with which they introduce new foods. And when they do add them, rotate. For instance, instead of feeding a mixed cereal three times a day, give oats once every four days, rice once every four days, wheat once every four days and so on. A Rotary Diet should be used from infancy on.'

In other words, food allergies may run in families – but they don't have to.

Your strategy against food allergies will be all the more successful if you pursue it as a game in which you are pitted against a crafty but not invincible opponent. Using the tactics and 'inside information' given here, you can score a victory.

CHAPTER 4

CLEARING THE AIR

Every day, each of us breathes in two heaped tablespoons of assorted particles – dust, pollen, mould, smoke, carbon, tar, rubber, metals, bacteria – to say nothing of countless chemicals. Two tablespoons is a lot for the body to deal with. Most of us, however, can cope with those particles; our respiratory tracts are equipped with tiny fibres called cilia that help push pollutants back out of the body.

But a highly sensitive person *can't* cope. A small amount of those same particles can put him in the hospital with a life-threatening attack of bronchial asthma. Other, moderately sensitive people will suffer lesser degrees of misery. In some cases, allergic people can breathe small particles, but other particles such as dust and pollen make them sick. Other people only react to airborne chemicals. A few react to *everything*.

Apparently, allergic individuals just can't handle all the debris in our air, minuscule as it may seem. And more people than ever are suffering from these 'inhalant' allergies – for a number of reasons. To begin with, converting forests and grasslands to fields of concrete has removed natural means of air filtration for pollen and dust. That, in turn, has fostered growth of more primitive vegetation such as moulds, yeasts, fungi and bacteria – all highly allergenic. Added to that is the chemical free-for-all generated by home and industry: vapours from household cleaning products, furnaces, and solvents in furniture – to name a *few* sources. (See Table 13 for a complete list.)

If there were plenty of fresh air to dilute the load on their lungs, allergic people would stand a far better chance of tolerating it all. But high oil prices have led us to tighten up homes and office buildings, piling on insulation and sealing cracks with weather stripping. In these energy-efficient buildings the total volume of air in a room – pollutants and all – is completely replaced only *once every several hours*; in a 'leaky' building without loads of insulation, the air is replaced every hour or two. So if you live or work in a tight building, you spend a lot of time in a place peppered with pollutants – which provoke itchy red eyes, coughing fits, swollen joints and various other health complaints.

'Indoor air pollution is eight or ten times more troublesome than outdoor levels of air pollution in causing chronic illness,' says Theron Randolph, author of two books on environmental illness.

Three possible avenues of relief exist. One is to clean up the environment as a whole. That's a task we can't even *begin* to address here. Equally important – especially for allergy sufferers – is to create a clean environment *indoors*, where most of us spend the majority of our time. Third, you can create an unpolluted room in your home – a personal 'oasis' where you can take refuge from allergens, be they dust, pollen or chemicals. Combining the last two steps will help you to tolerate better the outside world.

'If we take an allergic person and put him or her in a clean room at home and clean up his or her office as much as we can, we can diminish his or her allergy by an enormous degree,' says Joseph J. McGovern, Jr, an allergist in Oakland, California, who specializes in environmental illness.

The more pollutants you can avoid, the better you feel. So along with an in-depth focus on several of the most troublesome allergens in the air, this chapter will offer useful advice on how to clear them out of your personal environment. We'll also show you how to increase ventilation and purify the air (without wasting energy). *Keep in mind that whether you're allergic to one inhalant or fifty, the key to relief is to reduce your overall exposure as much as possible, using the most practical and effective means available.*

Dust is everywhere

Do you notice that you feel worse:

– when the house is being cleaned?

TABLE 13

Common Sources of Odours, Fumes and Airborne Particles That Can Trigger Allergy

Many airborne particles can also cause allergic reactions if they're touched. Pollen, for instance, can cause eczema and rashes on the face (especially the cheeks) if you're outdoors during a heavy pollen barrage. Cosmetics, of course, are notorious for wreaking havoc with skin and eyes either by direct contact or from the fragrances they emit. Clothing, too, can cause both contact and inhalant allergies, due to detergents, factory treatments, bleaches, dyes, dry-cleaning processes and so on. (See Chapter 7, Contact (skin) allergies, for more details on cosmetic and clothing allergies.)

Dusts

Attic	Chalk rubber	Feed mill
Broom	Chicken coop	Rugs
Carpet sweeper	Construction	Toys
Carpeting	Curtains	Vacuum cleaner
Cellar	Dusty books	Wrestling on floor rug or gym mat

Mould and Mildew

Any place that harbours water – leaky pipes and taps, sluggish drains, damp or flooded basements and crawl spaces.

Damp towels and clothing	Old, peeling wallpaper and paste	Refrigerator drip trays and rubber door gaskets
Foam rubber pillows	Overstuffed furniture	Roof leaks into attics or behind walls
Hay and grain fields	Paint	Vaporizers
Leather goods	Pet litter	Vegetable bins
Old caulking around sinks and tubs	Poorly vented wardrobes	Woodpiles
Old mattresses	Potted plants	

Pollen and Flowers

Flowers related to ragweed (goldenrod and chrysanthemums)	Pungent odours of some flowers (roses, violets, lilacs and others)
Grasses	Trees
	Weeds

Animal Fur and Feathers (Dander)

Animals – dog, cat, bird, horse, rabbit, cow, gerbil, hamster, hog, sheep, goat (mohair) and others
Feather pillows
Visit to zoo, circus or farm
Wool blankets

Fumes

Asphalt and tar (roof application, hot roadways)
Bus stations
Car exhaust
Chlorinated swimming pools
Dry cleaning fluids
Fuel oil
Garages
Gas appliances
Kerosene
Lighter fluid
Lubricating grease and oil
Machinery
Motor boat exhaust
Naphtha
Oil furnace
Petrol stations
Refineries

Household odours

Ammonia
Bleaches
Bubble bath
Cedar bags
Cedar wardrobes
Chalk
Cleaners (especially those containing carbon tetrachloride)
Sandpaper
Detergents
Disinfectants
Dyes
Fabrics (wash & wear)
Floor wax
Furniture polish
Glue
Insect sprays
Magazines
Moth balls and crystals
Newspapers
Paper tissue
Particle board
Perfumes
Plastics (soft)
Room deodorants
Scouring powder
Shoe polish
Soaps (powder and bar)
Starch
Window cleaner

Paint Odours

Enamel
Lacquer
Latex paint
Mineral spirits
Oil paint
Paint remover
Rubber-based paint
Shellac
Spray paint
Stains
Thinner
Varnish

Smoke

Charcoal
Cigar
Cigarette
Coal
Fireplace
Incense
Leaf fire
Pipe
Tobacco
Rubbish fire
Wood fire

TABLE 13 – *Continued*

Wood Smells		
Evergreen (including Christmas trees)	Lumber	Sawdust
	Sanding dust	

Cosmetics and First-Aid Products		
After-shave lotions	Hair removers (depilatories)	Perfumes
Antiseptics	Hair sprays	Powders
Astringents	Hair-waving lotions	Rouge and blushers
Cold creams	Lipsticks	Rubbing alcohol
Colognes	Lotions	Sachets
Deodorants	Mascara	Shampoos
Eye shadows and pencils	Mouthwashes	Shaving creams
Face creams	Nail polish	Tanning creams
Face powders	Nail polish remover	

Office and Industry		
Asphalt	Ink	Rubber goods (tyres, sheeting, hose, etc.)
Carbon paper	Marking pens	Smoke
Carpeting	Metal shops	Stencils
Correction fluid	Mill dusts	Sulphuric acid and hydrochloric acid fumes
Duplicators	Paints	Tar
Felt-tip markers	Paper	Typewriter pads
Formaldehyde	Perfumes	Typewriter ribbon
Fumes from galvanizing plant	Photocopier	Warehouse dusts
	Photographic materials	
	Plastics	

Food Smells		
Beans	Fish, prawns	Spices
Beer	Flour	Starch
Coffee	Frying odour	Vinegar
Egg	Onion	

– when the first cold snap of autumn prompts the heating to come on?
– in libraries, storerooms or other dusty areas?
– when bedding is being changed or the mattress turned?

If you answered yes to any of those questions, there's a good chance you're allergic to dust.

Plain ordinary house dust is one of the most common causes of allergy – especially respiratory allergy. A mere speck of the stuff may contain items as numerous and varied as algae, bacteria, cosmetics, cotton linters,* feathers, hair, house dust mites, insect particles, kapok,* lead, mould, paint chips, plaster, pollen, skin scales, street dirt, wallpaper flakes and wool particles – in short, whatever happens to be floating in the air.

Probably the most allergenic ingredients of house dust are mites – minute creatures that feed on the flakes of skin we normally shed every day. House dust mites absolutely love humidity, so bedding and upholstery in damp rooms set up an ideal climate for them to thrive. Since no odourless, non-irritating, non-toxic mite-killing products exist, the best strategy against mites is to eliminate sources of moisture: repair leaks, air out damp spots and, if those methods don't work, use dehumidifiers. And while lower humidity keeps mites in check, it also controls dust, since dust tends to cling to moisture in the air. (Controlling humidity will also help to relieve mould allergy, which we'll discuss shortly.)

As you may know, regular dusting and vacuuming is a large part of dust allergy relief. Without it, rugs, curtains, toys, bookshelves and knick-knacks collect dust like magnets, providing allergic people with regular snootfuls of the stuff. So does furniture, but while overstuffed couches and chairs trap loads of dust, spare designs such as Danish modern accumulate far less. Keeping clutter to a minimum also helps.

Dust control in a child's bedroom is especially important, considering the number of hours he or she spends sleeping and playing there. In fact, the housekeeping routine required by most allergy doctors is so rigorous it makes Army standards seem lax by comparison. The child's room must be stripped to the barest essentials. Rugs and curtains are the first to go. Only

* *Plant fibres used in furniture, bedding, pillows, sleeping bags, mattresses, carpet padding, coat lining and stuffed toys.*

washable, cotton curtains are allowed on the windows. Absolutely nothing can adorn the top of the dresser. Stuffed toys are out. Mattresses must be wrapped in zipped, dust-proof covers. Wardrobes are to be emptied of everything but the child's own clothing – hung on hangers, not stacked on the shelves. Last of all, the entire room must be dusted daily and wiped from top to bottom with a mop and damp cloth twice a week.

Sounds like good advice. Only problem is, few parents have the time or energy to follow it.

'Most mothers won't do it, even if they say they will,' says Constantine J. Falliers, an asthma and allergy specialist in Denver, Colorado, and editor of the *Journal of Asthma*. 'Complete control is impossible.'

'It's impossible to do every last thing, day in and day out,' agrees a mother of a highly allergic child. 'I'd have to do nothing but clean. Besides, the kid goes to school and is going to run into dust sooner or later. So I do the best I can and let the rest slide. That's all you *can* do, really. Dust is everywhere.'

Actually, there's plenty you can do to control dust without becoming a full-time scrubwoman. All it takes is a few basic changes around the house. In many homes, 'dust is everywhere' because forced hot-air heating systems generously spread it around the house. If you have forced hot-air heat, you can check your own heating system by placing several layers of cheesecloth over the air vents for a few days. If the system is properly filtered, the cheesecloth will remain clean. But since most conventional furnace filters remove only 5 to 10 per cent of the dust, your cheesecloth may very well come up sooty – telling you that you're breathing dust-laden air. In that case, you can place charcoal filters or washable, all-metal or cloth filters on all the hot-air ducts – or at the very least over those leading into the bedrooms and any other rooms where the dust-sensitive person spends a lot of time. Also, have the furnace and ductwork vacuumed by a professional furnace cleaning firm once a year, just before the winter heating season begins. And you can attach either a HEPA-type air filter to your heating system or plug in a portable model or two around the house. Either one allows you to let up on stringent housecleaning requirements. (For more on air filters, see the section on air cleaning equipment later in this chapter.)

The type of vacuum cleaner you use can also make a great

deal of difference in dust control. Most conventional air-bag-equipped vacuum cleaners work against you: they vent dust out of the exhaust hatch – and into the air again – while you zealously go after every last nook and cranny with the front end. And there's hardly a housekeeper alive who hasn't nearly choked on the cloud of dust stirred up every time the bag is changed – an utter disaster if you're allergic.

In contrast, central vacuum cleaning systems get rid of dust for good – as long as the exhaust is vented well away from living quarters. A more convenient and affordable solution – especially for people who rent their house or flat or move frequently – is a water-trap vacuum cleaner. This model collects dust in water instead of an awkward air bag, so dust isn't continually recirculated into the air you breathe. An added advantage: water-trap vacuum cleaners don't lose power the way bag-equipped models do when the pouch begins to fill up. Without that power loss, you can pick up more dust in the first place.

'They really do the job – and they do help allergies,' says Robert W. Boxer, an allergist in Chicago who recommends water-trap vacuum cleaners to his patients. 'We've had one in our house for about fourteen years and it's very effective,' he adds.

A bonus to the chemically sensitive is that water-trap vacuum cleaners offer attachments that allow you to shampoo rugs and upholstery with nontoxic cleaning products, rather than having to hire professional cleaners who use strong chemicals.

Here are a few additional dust control tips to make your life as easy and dust-free as possible.

- Purchase only stuffed toys that can be easily laundered.
- Avoid furniture, pillows, cushions, quilts and sleeping bags stuffed with kapok. (Check labels.)
- Wear a dampened cotton surgical mask over your nose and mouth while dusting, vacuuming or mopping. (See the Appendix for purchase sources.)
- To cut down on dust accumulation in wardrobes, hang clothing in zippered garment bags. Use the compartmentalized ones for shoes and sweaters.
- If your house has baseboard heat, detach the front and side panels (if they're removable) for vacuuming. 'Fried dust' can be very allergenic.

Pollen: when spring breezes bring the sneezes

Do your symptoms follow a definite seasonal pattern, mushrooming in the spring and subsiding in winter? You could be allergic to pollen – the powdery mass of tiny grains that burst from trees, grasses, weeds and flowers every spring and summer, and that are carried *everywhere* by the wind (and sometimes by animals).

Not all pollens cause allergy. Pine tree pollen, for instance, doesn't seem to cause allergies, despite the fact that pine trees produce tons of it. Ragweed, on the other hand, produces the most widespread and allergenic pollen in North America. Table 14 shows the other most common types of allergy-provoking pollen. Because trees, grass and weeds produce microscopic pollen that's easily carried off by the wind, their pollen is much more apt to trigger allergies than flower pollen, which is large, sticky and for the most part toted from plant to plant by insects. However, tree and weed pollen can land on flowers – something to keep in mind when bringing cut flowers indoors. (Some people react badly to the mere fragrance of roses and other highly scented flowers.)

While pollen counts are usually higher in the countryside, large cities are not entirely pollen-free – thanks to the wind which can carry pollen hundreds of miles. Generally, however, the seashore and high mountains have the least pollen.

We can't usually see pollen. But those allergic to it are only too aware of nature's seasonal bombardment. Leafy trees like birch, elm, maple and poplar generally pollinate in early spring; grasses in late spring and summer; weeds in late summer.

Pollen is worse on a dry, windy day and better when it rains, since the water washes it away. Pollen levels are highest in late evening and early morning. Staying indoors with your windows closed – especially while you sleep – can help you avoid the worst of it.

Obviously, you can't cut the grass, clear weeds and brush or play in a field during pollen season without stirring up a flurry of it. But there are steps to help you win out against pollen.

- Air conditioning is a natural way to help defend your home against pollen. And buying a car with air conditioning or having

TABLE 14
Common Sources of Allergy-Provoking Pollen

Weeds	Trees	Grasses
burning bush	Alder	Bahia
Careless weed	Beech	Bermuda
Dandelion	Birch	Bluegrass (some)
English plantain	Cottonwood	Brome
Firebush	Elm	Common reed
Goldenrod	Eucalyptus	Johnson
Lamb's-quarters	Hazel	Meadow fescue
Marsh elder	Hickory (especially pecan)	Oats (cultivated)
Mexican fireweed	Maple (box elder)	Orchard
Nettle	Mountain cedar	Redtop (bent)
Ox-eye daisy	Oak	Ryegrass (perennial and cultivated)
Pigweed (redroot, rough)	Olive	Sweet vernal
Ragweed	Poplar	Timothy
Russian thistle (tumbleweed)	Sycamore	Wheat (cultivated)
Sagebrush (wormwood and mugwort)	Walnut	
Sheep sorrel	White ash	
Spiny amaranth	White pine	
	Willow	

it installed will make a drive through the country more bearable. (See the section on air cleaning equipment later in this chapter.)

• During the summer, you should rinse your hair after coming in from playing or working outdoors and before going to bed at night. Otherwise, you could sleep in an air conditioned room and still have severe symptoms from pollen falling into your eyes and nose.

• Pets carry pollen on their fur. Discourage them from coming inside during the pollen season – unless you want to hose *them* down every night, too.

• Consider replanting a large part of your lawn with a less allergenic (and work-free) ground cover such as myrtle or crown vetch. Interspersed with azaleas, rocks and paths of crushed stone in the graceful style of Japanese gardens, your garden may turn out to be more beautiful than your neighbours' expanses of golf course greenery. At the same time, you'll cut down on the need for the chemical pesticides required to maintain picture-perfect lawns – a big plus for those sensitive to chemicals.

- Ridding the house of dust and moulds year-round will help the allergic person tolerate seasonal exposure to pollen. Again, it's a matter of treating a specific allergy by reducing the total load of related irritants.

Moulds and mildew

Do you feel worse:

– during periods of damp weather?
– when you walk into a damp, musty house or basement?
– if you sit in overstuffed furniture?
– if you're near hay or straw (in a garden, in a barn or at a circus)?
– if you're near a compost pile or leaf piles?

If you answered yes to any of those questions, chances are you're allergic to moulds. Another 'yes' clue:

Do you feel *better*:

– when there's snow on the ground?

Moulds are a type of plantlike growth called fungi. Like pollen, their spores ride on the wind and cause allergies. Mildew is the black or white growth produced by mould spores. Rubbish bins, shower curtains and damp basements are the most familiar mould habitats. But moulds aren't fussy – any place that is damp, warm, dark and poorly ventilated will do. And they're not just found indoors. (Table 14, at the beginning of this chapter, shows the most fertile breeding grounds for mould.) Check around your house for any leaks or damp spots that could harbour mould. The sooner you dry them out, the better. Also, see the box, How to prevent mould and mildew, for other tips.

Above all, reducing excess humidity in the house is the prime goal in controlling mould. One doctor reports that his own 'mould asthma' responded remarkably well to the addition of a dehumidifier in his bedroom. He managed to reduce the

HOW TO PREVENT MOULD AND MILDEW

GET RID OF DAMPNESS. **A wet basement can be a sign of cracked or defective mortar, cracks in the walls or inadequate drainage.**

CHECK YOUR RAINSPOUTS. **If your basement seems particularly damp after it rains, the roof downspouting could be depositing water too close to the foundations. In that case, extend the leader spout to carry the rainwater farther away and downhill from the house.**

USE ONLY LIGHT, WASHABLE RUGS INSTEAD OF HEAVY CARPETING, **especially in basements or other areas prone to dampness or water leaks. Wet carpeting is a lush haven for mould growth.**

VENT YOUR CLOTHES DRYER TO THE OUTDOORS **to help reduce excess moisture.**

THROW OUT ALL THOSE OLD, DAMP PILES OF ODDS AND ENDS YOU'VE BEEN HOARDING **in the basement, attic and backs of wardrobes – newspapers, books, magazines, old carpets, cast-off furniture, dingy pillows, broken-down toys and the like.**

KEEP THINGS CLEAN. **Never hang clothes in the wardrobes after they've been worn. Keep wardrobes, dresser drawers, bathrooms, and refrigerators as clean and dry as possible.**

SPREAD OUT DAMP TOWELS AND WASHCLOTHS IN THE BATHROOM. STRETCH OUT WET SHOWER CURTAINS.

CIRCULATE THE AIR. **When natural breezes are absent, use electric fans.**

SPRINKLE BORAX POWDER IN MOULD-PRONE AREAS, **like the bottom of the rubbish bin. This natural mineral compound happens to be a simple, effective anti-mould agent.**

AVOID WALLPAPER. **It's a haven for mould, especially in the bathroom. If you have your heart set on wallpaper, add borax or boric acid to the paste to retard mould growth.**

(See also Table 16 for more tips on fighting mould.)

humidity to 50 per cent in the face of outside moisture levels of up to 88 per cent in foggy, humid Ventura, California. With the drop in indoor moisture came a marked decrease in the mould level in his room – and discontinued use of steroid drugs for the treatment of his asthma (*Annals of Allergy*, February 1971).

Alfred Zamm, an environmentally oriented doctor in Kingston, New York, had this advice for mould sufferers; 'I recommend buying the largest-capacity [dehumidifier] available, one equipped with a control that automatically turns it off when the humidity drops to an acceptable level.' (*Why Your House May Endanger Your Health*, Simon and Schuster, 1980.)

Unlike pollen, mould is not strictly a seasonal problem, although moulds tend to flourish when the temperature rises and diminish during the cooler months. An exceptionally rainy summer will promote a bumper crop of mould. Fair weather activities like raking leaves, gardening and mowing grass stir up mould spores, making it easy to mistake mould allergy for pollen allergy. Burning leaves in the autumn can also bring on an attack.

Mushrooms and yeast are related to moulds, so eating them can trigger a reaction in mould-sensitive people. And it's not surprising that those same people can also develop symptoms after eating foods fermented with mould: sharp cheeses such as blue and Cheddar, baked goods, candied fruit, pickled or smoked meats and fish and soy sauce. The same goes for drinking beer, wine or cider, or using vinegar. (See Chapter 3, Finding your no-allergy diet, for more details.) Penicillin, too, is made from mould. If you're allergic to mould, you may be allergic to penicillin.

A pet peeve: animal allergy

Do you feel worse:

- whenever you are around animals?
- when you handle rugs, wear fur coats or down clothing, or sleep with a quilt or feather pillow?

If so, you're probably allergic to animal hair, dander and odour.

Allergy to pet dander – particles of hair and skin that cling to fur – can develop at any time, even if the same pet has lived with you for years. Cats are the worst offenders, with dogs running a close second. Less frequently, rabbits, gerbils, guinea pigs, hamsters or horses can set off allergies. So can parakeets, since feather allergy is closely related to dander allergy. And recent studies indicate that a pet's saliva or urine can also precipitate allergic attacks.

That seems to make goldfish just about the only truly hypoallergenic pet on the market! True, a person can be allergic to only one breed of dog or cat, but that's rare. And the popular notion that switching to a short-haired animal will alleviate allergy is true only in *some* cases.

'I've seen some long-haired dogs with silky fur that are no difficulty at all,' says Dr Falliers. 'And I've seen short-haired dogs whose dander is a big problem. So it depends. Generally, I'd say that a person with a lot of allergies should stay away from hairy pets. But a long-haired dog that stays outdoors is still better than *any* dog that sleeps next to a child's bed.'

Some families manage the problem by keeping the pet outdoors all the time and teaching allergic children to enjoy it from a distance. For others, a dog in the garden is still too close for comfort.

But removing the pet doesn't always relieve symptoms. Animal dander and other pet residue can linger in carpets or house dust for several months after the animal is gone. Or the pet may not be the only animal in the child's life.

'You have to be realistic, especially with children,' says Dr Falliers. 'The doctor can say, "No pets," But the child can still go next door and play with the neighbour's dog.'

Sometimes, it's the parent who must make the sacrifice – one way or another. Dr Falliers tells the story of a man who was allergic to the family dog, yet didn't tell his three kids because he knew they would resent him for making them get rid of it. 'So he took his allergy medicine and suffered,' says Dr Falliers. Without a doubt, giving up a pet is one of the most painful choices some families will ever have to make. Dr Falliers also relates the story of a family who refused to accept the fact that their dog was causing their allergies – until the pet was accidentally killed by a car and their allergies suddenly disappeared.

Occasionally, clothing made of mohair, alpaca, cashmere or

goat hair will trigger an allergic reaction. So can horsehair-stuffed chairs and couches. Or feathers and down stuffing. That means feather-sensitive people should steer away from down-filled quilts, sleeping bags and ski jackets. Doctors often recommend dacron-filled items as acceptable substitutes. Feather pillows can be replaced by a cotton pillowcase stuffed with rolled-up cotton T-shirts. Avoid foam rubber – it fosters mould growth.

Everyday odours and fumes

Do you feel worse after smelling:

- the odour of household cleaning products and detergents such as bleach, ammonia and polishes?
- the fumes from furnaces, car or bus exhaust, tarred roads, kerosene heaters, floor wax, petrol, coal smoke or other petroleum products?
- the fumes from recently cleaned clothing, upholstery or rugs?
- the odour of lighter fluid, moth balls or insect repellent?
- the vapours from chlorinated water?
- the fragrance of soaps, shampoos or bath oils?
- scented candles or decorations?

If you answered yes to any of those questions, you may be allergic to various chemical odours and fumes.

Some people, for instance, are allergic to the odours of trees, grass, weeds and flowers, rather than to the pollen itself. For some, the smell of pine panelling or a Christmas tree is enough to set off an attack. Other people are so allergic to fish, eggs or other foods that even the smell of those foods can make them sick.

What's the link between odours and sensitivity?

'The nose provides a direct route to the brain for odours,' explains Iris R. Bell, a psychiatrist in San Francisco who has a keen interest in environmentally induced health problems. In fact, the smell receptors in the brain are located right behind the uppermost cavities of the nose. And, for people who are sensitive, when the chemical fumes reach the brain, they tend to affect thinking and behaviour.

'Most toxic gases work in one way or another to reduce oxygen availability to the tissues,' says Francis Silver, an engineer from Martinsburg, West Virginia, who specializes in the effect of gases on health. 'With oxygen deficiency, the brain and nervous system is affected first and foremost, impairing judgement and causing other behavioural problems.'

But when it comes to being affected by chemicals, even the experts can't always tell whether a reaction is allergy or out-and-out poisoning. To complicate the matter, some people seem immune to a substance that makes other people ill, says Kendall Gerdes, an allergist in Denver, Colorado. 'On one end of the scale are people who could live in a chemical factory and never have any trouble,' he points out. 'On the other end of the curve are the people who can't live twenty miles away from that factory because they'd get sick. Most of us fall somewhere in between.'

So-called moderate exposure is where the real trouble starts.

'Many of our modern advances expose us to substances which are not lethal in small doses,' says Dr McGovern. 'But when you add up the amount of the chemicals you're exposed to daily in the pesticide sprays, the formaldehyde, the photocopier, et cetera, it often approaches toxic levels. Even though these may be small amounts, they add up to enormous doses in the course of the day. Once you exceed your tolerance for these chemicals in your system, your immune system becomes impaired. And you're stuck with allergies.'

Dr Gerdes told us, 'The highly sensitive people are the front line as we move into a more and more polluted society. The things that bother chemically sensitive people are no different from the things that, with a greater degree of exposure, will eventually bother the majority.'

Sensitivity sometimes goes unnoticed until an individual is blasted by a single large exposure that finally triggers a breakdown in health.

'A person may have only a slight sensitivity to chlorine, for example, and one day a tank accidentally ruptures in his or her town,' says Dr Gerdes. 'The toxic exposure may then change that moderately sensitive individual in some way so that from that time on, he or she can no longer tolerate chlorine – or any other chemical, either. The stress is additive.'

Doctors we spoke to agree that it's not all that important

whether you label the chemical reaction 'allergic', 'sensitivity' or 'toxicity'. The critical thing is to find out what bothers you and to do something about it.

Is your house gassing you?

Natural gas is touted as the clean fuel. And that's probably true in terms of its low contribution to polluted air in comparison with burning oil, coal or wood. But for chemically sensitive individuals, gas-fired furnaces and appliances are big trouble – they vent combustion fumes *back* into the household atmosphere. Pilot lights add to the problem. Burning nonstop, they continually discharge gas into your air – gas that contains carbon monoxide, formaldehyde, nitric oxide and nitrogen dioxide, as well as a group of compounds known as hydrocarbons (including benzene and acetylene).

No need to remember all those chemicals. Just follow the advice of Dr Randolph: 'The most important thing you can do is to get rid of the gas heat and range.'

Clothes dryers and cooking ranges should be electric and vented to the outside to reroute gas emissions. The same goes for a self-cleaning oven. Refrigerators, too, should be electric. In fact, Dr Zamm states strongly, 'A healthy house should not even be connected to a gas line.'

If you suspect gas fumes are a problem at your house, try this. Spend a few days at a friend's house, where there is no gas heat or appliances. If you feel better there, but experience symptoms again when you return home, gas may be the culprit. Perhaps you've already noticed an improvement while away on a business trip or holiday, or during the summer when the gas heat is turned off.

If you are sensitive to gas – or other fossil fuels, for that matter – consider converting to an electric hot-water heating system and electric appliances. If you rent or for some other reason cannot easily convert, here are some alternatives.

- Ask your gas company to turn off the pilot light on your stove so it doesn't needlessly give off fumes when it's not in use. Light the stove with a match when you want to cook.
- Install an exhaust hood above the gas stove. This can eliminate up to half of the fumes generated while you cook.
- For the remaining fumes, use an air filter in the kitchen

during and after cooking meals. (Air filters are discussed at the end of this chapter.)

- Ask a furnace installation firm to ensure that your gas furnace is equipped to funnel all exhaust fumes up the chimney so that no vapours are allowed to escape into the house or ductwork.
- An air filter hooked up to the central heating or cooling system will also help dissipate gas fumes.

Are you allergic to housework?

Beyond keeping our homes dust-free and mould-free, many of us are probably *too* clean for our own good – especially when it comes to allergies. Furniture polishes, window cleaners, aerosol sprays of all types, disinfectants, floor waxes, moth balls – all contribute to an invisible mist of chemical vapours in our homes. Most of these products are a combination of petroleum-based or coal-based ingredients, fragrances and complex chemicals.

'One of the major factors in chronic illness today is the products we clean with,' says Dan R. O'Banion, author of the books *An Ecological and Nutritional Approach to Behavioral Medicine* and *The Ecological and Nutritional Treatment of Health Disorders* (Charles C. Thomas, 1981).

Dr O'Banion is talking about chronic illness from chronic exposure. We all have heard the horror stories of people who mixed chlorine bleach with ammonia and keeled over dead. But repeated *single*, smaller exposures to these and several other products pose hazards of their own. 'Even mild exposure to certain chemicals may lead to chronic bronchospastic reponses [such as wheezing] or allergic reactions in susceptible persons,' write Drs Rose H. Goldman and John M. Peters in the *Journal of the American Medical Association* (18 December 1981).

The two worst household offenders are probably oven cleaners and air fresheners. Oven cleaners because they're the strongest; anything that replaces good old elbow grease in battling six months of burned-on fat and pie drippings has to be pretty potent. And air fresheners – either scented aerosols or the perfumed ornaments slapped on the lid of a rubbish bin – because they *add* more chemicals to the home environment.

But you don't need either of these products. Keep your oven clean by always wiping it out soon after you use it (and it's still warm) or by scraping off dried grit with steel wool. And a far better – and cheaper – air freshener, suggests Dr Boxer, is an opened box of plain old baking soda. 'That will absorb odours, not add them,' he says.

Baking soda, in fact, is one of many simple, old-fashioned items that do the job of several expensive and odorous housekeeping supplies. (See Table 15 for a more complete list of safe substitutes for almost every household job.)

If you must keep strong commercial cleaners on hand, store them in a tightly sealed container, preferably outside the home in a detached storage shed. That includes: paints, solvents, lacquers, turpentine, lighter fluid, charcoal fire-lighters, glues, odorous soaps and detergents, polishes, mops and cleaning cloths, chlorine bleaches and ammonia. When you use them, be sure the windows are wide open and a fan is on. Afterwards, leave the area for several hours while the fumes dissipate.

When it comes to painting, refinishing and remodelling, you may not have much choice of products. All may be highly odorous. In general, however, alkyd-base paints are better tolerated than latex or epoxy paints, whose odour seems to linger for months. If you'd like to test your personal tolerance to a particular product before making it a permanent part of your home, there are some ways to get an idea of what you can and cannot tolerate. (See the box, Self-tests for allergy to household products.)

Get the bugs out – without pesticides

Pesticide spraying is by no means confined to overhead spraying of agricultural crops. Homes, schools, theatres, public buildings and camps are often sprayed – sometimes daily.

In fact, the smorgasbord of household pesticides sitting on the grocery shelf next to the mops and pet foods gives us a false sense of security about their safety. Few people realize they are applying highly toxic chemicals to their environment, so if we're going to beef about supermarket oranges blitzed with malathion, we shouldn't use pesticides in our own backyards and kitchen cupboards, either.

Exotic, six-syllable chemicals aren't the only pesticides that can cause trouble. Many household insecticides contain pyrethrum, a perfectly natural product made from the flower of a plant related to ragweed. If you're allergic to ragweed, you're

TABLE 15

Household Cleaning Aids

See the Appendix for manufacturers and suppliers of commercial nontoxic cleaning products.

Job or Household Product	Substitute Method or Cleaning Aid
Air freshener	
for refrigerator, wardrobes, basement, storeroom, garage, workroom	1. Opened box of baking soda 2. Activated charcoal. (Replace either one every three months or according to package instructions) 3. Blow odours out of a room or wardrobe with an electric fan
for rubbish bin	Wash with borax solution. Then sprinkle some dry borax on bottom of bin
for pet litter	Add borax to litter mix
Anti-mould products	1. White vinegar 2. Borax in warm water
Boot and shoe polish (for leather)	Small amounts of olive or lemon oil. Buff with soft cloth
Chrome cleaner	1. Apply cider vinegar with soft cloth, then buff with paper towel 2. Apply whiting* with damp cloth, then dry with soft cloth
Coffeemaker and teapot (non-aluminium) cleaner	Pour baking soda on a damp sponge and rub
Crayon mark removal	1. Apply white vinegar sparingly and rub. Then apply fuller's earth.† Remove after a few minutes 2. See also General cleaning compounds, below
Nappies	Flush and put in solution of 4 oz/125g borax and 2 gallons/9.6l warm water. Soak overnight to get rid of odours and stains, then launder
Disinfectant	Borax in warm water
Drain opener and pipe unclogger	

* *Calcium carbonate, available at paint stores.*

† *Available at hardware stores.*

Job or Household Product	Substitute Method or Cleaning Aid
sinks and tubs	1. Flush with: 4 oz/125g baking soda and 8 fl oz/240ml white vinegar or 3 tablespoons washing soda or equal parts of salt and baking soda 2. Unclog with plunger and plumber's snake, available at hardware stores
waste disposal	Sprinkle 3 tablespoons borax in drain. Let stand 15 minutes. Turn on disposal and flush with cold water for a few seconds
Electric iron cleaner (not for Teflon or other specially coated iron surfaces)	In saucepan, combine white vinegar and salt to make a thick paste. Warm slightly and, with cloth, rub mixture on bottom of iron to remove dark spots or scorched matter
Furniture polish	Rub thoroughly after applying: beeswax or olive oil or 100% lemon oil or beeswax and olive oil
General cleaning compounds (painted walls, woodwork, floors and tiles)	1. Combine 4 oz/125 g borax and ½ teaspoon dishwashing liquid in 2 gallons/9.6 l warm water 2. Borax in warm water
Grease spots on clothing	Sprinkle fuller's earth† on the spot. Remove after 15 minutes to 2 hours. Careful: Will lighten coloured fabric if left on too long
Grease stains on rugs and upholstery	Rub baking soda into spot with cloth or brush, then sweep away
Gum and tar removal from skin or hair	Vegetable oil, followed by soap and water

Job or Household Product	Substitute Method or Cleaning Aid
Jewellery	1. Costume jewellery, diamonds and gems: clean with warm (not hot), soapy water and a soft nailbrush or soft toothbrush. Dry with a very soft cloth 2. Pearls: rub on a few drops of glycerin (available at chemists) and shine with a very soft cloth
Laundry	
bleach	Use nonchlorine (oxygen) bleaches
detergent	Use enzyme-free laundry detergent, baking soda or borax
rinse	To remove all traces of detergent, add ½ cup borax or 4 fl oz/120 ml white vinegar to first rinse cycle
stain removal and whitener	1. Add 4 oz/125 g borax to wash load 2. Hang washed laundry in sunshine to dry
Metal cleaner (for brass, bronze, copper, pewter and stainless steel; not for silver, silver plate or jewellery)	1. Dampen table salt with lemon juice and rub 2. Combine 1 tablespoon salt and 1 tablespoon flour. Add 1 tablespoon white vinegar. Mix into a thick paste. Apply with a damp sponge or cloth and rub gently. Let dry for about an hour. Rinse well with warm water. Buff dry with a soft cloth
Mildew removal on fridge door and rubber gasket	Wipe with white vinegar
Miscellaneous surface cleanser (Formica, glass, marble)	Rub with salt and rinse thoroughly with warm water
Moth repellent	Store clothes with cheesecloth sachets of: dried lavender or a mixture of 8 oz/250 g rosemary, 8 oz/250 g mint, 4 oz/125 g thyme and 2 tablespoons cloves

Job or Household Product	Substitute Method or Cleaning Aid
Oven cleaner	1. Wipe with damp cloth while oven is still warm 2. Scrub with steel wool and washing soda
Percolator (non-aluminium) cleaner	Fill with water to full-cup capacity. Add 1 teaspoon borax for every cup. Let percolate, then stand for 20 minutes. Rinse thoroughly with warm water
Pot and pan scrubber	Soak in warm salt water, then rub with plain steel wool
Refrigerator cleaner	Sponge with a solution of 1 tablespoon borax and 1 quart warm water. Rinse with cold, clear water
Scorch stains in clothing	Saturate with white vinegar, then wash as usual
Scouring powder for sinks, tubs, bathroom tile, fibreglass	Sprinkle baking soda or borax on a damp sponge and rub. Rinse thoroughly with warm water
Silver polish	1. Place in aluminium pan with: 1 teaspoon cream of tartar and 2 pints/1.25 l warm water or 1 teaspoon baking soda and 1 quart warm water 2. Rub with whiting* on damp cloth
Window cleaner	1 tablespoon white vinegar in 2 pints/1.25 l warm water or 2 fl oz/50 ml white vinegar in 1 gallon/4.8 l warm water
Windshield cleaner	Apply baking soda with a damp sponge

SELF-TESTS FOR ALLERGY TO HOUSEHOLD PRODUCTS

SEALED JAR TEST

To test fabric, insulation or other material, place a small amount in a clean jar. Seal. Place in the sun or in a warm spot for two hours. (That simulates the warm, hermetically sealed environment most of us live in.) Then remove the lid and smell the air coming directly from the jar. Note any reaction you may experience. If you experience no symptoms, chances are you can use the product.

PAINTED BOARD TEST

To test paint, varnish, stain or sealer, apply a few strokes to an old board. Allow to dry thoroughly. Sleep with the test board under your pillow or near your bed for a few nights. If you experience any symptoms, you could be allergic to the product and should avoid it.

SNIFF TEST

If you are unable to obtain a sample of a product, simply sniff the one on display. Many chemically sensitive people have an acute sense of smell that tips them off to products they can't tolerate. If you find the item in question smells objectionable or makes you feel sick, don't buy it.

apt to be allergic to pyrethrum, too. All of which prompts Dr Randolph to warn, 'Never, never use a pesticide indoors.'

If it comes down to either having the termites in your house exterminated or waiting for the timbers to crash down around you, ask the exterminator to apply the chemicals directly to the nest rather than zapping the entire house. If the firm won't do that, find one that will. And have any extermination done right before you go on holiday so fumes have a chance to lie down while you're away.

Table 16 shows safe insect control methods you can use to fight everyday bugs around the house.

You may even be able to escape overhead spraying outdoors. A woman in Texas who is extremely sensitive to chemicals tells

TABLE 16

Home Pest Control

See the Appendix for commercial sources of non-toxic pesticides.

Insect	Control With
Ants	1. Sprinkle red pepper on floors and countertops 2. Plant mint at front and back doors of house. (Ants hate mint) 3. Put honey and boric acid* on small pieces of paper and place in strategic spots
Beetles (in food)	1. Freeze flours and grains for 48 to 72 hours after purchase. Then store, as in item 2 2. Store flours, grains, crackers, cereals, biscuits and macaroni in glass jars in a cool place. Add a bay leaf to each jar
Fleas	1. Vacuum pet's areas at least every other day 2. Wash pet's bedding at least once a week in hot soapy water 3. Bathe pet and apply a herbal rinse: add 2 oz/150 g fresh or dried rosemary to 2 pints/1.25 l boiling water. (For larger dogs, increase recipe by half.) Steep for 20 minutes, strain and cool. Pour evenly over animal. Let fur air dry 4. Bathe pet and apply a lemon rinse: thinly slice a lemon, including peel, and place in 1 pint/600 ml boiling water. Steep overnight. Strain. Sponge solution on pet. For severe flea problem, apply daily 5. Add brewer's yeast or thiamine (a B vitamin) to your pet's food
Flies	1. Cover rubbish or enclose in bags 2. Hang flypaper 3. Use outdoor 'electrocutors' 4. Compost all manure
Garden pests	1. Intersperse vegetables with strong-smelling herbs such as basil, chives, garlic, lavender, onions, pennyroyal, peppermint, rosemary, sage and flowers such as chrysanthemums and marigolds 2. Combine 3 large onions, chopped; 1 whole garlic clove, chopped; 2 tablespoons hot red pepper and 2 pints/1.25 l water. Mix in blender. Add 1 tablespoon soap and stir well. Strain and spray

Insect	Control With
	3. Sprinkle diatomaceous earth† and wood ashes around plants
	4. Purchase friendly predators: ladybird, green lacewings (aphid lions), praying mantis and trichogramma wasps
Mites (on house plants)	Spray with a mixture of 1 lb/450 g flour and 4 fl oz/100 ml buttermilk in 5 gallons/24 l water
Mosquitoes	1. Discourage breeding by emptying stagnant water from cans, old tyres and clogged or improperly sloped spouting
	2. Use outdoor 'electrocutors'
	3. Purchase praying mantis, a natural predator
Moths	1. Wear clothes once a week or give them a good stiff brushing to disturb eggs and prevent hatching
	2. Washing clothes kills all forms of moths
	3. Wrap clothes in paper and freeze for 3 to 7 days before storing
Cockroaches	1. Keep home dry and free of food crumbs and scraps
	2. Sprinkle boric acid* liberally in crevices, corners, nesting places and around moulding
	or
	3. Mix 2 tablespoons flour, 1 teaspoon cocoa and 4 teaspoons borax. Place on small sheets of paper in strategic spots
Silverfish	Sprinkle mixture of boric acid,* flour and sugar on small sheets of paper and place in strategic areas. (These bugs love paper)
Termites	1. To prevent termite invasions, build with pressure-treated wood
	2. Apply mineral insecticides – copper chromate or cryolite (both poisonous) – to nests
Ticks	1. Swab each tick with a dab of alcohol. As the tick pulls its head out of the skin, grasp it with your thumb and forefinger, twist and yank out. Then destroy ticks to prevent spreading
	2. Apply vegetable shortening, softened butter or margarine to tick. Use enough to smother the insect. Then follow directions in item 1 above

** Boric acid is poisonous if swallowed. Do not use it if you have children or pets.*
† Available at hardware stores.

us: 'The little town I live in fogs for mosquitoes. I was hit with the fumes six times before I finally convinced them that they had to call me before they started fogging. I told them that if they hit me again, they might as well not send an ambulance, they should send the hearse instead. Now they have a sign on the fogger that says "Do not remove this machine from the garage without calling Mrs Scherzer, 278–4817."

'This year,' she continued, 'the town itself wasn't spraying, but the county was. And the county man would come around and knock on my door at nine a.m. and say, "We're going to fog this area at six o'clock this evening." That would give me enough time to leave town. I'd spend a couple of days with my daughter or mother-in-law until the stuff got out of the air.'

Ferreting out formaldehyde

Seven million pounds of formaldehyde are produced each year. Obviously, it's not all used to preserve lab specimens in school biology classes. The colourless, pungent liquid winds up in a variety of widely used products, from plywood and rugs to permanent-press clothing. (See the box, Products that commonly contain formaldehyde, for a more complete list.) Chemically, formaldehyde is fairly unstable – it easily breaks down into a toxic gas that seeps into the air and causes illness. The theory that explains formaldehyde sickness says that the inhaled molecules of the gas combine with a protein in the respiratory tract to form another substance capable of triggering the immune reaction we know as allergy.

Classic symptoms of short-term formaldehyde exposure are burning eyes, headaches, itchy skin or rashes, chest pain, a runny nose or nasal congestion, dry cough, nausea and a sore throat. Diarrhoea and asthma may also be a problem.

'Since [formaldehyde] is so ubiquitous, common respiratory diseases such as asthma and other phenomena such as allergic dermatitis may be more frequently associated with formaldehyde than is currently realized,' says Dr Ralph E. Yodaiken of the Centers for Disease Control, in an editorial for one of the most widely read medical journals in the US (*Journal of the American Medical Association*, 9 October 1981).

A case of formaldehyde-induced illness that affected *hundreds* of people occurred at a new administration building at a state college in Pennsylvania. After working in the office for three years, secretaries and administrators alike began to experience the symptoms described above. They would get progressively worse during the day, but feel better at night and on the weekends. When winter came and the heating system was turned on, people felt even worse. A squad of consultants was called in to conduct tests. The cause was narrowed down to formaldehyde gas generated by furniture and by bookshelves made from laminated chipboard and plywood (two common sources of formaldehyde).

As with so many new homes and office buildings, energy-saving measures had cut fresh air to practically nil. So part of the 'cure' was to open the windows, flooding the entire building with outside air for two weeks. The offensive desks and bookshelves were also replaced. After being left vacant for a full year, the building was eventually reopened. The staff resumed their work – without symptoms.

That scenario has repeated itself again and again in office buildings from Washington, D.C. to Los Angeles. And evidence now shows that long-term exposure to formaldehyde may cause cancer. Several doctors we spoke to express the hope that if consumers voluntarily avoid formaldehyde-laced products, manufacturers will be reluctant to put them on the market in the first place.

But for now, you'll have to be your own formaldehyde watchdog. Read labels before you buy. Look carefully: formaldehyde may be disguised as formol, methylene oxide or formalin. Here are some other tips.

- If you're doing any home building or remodelling, it may be worth your while to spend extra money for solid, genuine wood instead of chipboard and plywood.
- If your house already has lots of plywood and chipboard – in partitions, wardrobes, cupboards and furniture – paint the surfaces with a low-permeability paint. (See the Appendix for suggested sealers.)
- Instead of formaldehyde-soaked carpeting, use washable cotton rugs on your floors. (They also cut down on dust and mould.)
- Before buying a house, check to see if it's foam insulated. If it is, keep shopping – or plan to have the insulation removed.
- Ventilate your house (see the section on air cleaning equipment later in this chapter).

PRODUCTS THAT COMMONLY CONTAIN FORMALDEHYDE

Adhesives
Air fresheners
Antiperspirants
Carpets and curtains
Chemical fertilizers
Cigarette smoke
Detergents
Diesel fuel
Disinfectant
Facial tissues
Flame-resistant cloth
Grocery bags
Hair spray
Insecticides and fungicides
Insulation
Insulation
Nail polish
Newsprint
Paper products
Permanent-press clothes
Photographic chemicals
Plastic
Shampoos
Soap
Toothpaste
Wallboard
Wallpaper
Waxed paper
Wood veneer

Try to use fewer plastics and synthetics

In 1957, a House of Tomorrow was opened at Disneyland. The place was furnished from top to bottom in plastics.

That futuristic vision is now reality. Plastic and synthetic furnishings and building materials are rampant. So are plastic clothing and accessories – under the guise of words such as polyester, vinyl, Styrofoam, acetate and so on. Certainly, they're cheap and they last forever. But the problem for chemically sensitive people is that plastics, like formaldehyde, tend to 'outgas' – dispersing tiny molecules of whatever they're made of into the air, especially when they're heated. If you're surrounded by a lot of synthetic material – such as carpeting, clothing and furniture – you can eventually be overwhelmed by the insidious buildup of fumes, and not even know what's happening until you start to feel ill.

But there are simple ways to get round the problem – starting from the floor up.

'Next to getting rid of gas heat and gas-powered appliances, avoiding use of synthetic carpets and sponge rubber is the most important thing you can do to relieve chemical allergy,' says Dr Randolph. Next to go would be vinyl upholstery, tablecloths, curtains and polyester clothing.

As it happens, many people – and manufacturers – are

returning to natural building materials and furnishings: brick, wood, stone, clay, ceramic tile, terrazzo, quarry tile, stoneware, earthenware, terracotta, hemp, wicker, burlap, wool and cotton rugs, metals such as brass, copper and iron – all of which don't outgas. And all-natural fibres such as cotton, linen, silk and wool are once again giving polyester a run for the money.

As you shop, scout around for nonplastic versions of whatever you need. (See the Appendix for purchase sources of some nonsynthetic items.) If you must occasionally buy plastic, avoid new items. Outgassing tends to diminish after about two years, especially for hard plastics. Soft plastics, on the other hand, tend to outgas indefinitely. The harder the plastic, the safer you are.

'By all means, buy used wooden furniture rather than new synthetic material when you're trying to create a chemically clean room at home,' says Dr McGovern.

Where there's smoke, there's trouble

Some say smoke is an allergen. Others say it's just an irritant. But there's no doubt about one thing: people with allergies are also sensitive to tobacco smoke.

Smoking is nothing less than self-induced air pollution. And an assault on anyone within breathing distance. Cigarette smoke contains not only tar and nicotine, but also *1,500* other chemicals: benzopyrene, formaldehyde, carbon monoxide, nitrites, hydrocarbons, phenols, ammonia, aluminium, sulphur, aldehydes, hydrogen cyanide, pyridines and acrolein – just to name a few. No wonder cigarette smoke is murder on the sensitive airways of asthmatics!

Actually, cigarette smoke bothers asthmatics and non-asthmatics alike, according to a study conducted by allergist Dr Michael S. Blaiss and reported at the annual meeting of the American College of Allergists in January 1982. Whether smoking themselves or breathing the smoke of others nearby, both the seventy-two asthmatics and 322 non-asthmatics in Dr Blaiss's study experienced a drop in 'small airway function' – a medical way of saying they couldn't breathe too well.

If any of your children have asthma, you'll be doing them an enormous favour if you don't smoke. One study showed, for instance, that when their parents stopped smoking, nine out of ten asthmatic children improved dramatically (*Annals of Allergy*, March 1974).

But don't be surprised to hear your allergist tell you to stop smoking if you have any kind of allergy whatsoever. If you're the least bit allergic, smoke of any kind will make matters worse.

'Aside from cancer twenty years down the road, smoking is likely to be contributing to health problems you're having *right now*,' says Dr Bell.

You have more control over smokers in your own home than anywhere else. Tack up No Smoking signs if you have to. Should someone manage to sneak a light behind your back anyway, air out the place as soon as possible.

Wood smoke is related to cigarette smoke. If you have a fireplace in your house, keep the damper closed when it's not lit. Install glass doors across the front. Have the chimney and fireplace cleaned at the end of the season to stop smoky soot from filtering into your house – and your breathing space.

(Marijuana smoke is also an allergen, and has caused hives and asthma.)

Your personal oasis against chemicals

Creating a refuge against chemicals makes it easier for highly sensitive people to tolerate exposure to the rest of the chemical-ridden world. What's more, a personal oasis shores you up psychologically as well as physically, giving you confidence to venture out.

Dr McGovern tells his chemically sensitive patients: 'Select any bedroom in the house and make it "chemically clean". It's not hard to do. Remove the pictures from the walls. Take down all the curtains. Take out the rugs and carpeting. If there's hardwood flooring under the carpeting, so much the better. If not, it's best to cover the floor with ceramic tile. If ceramic tile is not available or too expensive, you may also use very inexpensive, hard vinyl tiles.'

The *in*expensive ones?

'The least expensive, self-sticking tiles tend to be harder and less toxic than the more expensive products. Take my word for it,' says Dr McGovern.

'Next,' he adds, 'you take out all the furniture. Use an

aluminium bed with springs – a folding cot – to sleep on. Instead of a mattress, use several 100 per cent plain cotton blankets. Wash them six or seven times in baking soda to remove any chemical treatment. Layer them to serve as a mattress.' For a pillow, Dr McGovern recommends cotton T-shirts, rolled up and stuffed into a washed, cotton pillowcase.

A pretty spartan sleeping arrangement. But Dr McGovern has a good reason to recommend it as some mattresses contain flame-retardant chemicals. Formaldehyde and pesticides are also employed in their manufacture and if chemically sensitive people sleep on such a mattress, they'll never get better.

For other furniture, Dr McGovern recommends nothing more extravagant than going to a second-hand shop. Finished furniture is okay, as long as it's a few years old and the fumes from paint or stain have had time to dissipate. And be sure to ask if it's been sprayed with pesticides. If it has been, don't buy it. If not, you're safe.

Do people actually make these kinds of changes in their homes?

'Nearly 400 of our patients are sleeping on metal beds,' says Dr McGovern, 'and making nice recoveries.'

'I've had 3,500 patients get rid of their gas stoves,' says Dr Randolph.

Dr William J. Rea, of Dallas, Texas, who has treated thousands of environmentally allergic people, adds, 'We don't recommend anything people won't do. It would be a waste of time.'

Taking the gas stove out of the kitchen and ripping out the carpeting at home are pretty much within our control. But what about going to work? Or travelling? Again, there's more you can do about these situations than you might think.

How to avoid a bad day at the office

Next to your bedroom, you spend the most time in your workplace. You might assume that people with industrial jobs have the most allergy problems. Not so, says Dr McGovern. Office workers – secretaries, clerical workers, administrative assistants, computer programmers and so on – suffer the lion's share of work-related allergic complaints.

'In almost every major office you will find people who are bothered by an allergy,' notes Dr Falliers. Not too surprising, if you glance around the average office. Carbonless typewriter ribbons give off petroleum fumes. Photocopy machines gas out a host of chemicals. Paper is impregnated with formaldehyde and other chemicals – to say nothing of the ink. Then you've got vinyl chairs, and formaldehyde in the panelling, rugs and ceiling tiles. Felt-tip marking pens. Correction fluid. Fluorescent lights. Cigarette smoke. Potted plants. Devout users of perfume and aftershave lotion. All in all, enough to match the fumes in any chemical factory if you're highly sensitive to chemicals.

Even if you could easily find a new job, you would have no guarantee the same problem wouldn't arise in your new workplace. So your best bet is to stay put and make the best of it, and here's how.

• Dilution is part of the solution. If you can, reduce the chemical content of your breathing atmosphere. Open a window and dilute the chemical concentration by ventilation. (Unless of course, a fleet of diesel trucks parks right outside your building. Or your office overlooks a parking garage.)

• Try to leave the building once or twice a day if the outdoor air pollution levels permit. Take a walk outdoors at lunchtime instead of spending the entire hour in the cafeteria.

• If you spend a lot of time on the phone, remove the wad of bacteria-killing cotton in the receiver. (Not all phones have it. To check yours, simply unscrew the mouthpiece on the receiver.)

• Cover the typewriter ribbon and well with a plain piece of cardboard.

• Plug in an air filter (see the section on air cleaning equipment later in this chapter for information on portable models).

Smokers in the workplace pose special problems. Banishing smokers to the rest rooms is really no solution at all, since nonsmokers eventually have to go to the bathroom, too. A lot depends on how co-operative your boss and co-workers are. Your doctor may be able to back you.

'I have personally written letters to employers on behalf of a patient saying: "This person should stay away from smoke," ' says Dr Falliers. 'Most companies are willing to accommodate. Maybe they can move the person to a different work station. I've had a couple of flight attendants as patients, who got sick if they served the smoking section of planes. So the airline lets them serve only the front and someone else serves the back. But there aren't always such easy answers.'

Of course, you may not necessarily be alone in your misery, and in an office situation, 'strength in numbers' can more easily bring about change for everyone.

'We've had buildings closed because 100 people got sick,' says Dr McGovern. 'Two people in one office would get sick, two others from the fourth floor would get sick, and so on, until one way or another they all wound up in my waiting room. In giving their history, they'd all say, "I work at such and such an address." And I'd say, "Wait a minute! Other people working in that building are also getting sick. Let's investigate." '

'So I tell people to go to their union. Or get the names of other people who are allergic. Or write to the company and ask them to improve the ventilation in the building. Sooner or later, companies will find they can't seal up the windows, blow smoke in everyone's face and allow toxic indoor pollution to accumulate in the workplace. Too many people are being permanently disabled. Lawsuits by people with environmentally induced illnesses are increasing.'

For some, just getting the home environment cleared up will be enough to enable them to go to work and do their job. 'Maintaining the home oasis can go a long way towards making unavoidable exposure in the workplace more tolerable,' says Dr Rea.

'After patients start to remove the chemicals in their office,' says Dr McGovern, 'and they clean up their house – mainly giving themselves a "safe" room – they'll improve within a few days or a week. They'll be able to think more clearly, or their joints will stop aching, et cetera, and they'll notice the difference.'

Smog by any other name is still hard to breathe

Sooner or later, we all have to venture outdoors – and deal with outdoor pollution. Certain areas are particularly bad. In

Denver, they call it 'the brown cloud'. Everybody else calls it smog.

Depending on the chemicals that form it, smog comes in two general types: London smog or Los Angeles smog. Los Angeles smog is typical of warm, sunny climates with heavy traffic. Its main ingredients are ozone, a toxic cousin of oxygen, plus nitrogen dioxide and the petroleum-produced chemicals known as hydrocarbons. London smog develops in industrialized cities and supplies its own brand of irritants. Either way, you can suffer anything from eye irritation, breathing problems and blurry vision to coughing, choking and fatigue – even if you're not allergic. Needless to say, smog is downright dangerous for asthmatics. Your doctor may be busiest – and hardest to reach – during an episode of heavy air pollution. It's important to be able to weather an attack on your own. (See the box, What to do during an air pollution episode.)

Tips for car travel

Even on a clear day, driving or riding in a car can expose you to one allergen after another: pollen, dust, car exhaust, asphalt fumes, industrial emissions. Rolling up all the car windows helps. Closing the windows *and* turning on the air conditioning (if your car has it) is even better.

According to a study conducted by Dr William Skellenger of the University of Michigan Medical School, Ann Arbor, rolling up the windows removes 90 to 94 per cent of noxious particles. Flicking on the air conditioner ups that to 97 per cent. Just be sure to have the system cleaned before you turn it on for the first time in summer – or periodically if you live in a warm climate. Otherwise, you'll get hit with a blast of dust. Also, have the vents cleaned and condensation water removed frequently to keep the system free of mould, or that too may trigger attacks of wheezing, hay fever or other respiratory troubles.

If chemicals are your problem, that 'new car smell' can drive you up a tree. Cars two years old or older usually pose less of a problem because the vinyl interior has aged somewhat. In any case, an air filter powered by the cigarette lighter can help suck up any lingering fumes. And – new car smell or not – an air filter is also helpful when driving in heavy traffic or polluted areas.

WHAT TO DO DURING AN AIR POLLUTION EPISODE

1. Try to stay indoors in a clean environment. Air conditioning (if available), air filters and face masks can be helpful.

2. Avoid smoking and smoke-filled rooms.

3. Avoid exposure to dust and other irritants, such as hair sprays, insect sprays and other aerosol products; paint; exhaust fumes, smoke from a fire of any kind and fumes in general.

4. Avoid unnecessary physical activity.

5. Avoid exposure to people with colds and respiratory infections, if at all possible.

6. If air pollution doesn't seem to let up – or if it begins to worsen – you may have to leave the polluted area temporarily until the air clears up.

7. If you are under a doctor's care for asthma or other allergies, ask him for specific instructions. Know what medication, if any, you should use. Know what symptoms should prompt you to call your doctor. Know when and where to go to a hospital.

SOURCE: *Adapted from 'Guidelines for the Asthmatic Patient during Air Pollution Episodes', by the Weather and Air Pollution Committee of the American Academy of Allergy,* Journal of Allergy and Clinical Immunology, *vol. 55, no. 4, 1975.*

Guide to air cleaning equipment

Say you find yourself in a setting where you're breathing one nasty allergen after another. You can't leave the room or remove the sources. Perhaps you can't even open a window – it's 10 degrees outside, or the window is bolted shut.

Enter the face mask. Lightweight, cotton surgical masks strain out particles such as pollen, dust and smoke. For chemical vapours you may need a charcoal-filtered mask (see the

Appendix for purchasing sources). Perhaps you'll only have to wear a mask in special situations, such as sitting in a meeting where everyone is smoking. Or you have a whole stack of papers to photocopy and can't tolerate the copier fumes.

Face masks are lifesavers, too, when the outside air is particularly bad, says Dr Phyllis Saifer, an allergist in Berkeley, California. Again, charcoal-filtered masks work best. 'Granted, other people are put off by seeing someone wearing a mask, especially if you sit next to them on the bus or the subway. But a mask can make the difference between feeling ill and feeling well. Just don't walk into a bank wearing a mask,' adds Dr Saifer. 'That makes people *really* edgy.'

For your own home or office – wherever you spend a considerable part of your day – it's worth looking into more elaborate equipment for ways of reconditioning the air you breathe.

Humidifiers and Dehumidifiers. People with asthma and other respiratory allergies feel better when they breathe moist air – it keeps the nose and bronchial passages from drying out. Cold dry air is also irritating to airways, which are already exceptionally sensitive in people with asthma. When the heat is turned on for the winter, you may need a humidifier. Too-high humidity in the house, however, promotes growth of house dust mites, moulds and fungi, and tends to carry more dust and pollen – all contributors to allergy and asthma. So in summer, you may need a dehumidifier.

Indoor humidity of about 35 to 50 per cent seems to strike a balance between personal comfort and preventing proliferation of allergens around the house. Be sure to get equipment with a humidistat that automatically shuts off when the desirable level of moisture is reached. And allergy doctors recommend that portable humidifiers and dehumidifiers be kept clean and mould-free by cleaning them frequently with a stiff brush rather than by adding strong disinfectants and detergents to the water.

Air-to-Air Heat Exchanger. As we said before, too-tight buildings with poor ventilation are a major cause of chemical fume buildup and mould growth. Air-to-air heat exchangers help solve the problem without sacrificing fuel efficiency. They work on the principle of 'good air in, bad air out'. Warm, outgoing indoor air and cold, fresh incoming air pass through ducts with a common wall. Heat from the indoor air is transferred to the fresher outdoor air. Should you have a heat exchange system installed, be sure that the outside air intakes are positioned where the air is the freshest – not drawing fumes from the garage or kitchen stove exhaust from your own or other buildings.

Air filters

Air filters range from small, inexpensive desktop models to whole-house air conditioning systems. Some do you a lot more good than others. Some, in fact, are worthless. The ones that work are a real blessing, though.

'I almost always prescribe air filtration,' says Dr Boxer. 'I feel it's helpful. I've seen asthma patients who were helped immensely by just using an air filter.'

'Air filtration is certainly a very natural way of controlling symptoms,' says Dr Falliers. 'There are dozens of products, and each has to be examined for what it does and doesn't do.'

Air filters may be installed in the ductwork of either your warm-air furnace or air conditioning system. Or you can buy portable models that sit anywhere in the room. Or even hook up to the cigarette lighter in your car. Portable units can sometimes be rented.

Activated Charcoal Filters. The odour-eating capacity of activated charcoal varies with the humidity and temperature of the air in the room, the concentration of fumes and the type of odours in the air. Dr Guy O. Pfeiffer, of Mattoon, Illinois, studied activated charcoal filters and found that they're generally pretty good for absorbing cooking and food odours (even from burned dinners and foods such as garlic, onions, cheese and citrus); cigarette and tobacco odours; diesel and petrol fumes; smog and ozone; and the odours from pets, mothballs and perfume. Charcoal is slightly less powerful against pollen, coal smoke, mildew, chlorine, fish odour and some noxious gases. And it's useless against carbon monoxide and formaldehyde. Installed piggyback with another type of filter, however, charcoal can be helpful; one catches what the other misses.

Electronic Air Cleaners. The most common type of electronic air cleaner is the electrostatic precipitator. Until a few years ago, electronic air cleaners were standard equipment for treating asthma and respiratory allergy. They act much like an electromagnet for air pollution: a fan draws in particles, zaps them with an electric charge and collects them on a plate. The charged particles are supposedly taken out of circulation. However, J. Gordon King, a consultant in air contamination, writes that although electrostatic precipitators are popularly advertised as being 95 to 99 per cent efficient, they're not. In reality, says Mr King, electrostatic air cleaners available for home use rarely trap more than 80 per cent of the particles in the air. What's worse, efficiency can drop to as low as 20 per cent within a short period of time – especially for bigger particles like pollen (*Respiratory Care*, March–April 1973).

That means electrostatic air cleaners are no more effective than putting a sheet of gauze over your mouth. And the charged particles that escape the filter build up on walls and furniture faster than if no cleaner was used at all. To top it all off, all electronic air cleaners produce ozone, a highly toxic gas which causes headaches in some people. So you may not want to bother with them at all.

HEPA (High Efficiency Particulate Air) Filters. These filters work a lot better than electronic air cleaners. Air that's been cleared by a HEPA is free of 99.97 per cent of all contaminating particles, according to the US National Bureau of Standards. That's about as clean as you can get in today's environment. And they maintain their efficiency throughout their operating life of two to five years. HEPA filters work well against pollens, moulds, yeast and other fungi, bacteria *and* viruses – a boon to allergy sufferers prone to frequent colds and flu attacks. HEPA filters have been known to relieve hay fever and asthma symptoms within ten minutes to half an hour. When potassium permanganate or activated charcoal is added, an HEPA filter can clear the air of jumbo particles like dust and pollen *as well as* minute chemical odours.

HEPA units with metal casings are better for chemically sensitive people than units with casings made of pressboard (which contains formaldehyde) or plastic.

HEPA filters did wonders for reducing nightly asthma attacks for asthmatic children at a summer camp in West Virginia, according to the camp's medical director Dr Merle S. Scherr. In his report, Dr Scherr emphasized that HEPA units are an important part of treatment of allergic asthma (*West Virginia Medical Journal*, July 1977).

HEPA units are also a godsend for preventing nightly asthma

attacks for asthmatic children at home in winter. Normally, cold nights require furnaces to work harder, so furnace fans circulate more dust – and trigger more asthma. But when HEPA filters were tested on eighteen children with hard-to-control asthma, the children collectively logged 140 nights of undisturbed sleep with use of the filter, as compared with only forty-five peaceful nights without the filter. 'This . . . not only relieved the parents of having to get up in the night and care for these children,' say the researchers who conducted the study, 'but we feel that the child, if well rested, felt better, performed better during the day and was probably more resistant to illness.' Several of the children were also able to cut down on their asthma medicine, and they no longer missed any school (*Annals of Allergy*, June 1973).

Air Conditioning. Pollen counts in a closed, air conditioned room plummet to around zero. In an unfiltered room, with the window open, pollen levels are about one-third the outdoor level – enough to aggravate symptoms in anyone with pollen allergy. So air conditioning definitely helps allergies. Whether one-room, window-mounted air conditioners or central, whole-house systems are better at filtering out pollen is not exactly clear. In general, pollen and mould levels tend to run lower in houses with air conditioning of *any* kind than in houses with no air conditioning whatsoever, largely because the doors and windows are closed. Whether you go in for a whole-house system or individual window units simply depends on what you can afford.

Backed up by a separate HEPA unit, air conditioning of any type is optimized. Be sure to clean the coils and filters, however, to prevent mould contamination. And don't run the air conditioner too high: too-cold air can aggravate respiratory allergy.

Negative Ion Generators. These gizmos generate negatively charged air particles (ions) – which are theoretically good for us – and thus replace positively charged ions – which are supposedly bad for us. Scientists haven't exactly rushed to support the health claims made for negative ion generators. But if you're allergic to particles such as dust, pollen or smoke, you may derive some benefit from their use. That's because negative ions travel around the room scavenging larger contaminants, which are then electrostatically attracted to walls, carpets, curtains, furniture and other surfaces closer to the ground – and away from our breathing space. Some do a better job of cleaning than others, however. The units equipped with a disposable collection pad are probably somewhat better.

Dr Falliers describes negative ion generators this way: 'In current scientific studies in which one group of asthmatics used a negative ion generator and another used a machine that did nothing, there was no significant difference in their symptoms. Yet individual cases of improvement are so impressive that I certainly would like to give anybody the benefit of trying one.'

Miscellaneous 'Tabletop' Air Purifiers. You may have noticed small portable fan and filter units – marketed as purifiers – in the housewares department of your neighbourhood department store or advertised on TV. About the size of a desk telephone, these appliances come in all shapes and colours. Most feature a small, electrically driven fan which draws air through a filter. Some contain activated charcoal or chemicals to absorb odours and contaminants. They sometimes claim to control formaldehyde.

We wish we could recommend these devices, but not much has been done to study their ability to clean the air. Considering their small size and the big job they're supposed to do, researchers say you'd probably be better off with an HEPA filter or air conditioning.

Every little bit helps

We'll be the first to admit that a pristine-pure environment – completely devoid of dust, pollen or chemicals – is unattainable. You can, however, realistically reduce your exposure to a variety of the most troublesome items. Start small, eliminating one source at a time. You should soon find yourself feeling better.

'Allergy is a reversible disease,' says Dr McGovern. 'If you give your immune system a chance, it will heal every time.'

CHAPTER 5

DON'T OVERLOOK DRUGS AS A CAUSE

Allergic reactions to drugs are usually mild or moderately severe – no more than some itching or a few hives. But occasionally a drug reaction can be fatal. That's why allergic people should learn *all* they can before they take any drugs, whether prescribed by a doctor or purchased over-the-counter.

Allergy or side effect?

Each drug has a number of known side effects – health problems caused by the drug, which doctors have learned to expect. An allergic reaction, on the other hand, is an *unexpected* reaction which people who respond to a drug with known side effects rarely have. One out of every four adverse reactions to drugs is allergic.

The chemistry behind drug allergies hasn't been pegged down as an antigen-antibody reaction, or any other identifiable immune reaction. Just the same, the possible symptoms are identical to those of other allergies: skin rashes, asthma, hives, shock. And reactions occur only after a prior, uneventful exposure to the drug or a chemically related substance. So doctors regard drug sensitivities as allergy in the true sense despite a lack of measurable immunological changes.

But how does your doctor know whether you are experiencing a side effect or an allergic reaction? For one thing, side effects, no matter how numerous and varied, are spelled out either on drug package inserts or in one of several reference books containing drug information, such as *The British Formulary of Drugs: A Handbook of Psychoactive Medicines.* More important, however, an allergic reaction follows a latent period – usually seven to ten days – after you first take the drug. In other words, your doctor starts you on penicillin today, but you may not react until next week. Then the next time you take penicillin, you may react immediately – and explosively. And if you're allergic, you'll react no matter how small the dose.

The skin is the organ most likely to suffer when you swallow a drug or get an injection that doesn't agree with you. (Contact allergy to topically applied drugs is addressed more fully in Chapter 7, Contact (skin) allergies, under the sections headed 'A note about skin medications' and 'Preventing skin allergies in the first place.') Here is a list of possible symptoms.

Itching. Alone or with other symptoms, itching is so characteristic of drug allergy that if you don't itch, you probably aren't really allergic.

Hives. Huge hives all over the body are almost a sure sign of allergy to certain drugs – notably penicillin, aspirin and related compounds (salicylates) or even allergy treatment extracts. Appearance of hives is probably due to histamine release, explained in Chapter 1, What is an allergy?

Rashes. Drug-induced rashes come in a variety of shapes and hues, from bright red, itchy patches to bumps or scattered spots that resemble measles. Occasionally, the rash takes on a bluish tint. Whatever the form or colour, it usually centres on the trunk.

A mixed bag of eruptions known as erythema multiforme is the ultimate in drug-induced rashes. The blotches vary in size, shape and appearance, are usually distributed on the backs of the legs or forearms, and are frequently accompanied by fever, general discomfort, stomach and abdominal upset, and joint pains. It's reassuring to know that all clears up when the drug is discontinued.

Generalized Swelling (angioedema). This often affects the eyelids, lips, hands and feet.

Broken Capillaries (purpura). These red or purple threadlike squiggles beneath the skin surface are less common but occasional signs of drug allergy.

Photosensitivity. Sunlight presumably alters certain drugs so that they readily form allergy-triggering substances in the skin. The resulting flareup resembles contact dermatitis or eczema, and may not appear until days or months after the sun/drug encounter.

Scaling and Shedding of the Skin (exfoliative dermatitis). Needless to say, this is one of the more drastic symptoms of drug allergy. Sometimes the hair and nails fall out, too. Fever, chills and overall discomfort go along with it. Don't worry about being taken by surprise, though; this problem doesn't develop overnight. The trick is to alert your doctor to any patches of scaly skin early on, before things get out of control.

While the skin takes the brunt of our allergic encounters with drugs, the rest of the body is not off limits. Bronchial asthma can be caused by aspirin. (Most people who get this already have regular asthma.) Fever – rarely a consequence of other types of allergy – can develop as part of a drug reaction, and can easily be mistaken for a symptom of the illness that's being treated. By far, though, anaphylaxis is the most severe and dangerous non-skin drug reaction, and one that's most commonly caused by penicillin. With little or no warning, blood pressure drops, the pulse weakens, the throat swells closed and the individual collapses – all within minutes or even seconds after getting the drug. Anaphylaxis, by the way, is far more likely to occur after an injection than after oral medication.

The most troublesome drugs

In one of the most comprehensive studies of drug allergy ever conducted – the Boston Collaborative Drug Surveillance Program – doctors collected data from patients in ten hospitals in the United States, plus eight foreign hospitals, covering 22,227 people in all. The results, presented in Table 17, show which drugs most often cause skin reactions (itching, rashes, hives and so on). It's important to note that women reacted 50 per cent more frequently than men, and that the severity of a person's illness had no bearing on how likely he or she was to react. What follows is a rundown of the most troublesome drugs.

TABLE 17

Drugs That Commonly Cause Allergic Skin Reactions
(as reported by the Boston Collaborative Drug Surveillance Program)

Drugs	**Reactions per 1,000 People Tested**
Penicillins	
Ampicillin (Ampicillin, Ampifen, Ampilar, Britcin, Penbritin, Vidopen, Ampiclox, Magnapen)	52
Semisynthetic penicillins (carbenicillin – Pyopen; cloxacillin – Ampiclox, Orbenin; methicillin – Celbenin)	36
Penicillin G (Crystapen, Bicillin, Triplopen)	16
Penicillin V (Crystapen V, Stabilin, Apsin)	16
Gentamycin Sulphate (septopal chains – Genticin, Cidomycin, Garamycin, Palacos R with Genamycin, Minims gentamycin)	16
Cephalosporins (cephalexin – Ceporex, Keplex; cephaloridine – Ceporin; cephalothin – Keflin)	13
Quinidine (Kinidin, Kiditard – as a bisulphate)	12
Heparin calcium (calciparine, minihep calcium)	7.7
Nitrazepam (Nitrados, Somnite, Mogadon)	6.3
Barbiturates	4.7
Chlordiazepoxide (Librium, Limbitrol, Libraxin)	4.2
Diazepam (Diazemuls, Atansine, Stesolid, Valrelease, Valium Roche, Alupram)	3.8
Isoniazid (Rimifom, Mynah, Rimactazid, Rifinah)	3.0
Guaphenesin (Bricanyl expectorant, Bricanyl compound, Sudafed expectorant, Dimotane expectorant, Franol expectorant, Actifed expectorant, Linctifed, Robitussin)	2.9
Chlorothiazide (Saluric)	2.8
Isophane insulin	1.3
Phenytoin (Epanutin)	1.1
Flurazepam HCl (Dalmans)	0.5
Chloral hydrate (Noctec)	0.2

SOURCE: *Adapted from 'Rates of Cutaneous Reactions to Drugs', by Kenneth A. Arndt and Hershel Jick,* Journal of the American Medical Association, *March 1, 1976.*

Penicillin. This is not one drug but a general name for a group of antibiotics. Different types of penicillin, made from special moulds, control specific types of bacterial infections – making penicillins the most useful and widely prescribed drugs in the world. Doctors find, however, that from 1 to 10 per cent of the population is allergic to penicillin. Fortunately, most reactions are mild. The chance of a dramatic, explosive reaction is relatively remote; the odds are somewhere between 1 and 4 in 10,000. Even then, only 2 in 100,000 of these result in death. The remainder are kept in check by emergency medical action. (Strangely enough, people who are allergic to penicillin moulds, such as those sometimes found in cheese or around the house, can generally tolerate penicillin.)

Doctors have begun to realize that many people who think they're allergic to penicillin aren't really allergic to it after all. Penicillin allergy, it seems, often fades with time if the drug is avoided. Researchers at the Clinical Research Center at Massachusetts Institute of Technology, for instance, tested 300 children who were reputedly allergic to penicillin, to find that only 19 per cent were indeed allergic. The authors conclude that the incidence of penicillin allergy is over-estimated, and that the allergy is not necessarily permanent (*Archives of Disease in Childhood*, vol. 55, no. 857, 1980).

In a similar study, a team of two doctors and a nurse tested nineteen children who had been judged allergic to penicillin three to five years earlier and found only five were still allergic (*Journal of Allergy and Clinical Immunology*, abstract no. 183, January 1982).

In still another study, researchers tested almost 800 people presumably allergic to penicillin. Nearly half of them were no longer allergic (*Journal of Allergy and Clinical Immunology*, September 1981).

These studies don't mean you should throw caution to the wind and disregard any bad experience you may have had with penicillin. On the contrary: it's important to know if you have an authentic, active allergy to penicillin. Certain conditions – for example, serious infections, a chronic disease such as cystic fibrosis or venereal disease – depend heavily on penicillin for their medical management. In such cases, doctors conduct a skin test with benzylpenicilloyl-polylysine (called Pre-Pen), which they consider to be the most accurate, lowest risk predictor available for penicillin allergy. Sometimes a doctor can manage penicillin allergy by giving stepped doses of penicillin to desensitize an individual to the drug. If using penicillin is out of the question, the doctor will look for a safe substitute.

Aspirin. Aspirin is the commonly used name for acetylsalicylic acid (ASA). Although aspirin didn't show up in the Boston study of allergic skin reactions, aspirin and related compounds are the second most likely drugs to trigger allergy.

Aspirin allergy (which, for some unknown reason, most often affects women) commonly afflicts the skin, resulting in hives. Until a few years ago, many doctors thought that nasal polyps were also a hallmark of aspirin allergy. Now, however, many doctors believe that's not so.

Aspirin *does* seem to produce asthma, though: one out of five asthmatics has aspirin to blame. Your airways tighten up. You wheeze heavily. Your nose continues to run like a broken tap. And quite often your skin reddens and you suffer giant, puffy hives. But the lungs and nose don't have exclusive rights to aspirin allergy. Occasionally, aspirin-sensitive individuals experience intestinal cramps or other abdominal discomfort, diarrhoea and vomiting. A few experience tremors, rapid heartbeat, constipation – even headaches. But runny nose, asthma and hives are the most common reactions, and the pattern is fairly predictable.

Aspirin allergy does not necessarily occur alone. In one study, 75 per cent of people allergic to aspirin were also sensitive to inhalants (such as pollen and dust), 74 per cent were allergic to some sort of food and 43 per cent were allergic to other drugs (*Annals of Allergy*, March 1981). As a matter of fact, it's quite common for allergy to aspirin to be accompanied by allergy to other pain relievers (analgesics), such as those listed in Table 18. (These dual allergies are called 'cross-reactions'.)

As we mentioned in Chapter 3, Finding your no-allergy diet, E102, or tartrazine, often causes serious problems in people who are allergic to aspirin. The two compounds seem to cross-react. To help you avoid tartrazine, Table 19 lists some of the common drugs that contain tartrazine. By law, drugs that contain tartrazine must list it on the label.

TABLE 18

Analgesics (Pain Relievers) That Cross-React with Aspirin

Usually Cross-React	Sometimes Cross-React
Fenoprofen (Fenopron, Progesic)	Naproxen (Synflex, Naprosyn)
Ibuprofen (Brufen, Apsifen, Fenbid, Motrin)	Sulindac (Clinoril)
Indomethacin (Imbrilon, Indocid, Indolar)	Tolmetin (Tolectin)
Phenylbutazone (Butazolidin, Butacote)	

SOURCE: *Adapted by permission of the publisher from 'Aspirin Intolerance in Asthmatics: Who Is Susceptible and Why?'* Modern Medicine, *January 15–30 1979, p. 65.*

People allergic to aspirin and aspirin compounds may also be allergic to certain foods containing natural salicylates (which have also been linked to hyperactivity). These foods include apricots, berries, cherries, cucumbers, currants, grapes, nectarines, peaches, plums and tomatoes. (See Table 25 in Part V.)

Children are not exempt from aspirin allergy. Dr Cecil Collins-Williams and a colleague tell of four children with poorly controlled asthma who began to wheeze within half an hour after taking aspirin. 'When [aspirin] compounds were removed from their diet, there was a dramatic improvement in their asthma,' write the doctors (*Annals of Allergy*, abstract no. 1, August 1981).

Aspirin shows up in a variety of over-the-counter remedies for headache pain, menstrual discomfort, sinusitis, backaches, stomach upsets and other aches and pains, as you can see from Table 20. Read all the labels of over-the-counter products if you are allergic to aspirin. And quiz your dentist about any treatments you receive; some dentists insert aspirin-containing wicks into tooth sockets during dental repair work.

Vaccines. Flu shots, made from influenza virus cultures on egg, provoke a reaction in anyone who is highly allergic to eggs. Although these vaccines are highly purified, traces of egg occasionally cling to the virus. For this reason, authorities at the national Centers for Disease Control in Atlanta say that people who are highly allergic to eggs shouldn't receive flu injections.

TABLE 19

Drugs Containing Tartrazine (E102)

Aminophylline (Phyllocontin, Amesec)
Anusol (suppositories)
Ascorbic acid (numerous trade names, not all of which contain tartrazine, although three common ones that do are Ketovite, Multivite and Abidec)
Bactrim
Colchicine
Decadron
Dimotane
Dulcolax
Ferrous Sulphate (many trade names, but the only ones which contain Fesovit, Fefol-vit and Fefol)
Hydrochlorothiazide (Co-Betaloc, Dyazide)
Ilosone
Intal (in gelatine capsules) and Intal compound
Keflex
Lonxin PG
Methotroxate
Phenergen compound expectorant
Phenobarbitone tablets and elixir
Potassium Chloride (many trade names, but those that contain tartrazine include Slow K, K Contin, Navidrex K, Diumide K and Kloref)
Prednisolone (Deltacortoril Enteric)
Premarin (but only the 1.25 mg tablets)
Seconal sodium
Tedral elixir

SOURCE: *Adapted by permission of the publisher from 'Aspirin-Induced Asthma in Children', by Y. Tan and C. Collins-Williams,* Annals of Allergy, *January 1982, p. 4.*

TABLE 20

Common Drugs Containing Aspirin (Acetylsalicylic Acid)

Alka-Seltzer	Codis	Migravess
Antoin	Dolasan	Myolgin
Aspar	Doloxene compound	Napsalgesic
Aspellin	Equagesic	Payrocin
Breopin	Hypon	Robazisal forte
Caprin	Labropin	Solprin
Claradin		Trancoprin

That applies to people who, when they eat eggs, develop swollen lips or tongue, have dramatic breathing difficulties or collapse in shock.

Insulin. During the first few weeks of insulin therapy, many diabetics experience a slight skin irritation at the site of the injection that usually subsides in a matter of time. Some diabetics, however, experience larger, more troublesome reactions that never let up. The injection site can be itchy, watery or painful to touch. Worse, the person may feel sick or go into anaphylactic shock. Insulin is made from extracts of either beef or pork pancreas, so if a diabetic seems to be allergic to insulin from one animal, doctors may test insulins from the other. If that doesn't do the trick, some diabetics are able to control the disease by eating a carefully planned diet or by using less powerful drugs that are taken by mouth, or doing both.

Drugs have additives, too

At times, the allergy isn't to a drug itself but to one of various additives. Artificial colours and flavourings are routinely added to drug compounds to make them both more palatable for consumers to swallow and easier for doctors, nurses and pharmacists to identify. Preservatives, fillers and coatings all show up. And an additive in a drug is just as likely to cause allergy as one in a food. For example, in his book *Why Your Child Is Hyperactive* (Random House, 1975) Dr Benjamin Feingold tells of two young women taking birth control pills who developed wheezing and coughing, watery eyes and laboured breathing. They were afraid they'd developed asthma. As it turned out, however, they were simply allergic to artificial colouring in the birth control pills. (Incidentally, the hormones themselves can cause allergylike symptoms – stuffy nose, itching, hives – even asthma.)

Many antihistamines, antihistamine-decongestants, corticosteroids, bronchodilators and theophylline (a muscle relaxer), among others, often contain the yellow dye tartrazine. Ironically, those drugs are the mainstay of medical treatment of asthma and respiratory allergy.

A capsule or tablet can also contain non-chemical additives you could be allergic to – for instance, starch derived from corn, potato, sorghum or other food. Or medications can have a binder made from pork, beef or lamb fat, a potential problem for anyone allergic to those meats.

Allergies to illegal drugs

Most people take drugs that are either prescribed or bought over-the-counter in a supermarket or chemist. Some drugs, however, are bought on the street – they're illegal. Aside from ruining health, abused drugs produce their share of allergic reactions. Barbiturates can trigger not only rashes but overall shedding of the skin, and can also raise large blisters around the mouth and at pressure points such as the hips and ankles. Amphetamines can cause rashes and asthmatic attacks. Cocaine, too, can cause serious asthma.

Marijuana harbours some of the very moulds that trigger allergy in asthmatics. If that's not bad enough, smoking marijuana releases some of the same nasty chemicals (such as benzopyrene and hydrocarbons) as regular cigarettes, making marijuana as abrasive to an asthmatic's lungs as tobacco. Even if a person doesn't have asthma, marijuana can cause red, inflamed eyelids (conjunctivitis), diarrhoea, dryness of the mouth, hypoglycemia, muscular incoordination, nausea, respiratory depression, spasms and urinary frequency.

Will you react?

Although no one knows the exact reason why one person develops sensitivity to a drug and another doesn't, certain recognized factors may alter your vulnerability.

Nature of the Drug. Some drugs, such as milk of magnesia, rarely cause allergic reactions. Others – namely penicillin, aspirin compounds and the sulphonamides – account for 80 to 90 per cent of all allergic drug reactions. Whether or not a drug will cause allergy seems to depend on its ability (or the ability of one of its byproducts) to latch on to a protein. And once you've had an allergic response to one drug, you're open to cross-reactions to chemically similar drugs. Remember, aspirin cross-reacts with other analgesics or the food colouring tartrazine. So anyone who has reacted to one drug is likely to react to new drugs.

How Old You Are. Children don't react to drugs as often as adults do, possibly because they use less.

Other Allergies. Some evidence suggests that people with allergic diseases (hay fever, eczema, asthma and the like) tend to react more readily to drugs. Other evidence says they don't. Nevertheless, when allergic people do react to drugs, they seem to react more seriously. For instance, an allergic person is three to ten times more likely to suffer an anaphylactic reaction to a drug than a non-allergic person.

Other Conditions. Doctors say that the risk of reacting is greater among people with a chronic illness. But, they say, that's probably not because the people are ill but because they take a *lot* of drugs.

How the Drug Is Taken. Perhaps because the skin is such a sensitive organ, drugs applied topically are more prone to cause reactions than those you swallow. Because of that increased risk, certain drugs, such as penicillin and sulphonamides, are no longer used in salves. Along the same line, you may react to an oral drug if you previously reacted to the drug when it was applied to your skin. For instance, if you once reacted to mercury-containing merthiolate painted on a scratch or cut, you could eventually react to a mercury-containing diuretic.

An injected drug, however, is more likely to cause an *immediate and severe* reaction, since it enters the system quickly.

Managing drug allergy

Recognizing a drug allergy for what it really is can be easy . . . or difficult. It's easy if:

- you show symptoms while you take the drug or a few days after you stop;
- symptoms disappear a few days after the drug is discontinued;
- your symptoms resemble those experienced by others who are allergic to the drug; or
- you've reacted to the same drug before in the same way.

It can be difficult to diagnose drug allergy, however, if:

– you have previously taken the drug in question with no difficulty;
– your symptoms resemble the symptoms of your disease (for instance, drug-induced wheezing and bronchospasms may resemble respiratory problems from asthma);
– you are taking several drugs at the same time;
– the reaction persists for weeks or months after you stop taking the drug, as is the case with drugs that the body eliminates slowly, like Depo-Testosterone and other time-release hormones; or
– you're unknowingly exposed to unsuspected sources of the drug (for example, penicillin in milk, or aspirin in over-the-counter remedies).

Overcoming these difficulties with skin tests to uncover the allergy is not really an option. For one thing, skin testing for drugs is risky because of the danger of anaphylaxis. For another, they don't offer accurate clues (except for the skin test for penicillin we mentioned earlier in this chapter).

The biggest 'difficulty' is the first on our list: drug reactions that get lost among the symptoms of a basic, underlying illness. For instance, say you're given streptomycin for a virus and develop an allergic fever. The fever may be misinterpreted as a symptom of the virus, when in fact it is a reaction to streptomycin. And that could be dangerous.

'A minor drug reaction may progress, if unrecognized, to more severe, even fatal, reactions,' writes allergist Dr Richard D. DeSwarte, an assistant professor at Northwestern University Medical School in Chicago.

Common sense, then, says that if you're taking drugs of any kind you should immediately report any unusual reactions to your doctor, even if you stopped taking the medication a few days before. That's not only for your personal benefit, but it also helps doctors to keep track of reactions so that drugs can be used more safely and wisely.

For mild drug reactions, stopping the drug is all that's usually needed. For widespread skin eruptions, tepid colloidal baths (described in detail in Chapter 7, Contact (skin) allergies) can soothe and relieve the itch. For systemic reactions, like asthma, your doctor may prescribe a short course of antihistamines or corticosteroids to get things under control. By staying away from a drug for a few years, many people lose their allergic sensitivity to it and are once again able to take it if they have to.

Because immediate reactions are more dangerous than the gradual, delayed onset of symptoms, people with drug allergies (or drug allergies in the family) should read Chapter 14, What to do in an allergic emergency.

Prevention is the best medicine

The preventive measures outlined here apply to all drug reactions, including allergic.

Most important, if you have allergies, *don't self-medicate.* As you can see, some of the most common causes of drug allergy – aspirin and other pain relievers – can be purchased without a prescription at the supermarket or corner store.

When your doctor does the prescribing, the cardinal rule is careful and conservative use of medications: the lowest doses, for as short a time as necessary.

'The simplest way to reduce or prevent allergic drug reactions is to prescribe medication only when clearly indicated,' writes Dr DeSwarte in the book, *Allergic Diseases* (J. B. Lippincott, 1972). 'Medications, especially antibiotics, are often used inappropriately, too frequently and over a prolonged period of time.'

Too many people demand a 'penicillin shot' for every little cold or sniffle – unnecessarily upping the odds for an allergic reaction. Dr DeSwarte says that out of a group of thirty people who died from penicillin-induced anaphylaxis, only twelve really required penicillin.

Chances are, though, that sooner or later you will have a legitimate need for medication. Ideally, your doctor should be well versed in adverse reactions to the drugs he or she selects. But a quick glance at the cumbersome volumes which list dozens of possible reactions to thousands of drugs, makes it obvious that no doctor could possibly keep abreast of it all. They must be particularly cautious with newly introduced drugs, and be prepared for reactions which have not yet been reported. Penicillin, for example, was initially regarded as a very low-risk drug. As time passed and more doctors prescribed it, reactions appeared.

You can help your doctor guard against problems by looking

up possible side effects yourself. My husband and I, for example, were planning a holiday in the Caribbean, so we asked our family doctor for an antibiotic to take along in the event we came down with Montezuma's revenge or some other traveller's scourge. He prescribed Minocin (minocycline hydrochloride), an antibiotic which he told us to take prophylactically – starting three days before we left – to stop any trouble before it began. He said that Minocin was widely used by people like ourselves who were headed for the tropics.

Before going to the chemist to have the prescription filled, I looked up Minocin in *Physicians' Desk Reference*,* which said that the drug can induce photosensitivity – a skin reaction to sunlight. That could be bad news for two people looking forward to a week of swimming and beachcombing. We took the drug anyway, but the knowledge of a possible reaction prepared us to discontinue its use at the first sign of red or itchy skin.

If you, your child or an elderly parent ever experience a drug reaction of any kind, be sure to jot down the name of the drug (both trade name and chemical name) and how you or they reacted. Ask your doctor or chemist for the names of suitable alternatives and possible hidden sources of related chemicals. Add that information to your home medical file and bring it to the attention of medical personnel should you or your relatives land in a hospital casualty department or change doctors. (That includes dentists.) Better still, buy a tag or card designating drugs to be avoided.

And last, when your doctor takes your medical history and asks if you're taking any drugs, don't forget to mention things like mouth-washes, vitamins, birth control pills, menstrual aids and suppositories. When it comes to drug allergy, you just can't take anything for granted.

With these preventive measures, drugs should do what they're meant to – help you get healthy again.

* English equivalents are *Medicines: A Guide for Everybody* by Peter Parrish, Penguin Books, 1984, and *A Handbook of Psychoactive Medicines* by DuQuesne and Reeves, Quartet 1982

CHAPTER 6

WHAT TO DO ABOUT INSECT ALLERGIES

Most people suffer only momentary discomfort when stung by a bee: a pin prick of pain; a red welt at the site of the sting surrounded by a paler, whitish area; and maybe a fierce itch. In a couple of days, all is forgotten.

Allergic people (and 1 out of 250 people is allergic to insect bites or stings) don't get off so easily. The area around the sting may swell and remain swollen for up to a day. That's no real cause for concern unless the swelling persists or the whole arm or leg swells. Then you need to see a doctor – if for no other reason than to determine whether or not you are at risk for a reaction that involves your whole body (doctors call it 'systemic') and may even be life threatening.

That type of reaction can *begin* mildly enough: a dry cough, itching and swelling around the eyes, sneezing, wheezing and widespread hives. And if you're lucky, that's where the symptoms stop. But in 4 out of 1,000 people, the pulse becomes rapid, the skin pale or flushed, and blood pressure falls – followed by constricted breathing, and possibly abdominal cramps, diarrhoea, nausea, vomiting, chills, fever and loss of consciousness – all within fifteen minutes of the sting. That's anaphylactic shock; unfortunately, it kills forty people a year. So even the first mild symptoms should be treated as an emergency if you've had a severe reaction at any time in the past. (See the accompanying box, Allergic and non-allergic reactions to insect stings and bites.)

A few individuals suffer not only an immediate reaction but a second, delayed reaction ten to fourteen days later. Symptoms can include a headache, general malaise, fever, lymph gland discomfort and painful joints.

Know thy enemy

Insects that cause allergy are of two general sorts: stingers and biters.

Stingers include bees, hornets and wasps. The females of the species are the troublemakers. Equipped with stingers mounted on their hind sections, they inject their venom much as a doctor injects you with a hypodermic needle. Stinging insects produce more severe reactions than biting insects.

Biters include ants, mosquitoes and flies and dispense venom through their saliva.

As the victim, however, you probably won't know what bit you, let alone notice what end it used. Still, it's helpful to know something about the habits and habitats of these tiresome creatures, in order to keep out of their way.

Bees

Bees differ not only in appearance but in temperament. Honeybees are mild-mannered and usually will not sting unless stepped on or otherwise disturbed, or unless their hive is threatened.

If you're approached by a solitary bee, your first reaction is probably to flail your arms wildly to shoo it away. *Don't.* That will only get it excited. Instead, slowly walk to the nearest building or car for cover. Incidentally, do not crush a bee near its nest. Doing so may release an odour that signals the colony to swarm out in revenge. And if one sting is bad, many are disastrous. If you inadvertently disturb a nest while trimming the hedge or painting the house, make a *fast* beeline for cover.

Ants

Fire ants are the biggest problem for allergic people (they're no picnic for non-allergic people, either) but fortunately they are not found in the UK. They are usually red, but they can blend into the surrounding soil like chameleons. When disturbed, fire ants can literally explode from their mounds, which they build in farm fields, playing fields, schoolyards, parks and lawns. Their stings burn like fire and cause symptoms that are decidedly different from the symptoms caused by stings of other insects. A welt rises at the site and then expands. Within four hours or so, the wound is surrounded by small blisterlike sacs filled with a thin, clear fluid. As the fluid drains, it is displaced by cloudy pus. Twenty-four hours after the sting, the wound is surrounded by a thin, red circle or painful swelling. The lesions can remain for three to eight days. Crusts develop. Scar tissue forms. All in all, an unsightly affair. And in highly sensitive people, fire ant stings can be fatal. Immunotherapy (which we'll get to a little later) is 90 to 95 per cent effective. Not bad, but not 100 per cent. So if you live in fire ant country, it's important to know what to do if you're stung. (See the box, What to do for insect stings and bites.)

Mosquitoes

It's hard to believe that anything so small can cause so much misery. You might assume the discomfort of a mosquito bite is from the bite itself. And that's certainly part of it. But for allergic people, the real problem is the saliva the mosquito injects with the bite to dilute the victim's blood and more easily suck it up through the tubelike proboscis. Allergic substances in the bugs' saliva can cause nausea, dizziness, hives, swelling, headache and lethargy. Not as severe as those reactions produced by its stinging cousins, to be sure. But more than a mere nuisance, nonetheless.

Flies

The flies that commonly cause allergic reactions are biting midges and houseflies.

Biting midges are also known as sand flies and gnats. A good steady breeze can cart them off, but they return the minute the wind dies down.

While horseflies usually dine on horses, cattle and deer, they are not averse to human fare. And they're vicious biters. Systemic reactions are rather frequent.

Aside from allergy, infection from scratching a bite is a serious concern, since flies are well known for their filthy habits. Be

ALLERGIC AND NON-ALLERGIC REACTIONS TO INSECT STINGS AND BITES

NORMAL

Momentary pain. Redness at site of sting or bite, surrounded by a whitish zone or red, hivelike spot. Itching. Irritation. Warmth. All traces of discomfort disappear within a few hours

LOCAL REACTION

Unusual amount of swelling, pain and redness at the site. Again, symptoms vanish in a few hours.

ALLERGIC, OR GENERAL SYSTEMIC REACTION

***First-degree symptoms*: Itching around the eyes. Dry hacking cough. Widespread hives. Constriction of chest and throat. Wheezing. Nausea. Vomiting. Abdominal pain. Dizziness.**

***More severe*: Difficulty in breathing. Hoarseness and thickened speech. Difficulty in swallowing. Confusion. A sense of impending disaster.**

***Anaphylaxis*: Cyanosis (skin turns blue). Blood pressure falls. Incontinence. Unconsciousness or collapse.**

TOXIC REACTION TO MULTIPLE STINGS OR BITES

Headache. Diarrhoea. Faintness. Fever. Drowsiness. Swelling. Unconsciousness. Convulsions.

wary of any signs of inflammation, redness, swelling, fluid leaks and pain from a fly bite. And try not to scratch.

Natural insect repellent

The most effective insect repellents contain Deet (diethyltoluamide). Repellents do not actually repel flies and mosquitoes, they simply fog their radar. Mosquitoes are guided to their victims by the sensations of moisture, warmth and carbon dioxide – exactly the qualities people exude while exercising or working outdoors on a hot, humid day. Repellent sprays or lotions give off fumes which block the bugs' sensory pores on

DELAYED REACTION TO STINGS OR BITES

Headache. Malaise (general uneasiness). Hives. Aching joints. Lymph gland involvement.

PSYCHOLOGICAL REACTION

Rapid heartbeat. Rapid, shallow breathing. Weakness. Dizziness.

You should consult a doctor without delay—

- **when a local reaction exhibits undue swelling covering two joints of leg, arm or hand, or when a sting causes swelling in the throat, nose or eye, particularly the latter. A sting close to the eye should be seen by a doctor because resulting complications can threaten eyesight.**
- **when a sting results in symptoms of a generalized systemic reaction, no matter how mild.**
- **when multiple stings produce signs of a toxic reaction.**
- **when the swelling accompanying a normal or local reaction persists. (Infection may have set in.)**
- **when symptoms of a delayed reaction appear.**

SOURCE: *Reprinted by permission of the publisher from* Insects and Allergy and What to Do about Them *by Claude A. Frazier and F. K. Brown (Norman, Okla.: University of Oklahoma Press, 1980), pp. 57–8.*

their antennae. So as bugs approach you, they get confused and hover out of striking range.

Sounds great. Except for two problems. While repellents turn off biting insects, they *attract* some bees and stinging insects. And some people may be more sensitive to the chemicals in repellents than they are to mosquito bites themselves.

To get around those problems, some doctors recommend taking tablets of thiamine (a B vitamin) as an internal insect repellent. It seems that when we consume large quantities of thiamine, some is excreted in our perspiration, creating an odour that repulses bugs. (Humans can't smell it.)

WHAT TO DO FOR INSECT STINGS AND BITES

Mild local reactions require little or no treatment. Allergic or toxic reactions, however, demand appropriate care.

- **Scrape out the stinger, if one is present, with your fingernail or a dull knife. Do not try to pull the stinger out – squeezing it will only inject more venom into the wound. (Bumblebees, wasps and hornets leave behind no stinger since their stingers are not barbed. Mosquitoes and flies have no stinger.)**
- **Wash the site well with soap and water. Follow with application of an antiseptic if bitten by a fly.**
- **Apply an ice pack and/or a paste of baking soda and water to relieve pain.**
- **Elevate the arm or leg to reduce oedema (fluid retention) and swelling.**
- **Be alert for symptoms of systemic reaction or unusual swelling, especially swelling that extends far beyond the sting site. If reaction looks at all serious, use an insect-sting kit as directed, then rush the victim to the nearest doctor or hospital.**
- **Avoid using tourniquets, sucking venom from the wound or cutting at fang marks.**
- **If possible, take the dead insect along with you to the doctor so that the insect can be correctly identified.**

***Note*: Allergic or not, consult a doctor without delay if you are stung on the face, nose, mouth or throat, areas which are especially susceptible to sting injuries.**

SOURCES: *Reprinted by permission of the publisher from* Insects and Allergy and What to Do about Them *by Claude A. Frazier and F. K. Brown (Norman, Okla.: University of Oklahoma Press, 1980).*

Monograph on Insect Allergy, *Macy I. Levine and Richard F. Lockey (Hartland, Wis.: Parker Printing of Hartland, 1981).*

In addition, you can wear light-coloured clothing (such as khaki or tennis whites), with long trousers and sleeves to expose as little skin as possible. Put up good screens, Discourage mosquitoes from breeding by eliminating, filling in or draining watery areas around your house: rain barrels, old cans and tyres, stagnant puddles, ditches, hollow trees and stumps, and marshy ground. Install an electronic bug zapper near your front door or in the garden. Or buy non-toxic insect traps (purchasing sources are listed in the Appendix.)

Will you react?

The questions most people ask about insect allergy are: How do I know if I'm allergic to insect stings? How can I tell if my child is allergic to them?

No one experiences a life-threatening reaction the first time they're stung. A severe local reaction, however – exaggerated swelling, nausea, weakness and so forth – is almost a certain harbinger of potential and more severe systemic reactions. And, as is the case with other types of allergy, whether or not you ever experience that ominous first reaction depends on a number of factors:

What Bit You. Anyone who is allergic to bees is apt to be allergic to wasps, hornets and ants. However, the potency of insect venom varies from species to species, so some can cause more of a problem for you than others.

The Amount of Venom. Naturally, the more venom injected, the more chance for a reaction. And more stings mean more venom. But venom levels can also vary for other reasons. In the early spring and late autumn, for instance, honey-bees carry around far less venom than they do at the peak of summer.

Other Allergy. Nearly one-third of people who are allergic to insects are allergic to drugs, especially drugs that are injected, like penicillin. Other than that, coexisting allergy doesn't seem to have much bearing on susceptibility to insect stings.

Your General State of Health. Although it has no bearing on whether or not you're allergic to insects in the first place, your general state of health may influence how well you tolerate a sting or bite. If you've ever had a run-in with any insect that resulted in anything more than a slight swelling, you should be on your guard against future encounters. And you should tell your doctor all the details. Don't be macho – mild reactions are the best clues for predicting life-threatening reactions and shouldn't be played down. The information can save your life.

Your doctor will also need to know what bit you. The problem is, most of us don't know one insect from another and assume anything that stings is simply a bee. So if you possibly can, take

HOW TO AVOID BEE STINGS AND INSECT BITES

Staying clear of our lively winged assailants isn't always easy, but there are several steps you can take to minimize the chances that you will tangle with a stinging or biting insect.

HOW TO AVOID BEE STINGS

- **Stay away from beehives and known nests. Call a beekeeper or the local council if bees choose your immediate environment to form a colony.**
- **Have wasp and hornet nests removed while they are still small enough to handle.**
- **Persons allergic to insects should be wary of power mowing, hedge clipping, scything and the like.**
- **Avoid looking and smelling like a flower during bee-sting season: avoid bright-coloured clothing. Light green, white, tan and khaki are the safest colours. Forswear perfumes and sweet-smelling lotions, creams, shampoos and hairsprays if you plan to be outdoors.**
- **Don't wear floppy clothing, and do tie up long hair; both can entangle the stinging insects and anger them into doing their worst.**
- **Don't go barefoot or wear sandels – the foot is vulnerable. Stay away from clover patches, flower gardens and other places where bees are busy.**

the insect's body to the doctor with you, even if it's squashed. Lacking a body as evidence, some doctors stock photos of common stinging and biting insects – rather like mug shots used to help identify criminals.

Skin tests

In addition to taking account of previous stings and how you reacted, your doctor may do a skin test. A bit of extract is either rubbed into a tiny scratch in the skin or injected. As you might have guessed, the injected (intradermal) test runs some risk of triggering a severe reaction in anyone who is highly allergic to insects. So it's generally reserved for people who show a negative scratch test but for some reason still seem to be allergic. If either test produces a red welt like a hive or a mosquito bite,

• Keep an insecticide spray in the glove compartment of the car (along with the insect-sting kit) for use if a bee flies in, a very common occurrence.

• If an attack seems imminent, do not swat at the bee or bees and do not flail your arms. Retreat slowly, keep calm and make no sudden movement. If retreat is impossible, lie down and cover your head with your arms.

• Be wary of litter bins and rotting fruit under trees – favourite attractions for bees and wasps.

• Discourage allergic youngsters from eating sweets, ice cream cones and drinking soft drinks outdoors during warm months. They attract bees, wasps and hornets.

HOW TO AVOID ANT STINGS

• Avoid anthills and mounds.

• Keep arms, legs and feet covered since they are the areas most frequently stung.

• Do not leave food uncovered or uncontained within the house, since this is an open invitation to ants.

SOURCE: *Reprinted by permission of the publisher from* Insects and Allergy and What to Do about Them *by Claude A. Frazier and F. K. Brown (Norman, Okla.: University of Oklahoma Press, 1980), pp. 66–67, 76–77, 88, 131.*

that indicates allergy. And the bigger and redder the welt, the more allergic you are.

Like any tests, skin tests for insect allergy aren't foolproof, but combined with your history, they can be somewhat useful.

Surprisingly, four out of ten people with both a history of sting allergy and a positive skin test will never again react to stings or bites in the future.

Once stung, twice shy

You can stay away from insects. The trick is persuading them to stay away from you. You can reduce your chances of a disastrous encounter by following the steps in the earlier box.

Given the numbers and agility of our flying and crawling pests, however, you can't be sure you will never experience a surprise attack. To be on the safe side, doctors recommend that anyone who has a past allergy to venomous insects and who shows a positive skin test receive immunotherapy (also called hyposensitization or desensitization). Immunotherapy is vaccination against bites and stings. Starting with a weak dose, extracts of insect venom are injected regularly, and increased in strength until you can tolerate the amount expected from a bite or sting. Then you receive regular injections to maintain tolerance – weekly during the insect season and every two or three weeks the rest of the year. (Immunotherapy for mosquito bites is fairly successful, but less effective than injections for bee stings.)

Immunotherapy with insect venom is fairly safe, even for children. Nevertheless, it's reserved for people prone to severe, life-threatening reactions. And since no medical treatment is 100 per cent effective, allergists strongly urge allergic people to carry insect-sting kits (available by prescription) as a backup even if they're receiving immunotherapy. The kits contain adrenalin and other emergency drugs to stop a reaction. Other doctors go so far as to advise anyone who has suffered even mild symptoms of an allergic reaction to bites or stings to carry the kits. Keep one handy all the time: in your home, in your car and so on.

It's also wise to wear a medical warning tag or bracelet to alert medical personnel that you are indeed allergic to insects. In the event that you pass out or become incoherent after a sting or bite, precious time will be saved. Your symptoms won't be confused with those of a heart attack or other illness.

We realize that even with an insect-sting kit tucked away in the picnic basket, anyone who is allergic will still recoil at the sight of a bee or mosquito. But knowing exactly what to do should take some of the anxiety out of venturing into their domain.

CHAPTER 7

CONTACT (SKIN) ALLERGIES

Few people are happier than those who have found lasting relief from skin allergy. Food and airborne allergies are certainly no fun, but skin allergies can be downright depressing. After all, if your eyes are swollen, your face is blotchy or your arms are patchy and dry, you won't feel much like going to work, playing sports or even socializing. And the constant urge to scratch can drive you crazy!

Skin allergies go far beyond a simple summertime clash with poison ivy. Add up the cosmetics and grooming aids, soaps, detergents, clothing, jewellery, hobby and office supplies we run up against every day, and you get a pretty good idea of the number of things that can cause skin allergy. But figuring out your problem and finding relief can be easy once you know where to start.

Mix-and-match symptoms

If you have a skin allergy, you probably know it. But just in case you don't, the symptoms are easy to spot because they always follow a variation of one general pattern. (The following description of the pattern includes medical terms in parentheses so you'll be able to understand your doctor when he or she talks to you about a skin allergy.)

Reddening (erythema) is the first sign of trouble, sometimes accompanied by bumps or pimples (papules) or blisters (vesicles) that may weep and ooze. Then the itching starts, and after a few days the red spots and bumps give way to crusting, scaling and thickening of the skin. Should the problem persist – if you continue to use the cosmetic, soap or apparel you're allergic to – the scaliness and thickening take over completely, and itching becomes more unbearable than ever. The whole business is customarily called eczema, or atopic dermatitis, especially if it's caused by something you ate. If the culprit is something you've touched, it's called contact dermatitis.

The face – particularly the eyelids – is the most sensitive area. Not only are the eyelids prone to react to chemicals applied to and around them (mascara, eye shadow and the like), but they also react to anything near them. hair dye or shampoo on the scalp, perfume on the neck, poison ivy or not-quite-dry nail polish on the hands can precipitate puffy, inflamed or scaly lids.

The backs of the hands and the fingers also waste no time in letting us know that they're 'in touch' with a troublemaker. But the scalp, palms of the hands and soles of the feet are remarkably resistant to allergy in most people.

Skin reactions aren't limited to these areas, of course – but they don't always crop up where you expect to find them. Jewellery allergy, for instance, generally shows up on earlobes, neck, wrist and fingers. But a loose bracelet can affect the skin anywhere from the wrist to the elbow. or detergents can splash above the tops of gloves. And the offending substance isn't always obvious, either. The trunk, underarms, forearms and inner elbows all react to clothing and perfumes. Eczema on the thighs could be from garters – or from coins or keys in a pants pocket.

Irritation or Allergy?

At this point, you may wonder whether your problem is really a skin allergy or simply an irritation. Irritation can mimic the beginning stages of an allergic reaction: dry skin, with perhaps a mild rash and itching; or, if the problem continues, swelling and cracked skin. But the difference is quite clear: irritation is liable to show up in anyone who has an intense or prolonged contact with harsh chemicals or strong detergents, or whose hands are in and out of water all day. Irritated skin loses its fatty protective cells and becomes chapped and inflamed. Houskeepers, bartenders and dishwashers get 'dishpan hands' (or 'housewives' eczema,' as it's sometimes clled) from the sheer physical or chemical insult to their skin. And irritation is likely to develop in *anyone* under these conditions.

An allergic reaction, on the other hand, follows a contact with a substance that is perfectly harmless for most people. And there's usually a time lag of anywhere from a few hours to a day or two between the contact and the drematitis. For distance, eczema from hand cream usually appears a few days after a new brand is used.

Nevertheless, irritated skin is weaker and therefore more apt to become allergic. And irritation can aggravate existing skin allergy. So while there is a difference between them, allergy and irritation go hand in hand. In fact, a large part of successful skin allergy control involves avoiding any unnecessary irritation.

'Why Me?'

Some people can practically swim in poison ivy and suffer hardly an itch. Others break out after merely handling exposed clothing or animal fur. That's because sensitivity depends on several factors – and many of them are within our control.

First and foremost, how long and how frequently you come in contact with the offending substance makes a great deal of difference. Similarly, pressing or rubbing against it increases the intensity of contact and may prolong the reaction.

The health of your skin is also a factor. Infected, inflamed, burned or otherwise irritated skin is in no condition to defend itself against an allergic contact. skin that's overly dry or too alkaline (from washing with alkaline soaps) is also vulnerable. So is skin that's already in the process or reacting. (We'll tell you more about skin care later in this chapter.)

Perspiration can also fuel a reaction because it dissolves and spreads allergic and irritating substances such as nickel and clothing dyes. in fact, some people break out only when they sweat heavily.

Certain drugs such as antihistamines and antibiotics increase your sensitivity to sunlight, making you more easily sunburned and susceptible to an allergic reaction. Some topical salves and lotions can also cause reactions in the presence of sunlight. Antiseptics in some soaps, for instance, are allergenic only under sunlight.

Contact allergy most often erupts during or after middle age; eczema in children and younger adults is more apt to be triggered by food and inhalants. Many older people, in fact, are taken by surprise by a sudden allergy to something they've been using safely all their lives. Skin allergies also tend to be more stubborn and resistant to control the older you get. Part of the reason is that as we age, we tend to have drier skin. So we use more bath oils and lanolin-containing lotions to relieve dryness. Using more lotions, however, means we're exposing ourselves to more chemicals with allergic potential. So the older you are, the more tender loving care your skin needs, including blander lotions and soaps.

Not only does our sensitivity change as we age, but also the way we react. While itching is as bad as ever, older people experience less inflammation and fewer blisters. Instead, the skin tends to thicken and grow scaly – from the allergic process itself, from the drier skin of old age and from constant scratching.

Your hobby or occupation may also habitually expose you to chemicals and other substances. Many materials used in gardening, carpentry, painting, ceramics and sculpture are potent allergy triggers. Gardening usually demands handling weeds and applying fertilizer or insecticides, organic or chemical. Both organic pesticides (like pyrethrum) and chemicals (like malathion) are potential causes of skin allergy. The turpentine, epoxy resins, glues and adhesives of carpentry can trigger a skin reaction. Cashiers and sales clerks, waiters and waitresses may find that they react to the nickel in coins. Nurses, doctors and dentists are subject to allergic skin reactions from penicillin, antibiotics, antiseptics, metals and the like.

We're not saying you should abandon your hobby or quit your job. Just keep all your regular activities in mind when looking for clues to an unexplained skin rash.

Relief is on the way

Relieving the itch is the first order of business, an essential step to take before you even begin to scout around for the cause of your misery. Not only will you welcome the comfort of relief, but you'll also eliminate the danger of infection (and possible scarring) from continued scratching. There are plenty of effective ways to conquer the itch.

Ice cubes, rubbed on skin whenever you get the urge to scratch, take the fire out of inflammation.

Cold, wet dressings soothe eczema and help to stop not only itching but oozing. And the colder the dressing, the more effective, says Alexander A. Fisher, a professor of dermatology at New York University Postgraduate Medical School and author of a textbook on skin problems. 'Wet dressings consisting of water with ice, made to the consistency of sherbet and applied with a cotton cloth for five to fifteen minutes and reapplied as necessary, are often well tolerated and beneficial,' says Dr Fisher (*Contact Dermatitis*, Lea and Febiger, 1978).

We found an easy way to make Dr Fisher's anti-itch slush. To break up the cubes, empty a tray of ice cubes into a plastic bag and pound it with a wooden meat mallet. Then empty the cracked ice into a blender with two tablespoons of cold water and, in several short bursts, blend into a mush. Wrap in cotton and apply to irritated skin.

Dr Fisher isn't the only doctor who favours cold, wet treatment.

'Cool compresses or ice packs relieve itching faster and more safely than most medications,' says Nia K. Terezakis, a clinical assistant professor of dermatology at Louisiana State University.

Lotions of calamine and milk of bismuth, following wet compresses, bring down weeping, swelling and redness, says Dr Terezakis.

Night dressings of zinc oxide paste (available at chemists), applied on a closely woven cotton cloth, are also suggested by Dr Fisher.

Vinegar in water (2 fl oz/50 ml of vinegar in 2 pints/1.25 l of water) is soothing.

Lukewarm water baths are extremely soothing, especially for inflammation around the genitals and buttocks or for widespread symptoms. A soothing bath is also a good way to soak off ointments and medications once they've served their purpose. Dr Fisher recommends 10½ oz/280 g of colloidal oatmeal (available at chemists) to a tub of water. This mixture is called a 'colloidal' bath because the particles stay suspended in the water to soothe the skin rather than settling to the bottom of the tub. Other colloidals recommended by Dr Terezakis are: skimmed milk, powdered milk, cornstarch, baking soda, or a combination of any of these ingredients. (Colloidal baths do make the tub slippery, though, so be extra careful climbing in and out. A rubber bath mat is a good safeguard.) Depending on the extent of your problem, one to three baths a day should be helpful. As you heal, you'll need to bathe less frequently.

Soaking in tepid water is comforting, even without colloidals. Whatever you do, avoid hot baths and showers.

Moisturize your skin by always applying a bland, non-allergenic moisturizing cream such as Nutraderm or Nivea Lotion after bathing or showering to prevent drying, itching and further irritation.

Humidify the bedroom in winter and dehumidify in summer to keep your skin comfortable.

Arthur L. Norins, professor of dermatology at Indiana University School of Medicine, recommends some further steps to reduce irritation and control itching and other symptoms.

Substitute 100 per cent cotton clothing, sheets and blankets for synthetics or synthetic/cotton blends. (If you have trouble locating them in department stores, the Appendix lists some mail-order sources.)

Wash new clothing and sheets before they're worn to get rid of chemicals used to stiffen fabric. We know a woman whose whole body broke out in an itchy, disfiguring rash after she slept on brand-new sheets. After several washings, they were finally safe to use.

Rinse all clothing and sleepwear in clear water after washing. Don't use fabric softener or other laundry aids. And be sure to use low-suds detergents without enzymes, whiteners, bleach and other additives.

Avoid tight clothing, tight dressings and adhesive bandages. Anything that rubs against your skin is going to aggravate the situation, says Dr Norins.

Stay out of the sun. The last thing that red, inflamed or scaly skin needs is to be cooked with heat and light.

Rest. Healing takes energy. If your arm or leg is so bad that it's swollen and red from top to bottom, you may have to rest it completely for a few days so it can heal itself successfully. In fact, if it's your misfortune to have a whole-body skin rash, your doctor may order a few days of bed rest.

In more than nine people out of ten, reactions will be mild

or moderate. Only 3 per cent react severely. If your skin problems are severe and widespread, covering 50 per cent or more of your body, don't fool around with self-diagnosis. Body-wide involvement calls for medical attention and sometimes even special hospitalization to isolate the individual from *all* chemical exposure.

A note about skin medications

Your dermatologist may feel that your problem calls for a topical ointment or oral medication of some kind. Dr Fisher cautions that preservatives such as parabens and ethylenediamine and other common ingredients of topical salves are common causes of allergy and can therefore *prolong* rather than heal the disease. Another doctor tells of one person with skin allergy who was treated with one medication after another by many doctors, with no relief – until parabens were considered. 'Within twenty-four hours of application of a parabens-free cream, his skin began to heal for the first time in seven years,' says William F. Schorr, dermatologist at the Marshfield Clinic in Marshfield, Wisconsin [*Journal of the American Medical Association*, 3 June 1968).

Dr Schorr points out that benzocaine, widely used for dishpan hands and other irritating skin problems, is a very common cause of allergy. In fact, he strongly advises against use of any topical ending in 'caine'. So if treatment calls for a topical medication, it's important that doctors prescribe only creams that are free of potent allergens.

For a similar reason, doctors strongly discourage people with any kind of skin allergy from buying over-the-counter medicated lotions.

You should also stay away from corticosteroid creams or ointments – they may cause a non-allergic-type inflammation, further compounding skin problems. Yet some dermatologists are rather quick to prescribe oral doses of corticosteroids, like prednisone, for allergic skin problems. Non-drug approaches may make steroids unnecessary, says Dr Schorr.

'It has been my experience . . . that it is rarely necessary to treat the average patient with contact dermatitis with systemic corticosteroids,' Dr Schorr states. The one exception, he says, is poison ivy, poison oak or poison sumac, common in the United States. They're such intense allergens that the disease continues to spread long after the initial contact. And the blisters and swelling produced can keep you out of work or school for longer than most people can afford. Under those circumstances, Dr Schorr sees little risk in a ten-day to two-week course of prednisone, in decreasing doses (*Minnesota Medicine*, October 1974).

Another exception to the no-drug rule may be antihistamines prescribed to be taken in the evening. They prevent you from scratching in your sleep, which would delay healing.

Overall, though, you should try non-medical means of relief if at all possible. There certainly are enough tried-and-true means available. Total relief, however, is only possible if you stay away from the allergy-provoking items. After you've got the itching under control, the next step is to find out what started it in the first place.

Unmasking the culprits

In its simplest form, skin distress can easily be linked to its cause, allowing you to avoid the allergen. Many people, however, have no idea why their temperamental skin is always on the verge of breaking out – often despite their best efforts to keep it clean and pampered. The answers to a few key questions can provide helpful clues.

Where and when did the skin problem begin?
What kind of work do you do?
What are your hobbies?
What medications do you apply to your skin?
What household cleaners do you use regularly?

If your problems started just recently, ask yourself:

What purchases have I made recently? (Jewellery, cologne, perfume and other toiletries; new brand of detergent; new sheets or towels.)
What gifts have I received? (Scarves, furs, gloves, sweaters, plus any of the 'purchases' list.)
Am I wearing new clothing or cosmetics?
Has my house been sprayed recently with an insecticide? (Particles could settle on furnishings.)

Have I travelled abroad recently? (Soaps and detergents used outside the United Kingdom often contain metals like nickel or chemicals not used in the same products in this country.)

Next, consider the possibility that any of those contacts is exposing you to any of several notorious causes of skin allergy listed in Table 21. Of course, a complete list of every possible cause and its sources would fill this book, so you'll have to read labels carefully and use your own ingenuity.

Like identifying a food allergy, discovering the cause of a skin allergy takes a good bit of detective work – as one fifty-two-year-old business executive discovered. From time to time, he experienced mild burning in his mouth, for no apparent reason. One day, his lips and the fingers of his left hand broke out in an eczemalike rash. One month later, the entire inside of his mouth broke out in blisters, his lips became more inflamed and the palm and sides of the fingers on his left hand were severely irritated. When he really thought about it, he realized that each episode occurred during or immediately following an out-of-town business trip. In his travel bag, he kept a tube of red toothpaste that he never used at home.

He called his doctor, who did tests and eventually found that the culprit was cinnamic aldehyde, a cinnamon derivative found not only in red toothpastes but in many other dentifrices, plus foods and household products (*Archives and Dermatology*, February 1976).

Typists sometimes discover that they're allergic to carbonless copy paper – the kind that frequently comes in tablets and, when typed on, automatically gives you copies, especially duplicates or triplicates of business forms. A team of dermatologists report that of seventy people who had skin reactions on their hands – mainly reddening followed by burning and itching – all experienced total relief when they stopped typing on carbonless-type paper (*Contact Dermatitis*, vol. 7, 1981).

Not all allergy triggers are created equal. Some chemicals, metals or compounds may cause allergy in 5 to 10 per cent of the population, while others affect less than 0.01 per cent. And any list of common causes of skin allergy is subject to change as manufacturers reformulate products or new ones become popular.

The important problem, however, isn't so much how often a

substance causes problems, but how easily it can be overlooked in diagnosis. Parabens, for instance, are widely used preservatives and play a part in about 3 per cent of all allergic skin disease. But unless you know that parabens are vandalizing your skin, chances for complete relief are slim and you'll continue to flare up every time you apply a salve, lotion or cosmetic containing a paraben.

Certain categories of products – cosmetics and grooming aids, soaps and detergents, clothing, jewellery and food additives – are most likely to contain allergy-causing chemicals, metals or compounds, as you can see from Table 21. (If there seems to be no connection whatsoever between your skin problems and a contact, there's always the possibility that they're food related. In that case, Chapter 3, Finding your no-allergy diet, may help you locate the offender.)

Finding cosmetics that agree with you

Are your lips chronically dry, cracked, peeling or swollen?
Do mascaras irritate your eyes?
Do deodorants leave your underarms itchy?
Do certain creams or face powders irritate your face or your hands?

If so, you could be one of the millions of people – primarily women – with allergies to something in their cosmetics. And 'cosmetics' means face creams, lotions, rouge, blusher, powder, eyeliner and shadow, lipstick, nail polish and polish remover, as well as nail lengtheners, shampoos, hair dyes, hair waves, hair straighteners, hair removers (depilatories), shaving cream, perfumes, cologne, sachets, bubble baths, douches, mouthwash, toothpaste – even dentures!

It's easy to see why cosmetics and other personal grooming products are the most common cause of skin reactions. They're usually applied daily, directly to the skin. And, as we mentioned in earlier chapters, chronic exposure breeds allergy. Also, over 5,000 different chemicals and compounds go into these products – as bases, dyes, fragrances, preservatives and the like –

TABLE 21

Common Causes and Sources of Skin Allergy

These are the most common and potent causes of skin allergy and their most likely sources. In some cases, not all items in each category contain the allergen. For example, not all jewellery contains nickel, and not all medication contains benzocaine. Check all tems you use routinely to determine possible causes of skin reactions.

Plant, Compound or Chemical	Common Sources
MOST COMMON CONTACT ALLERGENS	
Paraphenylenediamine (may cross-react with benzocaine, procaine, para-amino benzoic acid [PABA] and certain dyes in foods, drugs and cosmetics)	Dyes in clothing, shoes and textiles (especially black, blue and brown); hair dyes; fur dyes
Nickel and nickel compounds	Jewellery, coins, keys, buckles, clasps, zippers, door handles, knitting needles, thimbles, hydrogenated fats (as a catalyst), detergents used outside the U.K.
Rubber and rubber compounds	Rubber gloves, rubber bands, adhesive tape and bandages, elasticized underwear
Ethylenediamine	Preservative in topical ointments; aminophylline and theophylline suppositories
OTHER COMMON CONTACT ALLERGENS	
Alcohol*	Rubbing alcohol, cosmetics, medicinal preparations
Antibacterial agents	Soaps
Azo dyes (such as E102 Tartrazine)	Foods, drugs, cosmetics, ballpoint pens
Benzocaine (ethyl aminobenzoate)	Cosmetics, medications, salves, suppositories
Carbonless copy paper	Office forms
Carbowax	Cosmetics

** Some people allergic to contact with alcohol may also experience overall redness when drinking alcoholic beverages.*

TABLE 21 – *Continued*

Plant, Compound or Chemical	Common Sources
Cinnamon oil (cinnamic aldehyde and other cinnamates)	Flavouring in toothpaste, mouthwash, sweets, soft drinks, ice cream, baked goods, condiments, meats, chewing gum, flavoured vermouth and bitters; aroma in perfumes, household deodorizers, air fresheners and sunscreens
Copper	Coins, metal alloys, insecticides, fungicides (anti-mould agents)
DDT	Insecticide
Formaldehyde (sometimes known as formalin)	Clothing (cotton or blends labelled durable-press, wash-and-wear, wrinkle-resistant, drip-dry, no-iron or permanent press), spun rayon, rayon-acetate blends, polyester blends, flameproof sleepwear and clothing, shrink-proof woollens; cosmetics, deodorants, insecticides, paper towels
Fragrances (balsam of Peru, wood tars, benzyl salicylate, phenylacetaldehyde)	Perfumes, soaps, detergents, scented toilet paper
Henna	Hair dye
Iodine compounds	Tincture of iodine, Ioprep
Jasmine	Perfumes and fragrances
Lanolin (wool fat, wool grease, wool wax)	Soaps, lip gloss
Linseed oil	Paints, varnishes, furniture polishes, putty
Mercury	Topical ointments, disinfectants, insecticides
Musk ambrette	Men's colognes and after-shave lotion
Newspaper print	Newspapers
Orris root	Fragrance in cosmetics
Parabens (methylparaben, ethylparaben, propylparaben)	Preservative in most drugs and cosmetics

Plant, Compound or Chemical	Common Sources
Para-red dyes	Coloured sections of newspapers and magazines
Potassium dichromate	Yellow paints, leather (tanned), matches, some bleaches, anti-rust compounds, varnishes, plaster filler and glues, ink, chrome plating, welding, linoleum, cement, caulking compound
Potassium iodide	Table salt, photography (emulsions)
Procaine (Novocaine)	Local and spinal anesthesia
Propylene glycol and butylene glycol	Face masks, hand cleansers, moisturizing creams
Pyrethrum	Insecticide
Resorcin	Cosmetics, hair tonics, leather (tanned)
Rosin (made from turpentine)	Brown soap, adhesive tape, furniture polish, varnishes, glue, floor wax
Sodium hypochlorite	Bleach, cleansers
Turpentine	Paint remover, polishes, cosmetics, insecticides, paints, varnishes, liniment

SOURCE: *Alexander A. Fisher,* Contact Dermatitis *(Philadelphia: Lea & Febiger, 1978).*

multiplying the odds that something is going to disagree with you, no matter how minuscule the amount.

No wonder one doctor estimates that 85 per cent of people who are allergic to cosmetics don't even realize which substances are causing the problem. Where do you start?

With creams and lotions. These accounted for almost half of all allergic reactions in a study of seventy people sensitive to cosmetics, according to Dr Schorr. It's not that creams and lotions are any more allergenic than other products, he says. People simply tend to apply them to already irritated skin – which is more prone to react. And they use them all over their body.

An American study of cosmetic reactions found that the most frequent reactions were to: deodorants/antiperspirants, depilatories (hair removers), moisturizer lotions, hair spray, mascara, bubble bath, eye cream, hair colour, dye or lightener, facial creams or cleansers and nail polish – in that order.

Is a woman with cosmetic allergies dreaming if she hopes to wear makeup? Must men swear off all grooming aids? Not at all. They merely have to choose products carefully and apply them with extra care.

Is it really 'hypoallergenic'?

You've probably noticed ads for cosmetics or grooming products that claim to be hypoallergenic, implying that they are safe for people with skin allergies. At one time or another, though, you've probably heard someone say, 'I'm allergic to hypoallergenic products.' Perhaps that's even true for you.

So what's the story?

There is no official standard for hypoallergenic claims in the UK other than that such a product must be less likely to cause adverse reactions than other similar products. For some manufacturers, that simply means omitting fragrance, the single biggest cause of cosmetic allergies. Others go to great pains to find safe substitutes for as many of the other common allergenic chemicals as they can. The ingredients, then, will vary from one manufacturer to the next, so that one hypoallergenic mascara, for example, may cause no difficulty, while another is a problem.

Even the so-called hypoallergenic products contain lists of ingredients that read like the index of a high school chemistry text – and any of them can start trouble for you. One of the leading brands of hypoallergenic cosmetics, for instance, contains parabens. So hypoallergenic obviously doesn't imply a product is free of all possible troublemakers.

Since the cosmetics are less than pure, manufacturers marketing their products as hypoallergenic must also test them on people. One of the major distributors of such products told us that they test their products by repeatedly applying the product to the skin of 600 people, under the supervision of a dermatologist. Only those products which produce no reaction within the test period are marketed as hypoallergenic.

But as you can see, hypoallergenic is a relative term. What's hypoallergenic for you may not be hypoallergenic for your friend. The best approach is to read labels carefully, follow directions for use, and conduct a patch test (see the box, Do your own patch test, later in this chapter) if you tend to react to cosmetics.

The following tips will also help enormously when it comes to using any cosmetics, whether they're hypoallergenic or not.

How to apply cosmetics safely

• The first thing to remember is the less fragrance the better. Perfumes and perfumed cosmetics are *the* major allergens. Besides the usual redness and irritation, they can do strange things in sunlight. A brownish or smoky streak may appear where perfume was applied to the skin, usually behind the ears or on the neck – a reaction unique to fragrances. Certain lipsticks and deodorant soaps, too, have been known to cause burning and irritation only under exposure to sunlight. If you still want to splash on a pleasant scent, make your own scented water by packing rose petals or lavendar in a jar of cold water. Add a tablespoon of lemon juice. After ten days, strain and use as a subtle, refreshing perfume.

• Lipsticks are usually made of oil, waxes, dyes and perfumes. If you like the 'wet look' on your lips but react to the lanolin in lip gloss, smooth petroleum jelly over applied lipstick. If the perfume causes trouble, look for unscented lipstick.

• Use a sponge applicator, not your fingers, to apply foundation, lipstick and eyeshadow. (Rubber-sensitive people should use latex or natural sponges.)

• Nickel-sensitive people should use only stainless steel eyelash curlers and tweezers. They may also have to avoid nail polish with a metal mixing ball – solvents in the polish may leach out nickel.

• Eye irritation is less likely if mascara is applied just short of the inner and outer corners of the eyes. Also, brush mascara only on the outer two-thirds of your lashes.

• When applying eye shadow or liner, leave a thin makeup-free zone along the edges. *Never* use liner on the inner rim of the eyelids.

• Wand-style applicators should be used for no longer than four months, to avoid the build-up of bacteria and the risk of eye infection. Also, do not spit on liner, mascara or eye shadow to moisten it – that, too, fosters growth of bacteria.

• If your makeup starts to wear off during the day, it's safer to patch it up than to remove it and start all over again. This minimizes exposure.

• Use plain mineral oil to remove eye makeup. Commercial eye makeup removers are generally composed of mineral oil and fragrance. Non-oily removers, on the other hand, are harsh and drying.

• Never go to sleep at night without removing your makeup.

• Above all, don't use any eye product that irritates your eyes in the hope that you will get used to it. The irritation will only get worse.

• If you find a product that agrees with you, stick with it. Jumping from one brand to another only increases the likelihood of exposing you to a new allergen.

• For a non-drying, alcohol-free astringent, combine four parts water to one part apple cider vinegar. Swab on with cotton balls.

• People allergic to corn should not use powders containing cornstarch.

• Apply nail polish carefully, to avoid bumping it against cuticle or skin. Also, nail polish is not allergenic once it has thoroughly dried, so allow ten to fifteen minutes before touching anything – especially your eyelids, face or neck.

• Be wary of cream and lotion collecting under your rings.

• Mouthwashes can create all kinds of problems on the soft, delicate tissues inside the mouth, including redness, ulcers and even 'bald spots' on the tongue. The reactions disappear as soon as the mouthwash is discontinued. If you feel you need a breath freshener, chew on a sprig of fresh parsley or suck on a whole clove.

• The hair dyes most likely to produce a reaction are the oxidation type and those containing the chemical paraphenylenediamine. The allergic reaction may occur a few hours after application and usually becomes full blown after one or two days – so a patch test done just before your hairdresser is about to dye your hair is really no predictor of reaction.

Other colouring methods – progressive dye, semi-permanent organic dyes (like henna) and hair rinses – seldom cause trouble. Ask your hairstylist to help you choose a less allergenic product.

• Sunscreen lotions are a must for sunbathing. But have you ever used a sunblock and got a reddened, blistery rash anyway?

You could be allergic to the fragrances or benzocaine in the product – or even to PABA, a highly effective and otherwise safe sunscreen ingredient. An effective alternative is sunscreens containing benzophenone.

• Fragrance-free deodorants and antiperspirants with aluminium chlorohydrate are less likely to cause allergic reactions.

Soaps and detergents

Housework is responsible for 10 to 15 per cent of the skin problems that send people to their doctors. Many scrubbing powders contain abrasives – pumice, talc, sand, borax, cornmeal or wood powder – that are dynamite against ground-in oil, grease, tar and other stubborn dirt but also very rough on allergic skin. Seventy to 75 per cent of laundry detergents in the UK contain enzymes, proteins with allergic potential. And practically all laundry soaps contain additives such as sodium carbonate, sodium phosphate, ash, borax or sodium silicate – which may irritate even if they don't trigger allergy directly. And of course, soaps and detergents contain fragrances, which are just as liable to cause allergy as the scents in cosmetics.

Besides causing allergy directly, soaps and detergents enhance other allergies. These cleansers break down keratin, the tough protein component of skin, and the protective surface oils, therefore speeding up the absorption of allergic chemicals through the skin.

One woman, who has been highly allergic to such substances as pollen, moulds and foods from early childhood, told us that she had been spared the miseries of skin allergies until around 1970, when enzymes became the 'in' laundry additives. Her legs broke out in oozing, weeping eczemalike rashes. She remains free of the problem, however, as long as she uses only enzyme-free detergents.

You, too, can spare yourself the agonies of allergy to soaps and detergents by following a few simple guidelines.

• Buy only white, unscented soap that's free of antiseptics, lanolin, enzymes and so forth. Baby soaps and soaps for washable woollens and fine fabrics are the safest.

• In general, simple, basic formulas are less prone to cause reactions than complex ones. Read labels.

• Even the mildest laundry soaps and detergents must be thoroughly rinsed from clothing and bedsheets.

• Pour or measure detergents or bleaches carefully so that they don't splash on to your hands and arms. Or buy bleach sold in tablet form or packaged in premeasured envelopes.

• During the winter, when dry air makes skin more easily irritated by clothing, presoak laundry and use about half the amount of detergent the manufacturers recommend.

• Remove your rings when washing or using soaps, waxes and polishes to avoid trapping soap next to skin.

• Better yet, use protective gloves to do any kind of housework. For wet jobs, use rubber gloves over powdered cotton gloves to prevent excessive perspiration. To reduce irritation, wear the gloves for thirty minutes at a time rather than pulling them on and off several times in the course of a day. Even with protective gloves, don't make the scrub water too hot; the heat will penetrate and irritate your hands.

• For dusting or other dry, dirty housework, wear cotton gloves to keep your hands from getting too dirty. That way you don't have to scrub your hands with soaps to get them clean again.

• Use long-handled brushes as much as possible to keep sensitive skin on arms from being splashed with hot, soapy water or paints, varnishes and lacquers.

Incidentally, the tips suggested above will be helpful whether your skin is allergic or just easily irritated. And they'll help you tolerate contact with other sources of chemicals besides soaps and detergents.

Clothing and shoes

When it comes to clothing, shoes and other apparel, allergic people are better off with natural fibres and materials than with synthetics. Cotton is about the best all-around fabric – affordable, durable and attractive. Watch out for permanent-press, wash-and-wear or other types of wrinkle proofing – they usually contain formaldehyde, a common cause of grief for people with sensitive skin. Same for cotton that's been sized –

coated with starch, glues, vegetable gums and (would you believe it?) *shellac* to give fabric a stiff, polished or glazed finish. Cotton clothes that are usually sized are organdy, piqué, costume fabric, some sheets and mosquito netting. Sanforizing and mercerizing do not leave any chemical residue on cloth and are usually safe.

Linen and silk are rarely allergenic – and not necessarily too costly, if you shop carefully.

Nothing beats wool for warmth and good looks. Allergy to natural, unprocessed wool is extremely rare. Itching from wool is caused more by mechanical irritation than allergy. Layering wool clothes over cotton undergarments or a scarf can reduce itching.

If you react to wool no matter how soft or fluffy it is, chances are you're actually allergic to either the dye or shrink-proof chemicals in the fabric, or to its dry-cleaning treatment. If you are truly allergic to wool or can't find untreated wool, substitute thick cotton sweaters, all-cotton corduroy pants, chamois cloth or suede. Try to wear those fabrics in layers. Mohair is also relatively non-allergenic.

For some reason, truly wool-sensitive people seem to tolerate coats made of Persian lamb, a great find at thrift shops. (By the way, people allergic to cat hair may not tolerate fur coats made of wildcat, ocelot or leopard – even if they can afford them.)

Synthetic cloth and apparel should not be part of your wardrobe if you have temperamental skin. They're treated with all manner of chemicals. And synthetics may be doubly irritating since they do not 'breathe' or absorb perspiration. The most familiar synthetic fibres are polyester, acetate, acrylic, nylon, rayon, rubber, spandex, triacetate and metallics, although they go by various trade names. Stick to the natural fibres mentioned earlier. They are available in most larger department stores and speciality boutiques.

Dyes, contrary to popular belief, are not a common cause of clothing allergy. The problem is more likely to be with one of the finishes we mentioned earlier, or with a laundry additive. But when dyes are in fact the problem, it's the darker, more concentrated colours (notably black and dark blue) that contain allergenic chemicals. Some people who react to dark-toned stockings, for example, find they can wear lighter shades with no difficulty. And the dyes that are used in synthetics tend to cause allergy more than the dyes used in natural fibres, cotton, linen or wool. So you see, allergy to one dye does not imply allergy to *all* dyes. And that variation also explains why so many people can comfortably wear natural fibres but not synthetics.

Although modern dyes are considerably colourfast, clothing dyes can be loosened by perspiration. You may find you can wear that bright pink T-shirt around the house with no reaction, but you itch like crazy if you wear it while playing golf in 90-degree heat.

Dry cleaning processes use any of various potent solvents – alcohol, petrol, kerosene, carbon tetrachloride, chloroform, acetone, benzene, naphtha, turpentine or ether. Air out dry-cleaned clothing and blankets thoroughly before wearing them. Sensitive people may have to wait up to three weeks to give fumes plenty of time to dissipate. If you still react, buy only clothing and blankets that are washable, laundering them yourself with Woolite or some other mild, fine-fabric detergent.

When the culprit is formaldehyde, no amount of washing will get rid of the problem. Sometimes you can actually smell the formaldehyde (sometimes called formalin) when ironing a garment or pulling clothes from storage. We spoke to one woman in Dallas who was so sensitive to formaldehyde that she couldn't take more than a few minutes to shop for apparel – rummaging through racks of formaldehyde-laced garments and trying on one dress after another triggered her symptoms. Because formaldehyde is used chiefly in synthetics or to make cottons wrinkle resistant, you can avoid the chemical by sticking to untreated, all-cotton fabrics.

Don't forget that shoes and accessories could be allergenic, too. If your feet give you trouble, they'll heal faster – and stay healed – if you wear all-cotton socks and change them at least once during the day, especially in warm weather. (If possible, change your shoes, too.) By all means, change your running shoes or sneakers after working out or participating in sports. And never wear tight boots, especially for long periods.

Occasionally, a person who is allergic to the chemicals used to tan leather will have to invest in custom-made vegetable-dyed shoes. The problem can be partially avoided, however, by wearing canvas shoes in the summertime.

Watch out for synthetic belts, hats, gloves, handbags, watch-bands, suspenders, bras, girdles and garter belts. Rubber-sensitive individuals may have no choice but to wear spandex, a non-rubber stretchable fibre, in bras, girdles and support hose. Look for chemical-free brands such as Lycra, by DuPont (sold by Warner, among others).

Suspenders, zips and other fasteners usually contain nickel, a very common cause of skin allergy. That problem can be remedied by coating fasteners with clear nail lacquer or placing cloth between the thigh and garter.

Pinning down jewellery allergy

Speaking of nickel, that metal is to blame for more skin allergies than any other metal – probably because it's so widely used. Everything from zips and poppers to coins and costume jewellery contains some nickel.

What's more, the salt in perspiration dissolves nickel. People who wear costume jewellery with no problem during the winter often find that in summer, the same jewellery will make them itch and feel prickly within just fifteen or twenty minutes. An hour or so later, they break out. Or they break out wherever pressure is great – where tight suspenders rub against thighs, for example. (Incidentally, tight clothing in general tends to be more troublesome – another good reason to keep your weight down.)

Nickel molecules also tend to affix themselves to skin cells, prolonging symptoms even after you've removed the article in question.

One in every ten women is allergic to nickel, and most of them, says Dr Schorr, are young women who have had their ears pierced and subsequently developed nickel allergy. The problem begins, obviously enough, on the earlobes, and later resurfaces on the wrist, neck or abdomen due to contact with nickel in watches, bracelets, necklaces, buckles and clips.

Nickel-sensitive people resort to various schemes to put a barrier between their skin and nickel. Earring fasteners can also be coated with clear nail lacquer (if you can wear it safely). You can wear powder underneath your necklace and clasp bracelets. And buy spectacle frames of plastic or with plastic sleeves on the stems.

If you're going to have your ears pierced, you can avoid nickel allergy by having it done by a doctor, and requesting that he or she use a stainless steel needle. Wear only stainless steel, stud earrings for the first three weeks, until the hole heals over completely. After that, you can wear any earrings safely, says Dr Fisher (*Journal of the American Medical Association*, 3 June 1974).

Stainless steel is non-allergenic, even if it contains nickel, because the nickel is bound in so firmly that even sweat cannot free up the metal. Certain other metals – especially copper and silver – corrode readily and can occasionally cause trouble, especially when dampened by perspiration.

Gold is far less apt to cause allergy than other decorative metals. Some people can wear no jewellery unless it's 24-carat (100 per cent) gold. But even 'pure' gold may be contaminated with traces of nickel or other metals. And sulphur and other chemicals in smog can tarnish gold. When a tarnished gold ring is slipped on the finger or a bracelet is placed on the arm, the tarnish may cause a reaction.

Food and food additives

Some of the same preservatives, flavours and colours that cause food allergy when eaten also cause skin reactions when touched – especially in cooks, bakers and homemakers who handle large amounts of food daily. One doctor, for example, found that hand eczema in a salad chef was due to sodium bisulphite – which, like metabisulphite, is used in many restaurants to prevent browning of fruits and vegetables. (Table 22 lists some food ingredients that commonly cause skin reactions.)

It's not unheard of for fruit and fruit juices, vegetables and uncooked meat to irritate the skin, aggravating allergic hands. If your hands are inflamed, avoid direct contact with the juice of onions, garlic, peppers, tomatoes, citrus fruits and raw meat.

Preventing skin allergies in the first place

Many of the remedies and avoidance tactics we've talked about in earlier chapters also double as preventive measures against

TABLE 22

Food Ingredients That May Cause Skin Reactions upon Contact

Not all the foods in the Common Food Sources category contain the additives they're matched up with, but there's a good chance they might. To know for sure, you have to read labels and do the type of additive-finding detective work described in Chapter 3, Finding your no-allergy diet.

Additive	Common Food Sources
Artificial colours	Many foods
Benzoyl peroxide	Flour
Gum arabic (acacia)	Creams and cheeses
Karaya	Sweets, pastry and other confections
Lanolin	Chewing gum
Nickel	Hydrogenated fats
Parabens (preservatives)	Tomato, meat and fish products, pickles, relishes, sauces
Sodium bisulphite	Fruit and vegetables
Vanillin	Artificial flavours

SOURCE: *Reprinted by permission of the publisher from* Contact Dermatitis, *by Alexander A. Fisher (Philadelphia: Lea & Febiger, 1978), p. 77.*

skin allergies. But there are a few additional guidelines you should follow.

1. To keep your skin from becoming dry and easily inflamed, avoid long hot soaks in the tub, leisurely showers or too-frequent washing. After washing, don't rub vigorously. Rather, pat the skin dry with a soft towel.

2. Use non-alkaline soaps to maintain your skin's natural acidity.

3. Don't allow your children to 'play grown-up' with your makeup. Early exposure to cosmetics increases the chances that when they do grow up, they will develop not only cosmetic allergy, but other assorted contact allergies, according to Guinter Kahn, a dermatologist in North Miami Beach. Cosmetics marketed to pre-teens are also unacceptable.

4. To reduce the number of potential offenders you come in contact with, use body care products with the simplest, most basic formulas.

TABLE 23

Common Sites and Sources of Nickel Allergy

Site	Nickel Source
Scalp	Hairpins, curlers
Earlobes	Earrings
Ear canals	Insertion of metal objects
Back of ears	Spectacle frames
Eyelids	Eyelash curler
Sides of face	Hairpins, curlers, dental instruments
Lips	Metal pins held in mouth, metal lipstick holder
Neck	Clasp of necklace, zip
Upper chest	Medallions, metal identification tags
Armpit	Zip (usually on one side only)
Breast	Wire support of bra cup
Palms	Handles of doors, handbags, umbrellas, keys
Fingers	Thimbles, needles, scissors, coins, pens
Wrists	Watch bands, bracelets
Arms	Bracelets
Inner forearm and elbow	Metal handle of handbag
Thighs	Suspenders, metal chains, keys or metal coins in pockets
Ankle	Bracelets
Instep of foot	Metal eyelets of shoes
Foot arch	Metal arch support
Pubic area and vulva (women)	Safety pin on Sanitary Towel
Bullet wounds	Nickel alloys in bullets and shrapnel (other than stainless steel)
Postoperative sites	Screws, bolts, plates in orthopaedic implants (other than stainless steel)

SOURCE: *Reprinted by permission of the publisher from* Contact Dermatitis, *by Alexander A. Fisher (Philadelphia: Lea & Febiger, 1978), p. 97.*

DO YOUR OWN PATCH TEST

Doctors sometimes test for allergy to specific chemicals or compounds by placing a dilute amount of the substance in question on the skin and observing any reaction. But because some products contain such a large number of chemicals and compounds, it's not possible or practical to test for every single one. So doctors find it easier simply to apply a sample of the cloth, cosmetic or other suspected cause of allergy to the skin. If there is no reaction, the result is considered negative. If there is redness or swelling, it's positive and the material must be avoided. This is called a 'patch test'. And you can do your own.

To test cosmetics, place a small amount of the suspected cosmetic on the more sensitive skin of the inner forearm, twice daily. If you are truly allergic, you'll react at the site within one to four days. You can patch test up to four cosmetics at a time, one on each forearm and one on the back of each knee.

To test sunscreens, rub a small amount on your forearm (protect the rest of your body with clothing), and spend about fifteen minutes in the sun. If you react, test again a few days later with another sunscreen until you find one you can use safely.

To test cloth, snip a small sample from an inside seam, corner, or other unobtrusive spot. (When buying through mail order, ask for sample swatches.) Affix it to the forearm with a non-allergenic tape.

Do not self-test for industrial-strength chemicals. You could get a very nasty chemical burn. It's also important that you test only when your skin has completely healed from an allergic encounter. If you patch test while you are reacting, you not only run the risk of aggravating the existing problem, but you will be more likely to get a false reading from the test.

5. Be on guard for the smallest symptoms any time you test a new product. If something does trouble you, try to determine from the list of ingredients which ingredient is the problem, and avoid other products containing that substance.

6. Relax! Some people break out only when they're tired, tense or upset, or under any strain that taxes the body's defence

system. (See Chapter 13, Mind over allergy, for a complete discussion on coping with allergy.)

7. Enlist your doctor's help to prevent skin reactions. He or she should avoid prescribing topical or oral medications which are known to cause skin reactions – benzocaine, furacin, neomycin, penicillin, sulphonamides, ammoniated mercury, thimerosal, dibucaine, cyclomethycaine sulphate, wool wax alcohol (lanolin) and turpentine.

8. If you're facing surgery, tell your surgeon if you're allergic to nickel. Some nickel-sensitive people react to surgical clips used to close incisions or to metal prostheses (artificial parts) inserted in limbs.

9. Use over-the-counter medicated salves cautiously, if at all. If you're allergic to a dye or a preservative (like parabens or formaldehyde) in cosmetics, you'll also react to that compound in medicinal creams and lotions. Also, avoid all of the '-caine' salves and ointments.

Skin allergies, of course, can coexist with other skin diseases, such as acne or psoriasis. If the problem persists in spite of all your efforts to control it, don't hesitate to make an appointment with a dermatologist.

CHAPTER 8

OTHER UNEXPECTED ALLERGIES

The driver of a cab I hired in Chicago told me that he was allergic to his new girlfriend. He didn't know what it was about her, but he broke out whenever he got near her. He was certain it wasn't anything obvious like perfume or cosmetics.

Far-fetched? Not at all. A few days later, I stumbled across a possible explanation. An allergist in that same city told me that sensitivity to human dander – hair and skin particles – has been written about in medical journals from time to time.

Of course, I never did find out how the cabbie fared. But his was just one of several types of odd allergies that I ran across while researching this book – allergies which I'll review here in case you or someone you know happens to have a very unusual problem. Some of these allergies are so rare that doctors have had little opportunity to develop any real therapy – other than to avoid the cause of the problem. (Unless it's something you're willing to endure – like your girlfriend.)

Sunlight

Allergy to light may sound like the ultimate in hypochondria. But it does occur. And not only in people who are taking certain drugs or handling chemicals that activate skin problems in the presence of light, as we discussed in earlier chapters. Once in a blue moon (or sun), along comes someone who really is allergic to light per se – and then only to certain wavelengths: artificial light or light streaming through a window is okay, but direct light is a problem. The person's skin gets red, swollen and tender, except for well-defined areas covered by sleeves, trousers or a hat – just like sunburn. But the skin flares up only moments after an exposure too brief to produce sunburn in most people. Sometimes the mock burn is accompanied by headaches, vomiting and burning eyes. *Very* rarely, light sensitivity can lead to anaphylactic shock.

People with allergy to sunlight don't go to many beach parties. But they don't have to go underground, either. Protective clothing is a must, of course. And sunscreens can be a tremendous help. Mildly sensitive people can build up their tolerance to sunlight by exposing small areas, a little at a time.

Cold Temperature

Some people break out in hives when they dash in and out of an air-conditioned store in summer. Or when they come into a warm house after shovelling snow. Or if they take a quick dip in a chilly pond or pool. Or even if they rinse their hands in cold water.

That's called cold urticaria, and while it's the drop in temperature that triggers the reaction, the symptoms appear as the body temperature warms up again. That increase in body temperature, it's believed, releases histamine and other allergy-triggering body substances (explained in Chapter 1, What is an allergy?). Hives may develop all over the body, but they're usually more prominent in the areas directly affected by the cold, such as uncovered hands or face. If very cold food is eaten, the lips and tongue may swell somewhat. And cold-induced hives may be accompanied by headache, vomiting, rapid heartbeat and fainting.

Cold urticaria is related to allergy to exercise, which also prompts a rise in body temperature, and is medically referred to as a 'cholinergic' allergy, which means that the allergy involves the nervous system. And cold allergy can be accompanied by water allergy, a rare and slightly different variation of cholinergic allergy.

It's not always easy to tell the difference between cold urticaria, exercise urticaria or water urticaria. Widespread hives that develop after swimming, for example, could be caused by cold water, exertion (if it's a heated pool) or by the water itself. To sort it out, doctors do what amounts to a patch test with an ice cube. If you don't react, you're not cold sensitive.

Allergy to cold temperature is very often part of one of a few other, underlying illnesses, and disappears when the disease is cured. In other cases, cold allergy simply subsides as mysteriously as it began. If not, common sense tells the individual to take precautions against exposure to cold. Where cold is unavoidable or the allergy is a major problem, many people have been successfully desensitized to cold temperature by gradual exposure to decreasing temperatures – either in a cold room or cold water – for progressively longer periods of time until cold can be tolerated.

If that doesn't work, antihistamines may help. While we don't encourage casual use of drugs, we do feel that in certain circumstances – such as this – medication is less of a hazard than the risk of a severe reaction to an unavoidable allergen. (For more on medical therapy, see Chapter 10, Allergy drugs and their alternatives.)

Exercise

'Allergy to exercise' may sound like a lame excuse to stay chair-bound. But there actually are a few rare individuals who swell up and break out in hives after even mild exertion. A couple of laps across the pool or a few minutes of jogging leave them not only red and itchy, but possibly even dizzy, nauseated and exhausted. In most cases, antihistamines can help.

Asthma attacks, too, may be triggered by strenuous exertion. But those breathing difficulties may be due to the direct effect of cold, dry air on sensitive airways and are in no way related to exercise-induced hives. (See entry on *Asthma* in Part V.)

Water

Water allergy (aquagenic urticaria) is extremely rare. Water of any temperature touches off itching and spotty hives. And like allergy to cold or emotional triggers, histamine release seems the basic mechanism at work. In one of the few cases studied, oral doses of hydroxyzine (an antihistamine) three times a day for one week effectively blocked the reaction to water.

Emotions

As a schoolgirl in Sweden, actress Ingrid Bergman was so shy that she used to break out when she had to recite in class. Her fingers swelled so badly she couldn't bend them. Her lips and eyelids swelled, too. The doctor said Ingrid was allergic to shyness. Fortunately for Ingrid and the film world, drama school eventually cured her. But her case is a good example of how we can be allergic to strong emotions.

Emotionally stimulated allergy may be triggered not only by shyness, but also anxiety, anger, fear, embarrassment – any emotion that prompts an increase in body temperature.

Sperm

A few women have been surprised to learn that they've suddenly become allergic to their partner's sperm. One woman experienced anaphylaxis while having sex with her husband – an extraordinary response by anyone's standards. Skin tests confirmed that her husband's sperm was provoking allergic antibodies. The woman's doctors were able to desensitize her in much the same way they desensitize other individuals against pollen. She and her husband were able to resume their love life safely (*Journal of Allergy and Clinical Immunology*, abstract no. 182, January 1982).

Condoms

Snicker if you will, but dermatitis from condoms isn't all that rare. A reaction usually begins with a swelling of the foreskin, which may spread to the shaft, scrotum and inner thighs. In most men, the allergy is to rubber – in which case they've probably had other unpleasant brushes with rubber in clothing or other articles. Switching to another brand of condom may help.

'Some men have found by trial and error that only certain brands of rubber condoms produced reactions, while others were well tolerated,' writes Dr Alexander A. Fisher (*Contact Dermatitis*, Lea and Febiger, 1978).

Occasionally, the problem isn't the rubber itself but a powder or lubricant it bears. Try a plain, untreated product. Otherwise, some rubber-sensitive men may have to switch to the original, old-fashioned condoms made from sheep's intestine.

And of course, a partner's condom should be suspected as a possible cause of an unexplained rash or other inflammation on the vulva or inner thighs of a woman, even if her partner isn't allergic to the device.

Spermicides

Allergy to vaginal spermicides (sperm-killing creams, foams or jellies) isn't common, but it happens nevertheless. The four most sensitizing chemicals in these products are phenylmercuric acetate, oxyquinoline sulphate, quinine hydrochloride and hexylresorcinol.

If a woman's chosen spermicide is making her itch or giving her other discomfort, she should look for an alternative with different ingredients. Before using a brand or type of spermicide for the first time, she can do a patch test on her arm to determine her tolerance. (See the box, Do your own patch test, in Chapter 7, Contact [skin] allergies.)

As with condoms, what's good for the goose may be bad for the gander: a woman's partner is also apt to react to contact with vaginal spermicides, even if she doesn't.

Feminine hygiene sprays

Aside from the fact that these sprays do little or nothing for vaginal hygiene, they may irritate and produce a burning sensation if squirted too close to the skin or vulva. Applied from a proper distance, the freon propellant presumably evaporates before it reaches its destination. Even then, the perfumes can cause trouble. And a woman's partner may develop a rash or burning sensation on his penis or scrotum if they have sex together soon after the spray is applied. So why bother with sprays at all?

Copper I.U.D.s

Copper-containing intrauterine birth control devices sometimes induce stubborn allergic reactions in women who use them. The classic symptoms are a recurrent rash on and around the vulva, lower abdomen and inner thighs. Less frequently, it may spread to the chest and lower back. Ointments, antihistamines and cortisone treatments provide only temporary relief. The only real cure is to have the I.U.D. removed and choose an alternative birth control method.

PART III

What Your Doctor Can Do for You

CHAPTER 9

ALLERGY TESTS: WHAT THEY CAN AND CANNOT TELL

Doctors have at their disposal a variety of ways to test for allergy. But trying to get a consensus of opinion on which allergy tests are the best is like trying to find out which car is the 'best'. Everybody has their own preference. For instance, some doctors say that the RAST test (a type of blood test) is the 'best' way to test for food allergy and that skin tests are the worst. Others say just the opposite. But whatever test your doctor uses, it's important to realize that *all* allergy tests have shortcomings, and that no matter what the results, you still must pay close attention to your diet and environment to help your doctor diagnose allergy correctly.

Skin tests

Traditionally, skin tests have been *the* techniques of allergy diagnosis. Here are several methods of skin testing.

1. Placing a drop of allergen extract (a diluted amount of the suspected substance) on the skin and scratching the surface of the skin (scratch test).
2. Pushing the test substance into the skin with a needlelike probe (prick or puncture test).
3. Injecting the test substance between layers of skin (intradermal or intracutaneous test).

When the allergen makes contact with the skin, mast cells (discussed in Chapter 1, What is an allergy?) release histamine and other allergy-inducing substances, which usually produce a 'weal-and-flare' reaction within ten to fifteen minutes if the test is positive. (If the test is negative nothing happens.) The raised weal, or welt, may vary in size from that of a mosquito bite to that of a large thumbnail; flare is simply another word for redness. To distinguish between irritation at being stuck with a sharp metal object and a genuinely allergic reaction, a separate test dose of plain salt water is applied also.

The scratch test is the least sensitive but the safest of the three skin tests, since the material can be wiped off if a severe reaction is unexpectedly triggered. And the scratch test is the least painful, although no one looks forward to any kind of skin test. (Children, especially, tend to fuss at encounters with needles.) Injected material, on the other hand, cannot be removed, but it most accurately reflects the allergic tendency, picking up levels of sensitivity so low that they often do not produce any symptoms.

The puncture test is basically a version of the intradermal test; once the fluid has been placed in the puncture hole, it essentially has been injected. And the puncture test is only slightly less sensitive than an intradermal test, without the added risk and discomfort. So unless your doctor can give you a good reason for choosing a scratch or intradermal test, the puncture test is the most preferable of the three skin tests.

None of these skin tests, however, is 100 per cent foolproof. In fact, the irony of skin tests is that they're more accurate for people who suffer immediate, severe reactions – people who probably already know what they're allergic to. They're not as useful for diagnosing the cause of hives or eczema as they are for diagnosing the cause of asthma, hay fever or other classic allergy symptoms.

What's more, skin tests can only be used to test for allergy to certain things. Except for penicillin, skin tests are not useful for diagnosing drug allergy. And even when skin tests for penicillin allergy are used, the only people to get tested are those who have a *known* allergy to penicillin but must take the drug for a serious infection. The only other use for a drug skin test is to establish the safety of egg-derived vaccine in children who have a history of egg, chicken or feather sensitivity.

As for detecting allergy to stinging insects, skin tests are notoriously poor. They're also fairly unreliable when it comes to food allergy. For instance, a person may have a 'positive' skin test for egg, but if he can eat eggs with no problem the test is meaningless; for all intents and purposes, no allergy to egg exists. (A 'positive' test means a person has the allergy; a 'negative' test means there's no allergy.)

In the case of pollen or dust, skin tests are not 100 per cent accurate. So the real proof is in the breathing.

Fasting

Some of the many doctors who find skin tests to be unreliable in revealing food allergy use fasting – no eating for a few days – as a test. After all, the simplest way to find out if you're allergic to food is to not eat any and see what happens. Usually, if symptoms are due to a food allergy of any kind they get worse during the first, second or third day without food, but disappear by the fourth or fifth. Then eating is resumed.

During a fast, drinking plenty of water is essential. The body can live off its fat reserves for several days, but it needs water daily. Distilled water is best during a fast, since a few people are sensitive to ingredients in tap water.

Still, going without food is stressful, and most physicians who use fasting as a diagnostic tool do not recommend that people try it on their own, especially if they have diabetes, hypoglycemia, are underweight or suffer any chronic illness. Ideally, a person on an allergy fast should be away from the home, school or work environment to avoid allergens which may be reinforcing (or confusing) any reactions to food. In some cases, that calls for hospital-controlled fasting.

Because of both the inconvenience and stress on the body, allergy doctors feel that fasting is best reserved for highly allergic people.

As an alternative to a total fast, some doctors will allow an individual just *one* food at each meal during the test period (three to five days). That's monotonous, but less gruelling.

Inhalation challenge (nasal and bronchial provocation)

Because skin tests sometimes miss the mark entirely, some doctors use an inhalation challenge for allergy to inhalants. To test for mould allergy, for instance, a small amount of dried, powdered, sterilized mould is placed on the end of a toothpick and sniffed. Symptoms are expected to appear within five minutes if the individual is allergic to mould.

So far, these tests all carry an element of anxiety – the fear that you will react. No wonder – that's the whole idea. The ideal allergy test, from the patient's point of view, is one that's accurate, yet doesn't risk a reaction. Enter the RAST test.

RAST (radioallergosorbent test)

The RAST test measures the amount of IgE in your blood. It's certainly safe, since the test is conducted on a blood sample in the laboratory. Anaphylactic shock, which occasionally occurs with skin testing, is impossible with a RAST test (although you still have to endure the discomfort of a needle). RAST is more sensitive than a puncture or scratch test.

'One of the criticisms of the RAST test is that it's expensive,' comments Dr Jonathan V. Wright, from Kent, Washington, who uses the RAST test a great deal. 'Unfortunately, no other test comes as close to it in accuracy.'

A RAST test measures the amount of IgE (allergy-provoking antibody) in the blood. In contrast, skin tests merely measure the weal-and-flare – indirect evidence of IgE activity. More precise measurement of IgE activity by RAST means that, if needed, allergy injections (discussed in Chapter 11, Immunotherapy – a matter of choice) can be started at a customized dose, and relief can be expected in three or four months. In contrast, allergy injections based on skin tests are begun at a lower estimated dose and gradually increased until the optimal dose is reached, which sometimes takes six months to a year. (Incidentally, IgE levels run higher in smokers than non-smokers, for some unknown reason. Be sure to let your doctor know if you smoke so that factor can be taken into consideration when interpreting your RAST test.)

For all its advantages, the RAST test is somewhat controversial. Aside from increased cost, doctors must resist the temptation to rely on it too heavily for diagnosis. For instance, many people react positively to both skin and RAST tests for cereal grains, but eat them routinely with no ill effects. Like any allergy test, the RAST is meant to supplement, not replace, a good, thorough medical history. Consequently, many doctors feel that the *most* accurate way of testing for food allergy is still elimination and rechallenge, described in Chapter 3, Finding your no-allergy diet.

Controversial tests

Within the field of clinical ecology, doctors have developed four more allergy testing techniques – all highly controversial, but showing some promise nonetheless.

Intradermal skin titration is much like traditional skin testing, but with a slight twist. Instead of using a standardized test dose, testing begins with a weak dose and measures the weal produced by each subsequent dose, until reactions reach a plateau and weals no longer grow progressively larger. Doctors who use this technique say that it not only determines the degree of sensitivity to the substance but also indicates how strong the treatment dose should be. (To eliminate the power of suggestion, patients aren't always told what they're being tested for.)

Intradermal provocation is a variation of intradermal titration. The idea is to produce not only a weal-and-flare but symptoms – which are then immediately neutralized with subsequent injections of the diluted solution. Patients may also be sent home with pre-measured doses of the allergen – either to neutralize unpleasant reactions or to prevent them. (See Chapter 11, Immunotherapy – a matter of choice.)

Mainstream allergy doctors who've tried these alternative methods of skin testing claim they do not give consistent, accurate information – contrary to what the tests' advocates claim. Doctors familiar with those same tests, however, say that other doctors get poor results because they don't follow the procedures correctly.

Sublingual (under-the-tongue) provocation is used primarily to identify allergy to foods and sometimes allergy to inhalants. Extracts are mixed half-and-half with glycerin and squirted under the tongue. If nothing happens within ten minutes, the next food is tested. If symptoms develop, neutralization is attempted with dilutions of the same food extract.

Over a series of several visits, dozens of foods can thus be tested – up to thirty or forty is usually adequate. You might say that sublingual provocation is comparable with a deliberate challenge with the food itself. And it's very controversial: the few doctors who use the sublingual method swear by it, saying it works very well and is just the ticket for fidgety children or people who hate needles. Traditional doctors who've tried sublingual testing say they can't get accurate results.

The cytotoxic test (or leukocytotoxic test) is also used to detect food allergy. A sample of blood is drawn and cells are added to a mixture of sterile water, then applied to microscopic slides smeared with food extracts in a base of petroleum jelly. The slides are examined several times – within ten minutes, after thirty or forty minutes, after one hour, after one and a half hours and after two hours. Certain changes in blood cells are interpreted as a sure sign of allergy to the food smeared on the slide.

The big plus of cytotoxic testing is that doctors claim they can diagnose allergy to many, many foods from one sample of blood. The problem, though, is that cytotoxic testing may not be as reliable or valid as its proponents crack it up to be.

'It may be reliable in the sense that two different lab technicians doing the same test on the same individual may get roughly the same result,' says Iris Bell, at San Francisco Veterans Hospital and the University of California at San Francisco. 'But there's not a lot of good evidence that it's valid – that a positive test really means you can't eat the food.'

'In other words,' continued Dr Bell, 'if the cytotoxic test shows you are sensitive to fifty items – and some show that – the question is, Can you *really* not eat all those foods without getting symptoms?' Conversely, the test may show no reaction to a food to which you are blatantly allergic. In other words, the cytotoxic test has the same potential (or possibly more) for false positive results as does the traditional skin test.

An additional drawback of the cytotoxic test is that it gives no indication of type of sensitivity, even when the test is accurate. 'There's no way to tell from looking at a slide if you're going to get a life-threatening asthma attack or break out in one hive,' says Dr Bell.

At present, the cytotoxic test is no better than skin tests in diagnosing allergy. In fact, in some ways cytotoxic tests are less accurate than skin tests.

'I see the cytotoxic test at the level it's been developed right now as being able to offer a hint that something may be going on,' Dr Bell says. 'But I don't think it can be used to tell you what you absolutely can and cannot eat.'

As this brief review clearly shows, allergy testing is not an exact science. Try as they might, doctors cannot always tell exactly what's going on in an allergic body. One thing that all these tests have in common is that they must be correlated with a complete and thorough medical history if they are to be interpreted correctly. No matter how sophisticated the tests become, there's no substitute for a doctor asking you for details about your diet and the environment in your home, school or workplace.

'My advice to young doctors is to listen to what the patient says,' offered Dr Constantine J. Falliers, an allergist and asthma specialist in Denver, Colorado. 'You can learn more from that than from doing the most expensive, fancy tests.'

CHAPTER 10

ALLERGY DRUGS AND THEIR ALTERNATIVES

Drugs do not cure allergy. At best, they *sometimes* relieve the more common symptoms: wheezing, runny nose, itching. And they're often very valuable in breaking the spiralling escalation of more and more allergic irritation and discomfort, which can worsen allergies. One thing about drugs is certain, however: they all have the potential to produce unpleasant – and sometimes dangerous – side effects. Table 24 lists some of the more common adverse reactions, so we won't repeat them in detail. It's enough to say that *no* allergy drug is perfectly safe, and all should be used cautiously. And in many cases, non-drug alternatives work just as well (if not better), especially when combined with a programme to avoid allergy triggers.

Some natural alternatives to asthma medication

The chief characteristic of asthma is wheezing. The lining of the air passages swells, the bronchial muscles around the airways shrink or go into spasm and the lungs produce more mucus. The chest feels tight and breathing is a chore.

The obvious solution is to avoid the allergic stimulus, be it pollen, dust, dog hair or something else. When that's impossible, an asthmatic is likely to be prescribed one or more of the following drugs:

– an expectorant to thin mucus and promote coughing to

eject it from the lungs (although use is increasingly less frequent);
– a bronchodilator, such as theophylline, to relax tightened bronchial muscles;
– cromolyn sodium, if exertion triggers the asthma (in nine out of ten asthmatics, it does);
– a corticosteroid (such as prednisone) to reduce swelling and inflammation of the lungs and mucous membranes.

But there are non-drug approaches that relieve asthma, especially in non-emergency situations (which most are).

First of all, drinking plenty of liquids helps keep mucus in the lungs thin so that it can be coughed up, thereby eliminating the need for expectorants. (A dry or sticky tongue in an asthmatic is a sure sign that the body needs more fluids.) Drinking half to one cup of liquid, once an hour, is a good guideline. (Don't drink cold liquids, though. Cold can stimulate sensitive airways and trigger bronchial spasms. Also, avoid any colas or beverages with food dyes to which you or your child may be allergic.)

Drinking warm liquids such as soup, herb tea or even plain warm water has another benefit: it *relaxes* bronchial muscles, says Dr Constantine J. Falliers, an allergist and asthma specialist in Denver. 'We've used it, and it works. We've had kids in the hospital for treatment, and when they can't breathe, we give them something warm to drink – water, or something with a little more flavour, like tea or hot cider or apple juice. They relax and don't need anything else. We control the panic and they start breathing quietly.'

Notice that Dr Falliers mentions emotional calm as a necessary step in controlling an asthma attack. That's because relaxation loosens up the bronchial muscles, in many instances replacing the need for bronchodilators.

'Many children breathe better as soon as a physician enters the room, before any medication has been given,' writes Dr Doris J. Rapp in her book, *Allergies and Your Family* (Sterling Publishing, 1981). 'They anticipate help and that alone relaxes the bronchial muscles.' Similarly, if the parent keeps calm, the child will be less panicky.

To make relaxation a skill rather than a hoped-for response, children and adults alike are often taught relaxation techniques and calming breathing exercises to nip panic in the bud and

TABLE 24

Allergy Drugs and Their Side Effects

Types of Drugs	Chemical Names	Trade Names
Antihistamines	alkylamine	Actidil, Actidil Elixir
	ethanolamine	Benadryl, Dramamine
	ethylenediamine	
	phenothiazines	Phenergen
	piperazines	Antepar, Pripsen
	miscellaneous	Atarax, Optimine, Periactin
Bischromones	cromolyn sodium	Intal
Bronchodilators	1. Adrenergic agonists	
	albuterol	Ventolin
	ephedrine	Argotene, Asmapax, Davenol, Frenol, Noradran, Rubelix, Tedral
	epinephrine	Adrenalin chloride
	isoetharine	Numotac
	isoproterenol	Medihaler
	metaproterenol	Alupent
	protokylol	
	terbutaline	Bricanyl
	2. Methylxanthines	
	aminophylline	Aminophyllin, Aminophylline, Phyllocontin, Theodrox
	oxtriphylline	Choledyl
	theophylline	Asmapax, Franol, Nuelin, Provent, Theodur, Uniphyllin, Contrin

Types of Allergy Treated	Most Common Side Effects
Hives (urticaria), contact dermatitis, eczema, hay fever (allergic rhinitis), gastrointestinal allergy	Drowsiness, nausea, abdominal discomfort, dry mouth
Asthma (allergic and exercise induced), gastrointestinal allergy	Throat irritation, hoarseness, coughing, wheezing. Safety during pregnancy not yet determined
Asthma, hives (occasionally)	Fear, anxiety, tenseness, restlessness, headache, weakness, dizziness, pallor, accentuated heartbeat, nausea, insomnia, tremor
Asthma	Irritation of stomach or intestines, nausea, abdominal cramps, heartburn, exacerbation of ulcers, temporary sleeplessness, nervousness

TABLE 24 – *Continued*

Types of Drugs	Chemical Names	Trade Names
Corticosteroids	1. Aerosol	
	beclomethasone	Becloporte, Beconase, Becotide, Propaderm, Ventide
	dexamethasone	Decadron, Dexa Rhinaspray, Maxidrex, Maxitrol, Orade, Sofradex
	2. Systemic	
	hydrocortisone	many trade names
	methylprednisolone	Methylprednisolone, Depomedrone, Neomedrone, Solumedrone
	triamcinolone	Adcortyl, Audicort, Kenalog, Lectorspan, Silderm
	cortisone	Cortisone acetate, Cortelan, Cortistals, Cortisyl
	dexamethasone	Decadron, Dexa Rhinaspray, Maxidrex, Maxitrol, Oradexon, Sofradex
	beta methasone	Betridan, Betrosol preps., Betrovate preps., Bextrasol, Fuabet, Vistamethasone
	3. Topical	
	betamethsone hydrocortisone prednisolone	variety of trade names

Types of Allergy Treated	Most Common Side Effects
Hay fever, nasal polyps, asthma	Dry mouth, hoarseness, fungal infections of mouth and throat **Rinse mouth thoroughly with water after each use**
All allergies, especially acute, chronic asthma; acute hives; drug reactions	Water retention, weight gain, susceptibility to bruising, stretch marks, more body hair, insomnia, uneasiness, leg cramps, 'moon face'. (Most minor side effects more likely after long-term use at high doses.) Supression of adrenal hormones
Rashes (especially eczema and contact dermatitis)	Burning sensations, irritation, itching, dryness, inflammation of hair follicles, acne, loss of pigmentation, thinning of skin, stretch marks, tendency to bruise easily, skin ulcers. (Side effects depend on potency, concentration and duration of use.)

TABLE 24 – *Continued*

Types of Drugs	Chemical Names	Trade Names
Decongestants	naphazoline	Antistan, Privine, Vasocan A
	oxymetazoline	Afrzine, Liadin-mini
	phenylephrine	Betrovate preps., Dimotane, Exypten, Hayphryn, Neoptryn, Minims Phenylephrine, Prefin, Zincfrin
	pseudoephedrine HCI	Actifed, Benylin, Congestese, Dimotan, Extil, Linctifed, Sudafed

prevent bronchospasms from mushrooming into full-fledged asthma attacks. (See the boxes, Basic deep-breathing exercise for asthma and How to relax away an asthma attack, pp. 204–5.)

Relaxation techniques, a calming presence or warm liquids are certainly more natural treatments than theophylline, a commonly used bronchodilator and a cornerstone of the medical management of acute, chronic and disabling asthma. Theophylline drugs are methylxanthines – compounds related to the chemicals caffeine and theobromine (found in coffee, chocolate, tea and other substances). Because some people – particularly children – are very sensitive to methylxanthines, doses of theophylline must be very carefully adjusted to individual tolerance. Otherwise, the drug makes you feel like you just drank thirty cups of coffee.

Cromolyn sodium is another drug for bronchospasms, but it's primarily used to help the many asthmatics who experience tightness and wheezing after exercise. When inhaled, cromolyn sodium desensitizes the tissues in the lungs and airways, making them impervious to the stress of exercise. As allergy drugs go, cromolyn sodium *seems* to be one of the safest. Taking

Types of Allergy Treated	Most Common Side Effects
Rashes – *Continued*	Contact dermatitis can result when cream, gel or ointment contains preservatives
Hay fever, gastrointestinal allergy	Nervousness, dizziness, nausea, rapid heartbeat Do not use nasal decongestants for more than 5 days. May prolong symptoms

cromolyn sodium can occasionally cause throat irritation, hoarseness, coughing – even *wheezing* (the last thing an asthmatic needs).

Studies have shown that many natural methods can also prevent exercise-induced attacks, thereby reducing the need for cromolyn sodium. Among them are: taking vitamin C; wearing a face mask; choosing the right type of exercise; and doing a pre-exercise warm-up. Let's look at them one by one.

Two scientists at Yale University discovered vitamin C's ability to relieve exercise-induced bronchospasms. Several of their patients were pretreated with 500 milligrams of vitamin C before an exercise test. The vitamin C significantly lessened the severity of the bronchospasms following exercise (*Chest*, September, 1980).

Dr E. Neil Schachter, one of the investigators, told us, 'Vitamin C has the potential to help asthmatics, without the unpleasant or dangerous side effects of drugs.'

The reason that exercise throws an asthmatic's lungs into spasm may be water loss from the air passages, breathing in pollen or other allergens, or cold air that shocks sensitive airways (or all three). A light, cotton face mask may help reduce those

BASIC DEEP-BREATHING EXERCISE FOR ASTHMA

Asthmatics tend to breathe with the muscles of the shoulders and chest but not with the diaphragm, the muscle of the abdomen. This fills and empties only the top part of the lungs – it's a type of breathing that's shallow, inefficient and unhealthy. Deep, complete breathing is just the opposite. By learning to fill the lungs completely and to exhale fully with each breath, asthmatics can ward off wheezing, chest tightness and shortness of breath.

Deep-breathing exercises followed for five minutes every day can reduce the need for bronchodilators and other drugs. They can be practised lying down, sitting or standing.

1. Think of the chest and abdomen as a container for air. As you (or your child) breathe in through the nose, slowly fill the bottom of the container first and keep filling until the stomach feels puffed up like an inflated balloon. To be sure you're breathing correctly, place your hand on the area just above the belly button. Feel your middle rise and fall as you breathe.

2. Exhale calmly through the mouth, as slowly as possible. The 'container' must be completely empty and the stomach flat before you slowly inhale once again.

3. Repeat. Inhale and exhale twelve times.

SOURCE: American Lung Association Newsletter, *May 1981.*

effects. Scientists at the National Asthma Center in Denver found that after exercising for six minutes wearing a face mask, ten asthmatic youngsters experienced much less asthma – or none at all. The researchers conclude that a 'simple face mask may be an inexpensive, [nondrug] alternative for the alleviation of exercise-induced asthma' and may also be practical for asthmatic runners and skiers (*Journal of the American Medical Association*, 14 November 1980).

Wearing a scarf over the mouth before going outside, especially in winter, accomplishes the same thing. And breathing through your nose, instead of your mouth, also helps to warm

HOW TO RELAX AWAY AN ASTHMA ATTACK

The American Lung Association teaches kids that if they learn to relax, they can ward off an asthma attack – or stop one in its tracks. The following exercise, practised for five minutes a day, can be 'turned on' whenever the chest starts to feel tight or other warning signals arise. And it works wonders for adults, too!

1. Stand up and make all your muscles *very* tight. Then take a deep breath. Point your chin up to the ceiling and grit your teeth. Hold your arms out straight. Keep your elbows tight, your fists tightly closed, your legs stiff and your toes stiff. Hold for a few seconds.

2. Now, let everything go, like a balloon that's being deflated. Completely relax all your muscles until you feel like a wet noodle or a rag doll.

3. Flop to the floor in a lying position and stay there. Close your eyes. Keep your arms limp and loose. Your face and feet are limp, too.

4. Picture yourself floating down a river. Concentrate on each muscle and how nice and floppy it feels.

5. Breathe softly and easily, as if you were cosy and fast asleep in your bed. Stay quiet and droopy, and feel how pleasant it is.

6. Open your eyes. Turn on the relaxed, 'wet noodle' feeling whenever you feel nervous or short of breath, or feel an asthma attack coming on.

---

and filter air before it reaches the airways, according to doctors at Brigham and Women's Hospital in Boston (*Journal of Allergy and Clinical Immunology*, April 1982).

The type of sport an asthmatic engages in may influence how well he or she tolerates exertion. Sports that involve brief spurts of activity, separated by rest intervals, are far less likely to cause an attack than is continuous exertion. An asthmatic who plays baseball or soccer, for instance, is less apt to suffer asthma than one who runs the mile, and is therefore less likely to need cromolyn sodium or other asthma medication. Swimming, too, is ideal for asthmatics, provided the water isn't too cold and proper rest breaks are taken.

Deep-breathing and warm-up exercises also help asthmatics

to handle exercise without stress. The American Lung Association recommends the following warm-up routine for kids with asthma. (Adults can benefit, too.)

1. Lie down and do twelve deep-breathing exercises (as described earlier in this chapter).
2. Bend your knees and bicycle slowly for a minute or so. Stand up.
3. Stretch each arm straight above your head, six times.
4. Touch your toes six times.
5. Put your hands on your head and twist your trunk from side to side, six times.
6. Do twelve jumping jacks.

Then go out and enjoy yourself!

Steroids: handle with care

Corticosteroids – cortisone and hydrocortisone – are hormones produced naturally in the body by the adrenal cortex (part of the adrenal glands, which are located on top of each kidney). It's not a steroid deficiency, though, that prompts the use of steroids (usually synthetic) to treat allergy. These steroids are potent anti-inflammatory agents, and are therefore useful in soothing the sensitive, hyper-irritable airways of asthma. But steroids present some real problems. As you can see from Table 24, steroids carry a higher risk of adverse effects than any other drug. It's important that they be used only when absolutely necessary, in as small a dose as possible, for as short a time as possible – one to five days. The main problem is that while a person receives synthetic hormones, the adrenal glands automatically slow or shut down production of natural steroids – and in some people, don't resume production until several months after all forms of corticosteroids (oral, inhaled, topical) are discontinued. With natural steroids cut off for long periods, the body loses its power to manufacture infection-fighting eosinophils and lymphocytes in the blood, depressing immunity to bacteria and viruses. Steroid therapy also thwarts the growth of children by slowing formation of collagen, a basic structural material of bone.

Those side effects – depressed immune response and impaired collagen formation – have responded to high doses of vitamin C. Dr Hiram C. Polk, Jr, and other researchers at the University of Louisville School of Medicine found that vitamin

C reversed cortisone's effect on the immune response and restored the ability of white blood cells to kill bacteria (*Journal of Surgical Research*, February 1977). And in Athens, doctors found that vitamin C normalized the rate of collagen formation in children on steroid therapy (*Archives of Disease in Childhood*, May 1974).

Besides taking vitamin C, other measures can help allergy sufferers against the effects of steroids.

• Asthmatics on long-term steroid therapy have suffered spontaneous fractures, cataracts and exacerbation of diabetes and stomach ulcers. Doctors have found, though, that those risks can be minimized when steroids are taken in single, morning doses – when the body's own adrenal activity is at its peak.

• Salt restriction and potassium supplements can reduce water retention, the most common side effect of steroid use.

• Gastrointestinal effects can be minimized if the drug is taken with food.

• Risk of skin effects, such as pigment changes and scarring, can be reduced by staying out of the sun if you're taking steroids.

• The risk of broken bones can be reduced considerably when vitamin D plus calcium supplements are prescribed along with the drugs, especially in postmenopausal women, who are highly prone to bone fractures whether they take steroids or not.

Doctors are also looking into the possibility of giving steroids only every other day, to further cut the risk of adverse effects. Aerosol steroids, a new form of the drug that can be sprayed directly into the airways and used in lower doses, may also reduce – or even reverse – the systemic effects.

'We have seen reversal of [steroid-induced] cataracts in children switched to aerosol steroids,' says Dr Anthony R. Rooklin, of Crozier-Chester Medical Center in Chester, Pennsylvania.

Several commonly used drugs speed up or slow down the elimination of steroids from the body, magnifying or diminishing their expected effects. So it's vital that your doctor take into consideration any other medication you may be taking, be it prescription or over-the-counter, before prescribing steroids.

For more on effective drug-free treatment of asthma, see the entry on *Asthma* in Part V.

Drug-free therapy for hay fever

Antihistamines, as you might have guessed, block the release of histamine from mast cells, thereby reducing classic allergy symptoms such as headaches, itching or runny nose. In fact, they may be employed for any allergic reaction that's blamed on histamine release, like hives. Too much antihistamine, however, can make a person sleepy. And antihistamines tend to dry out mucous membranes. The secretion of those membranes becomes so thick and dry that it can't be expelled by coughing or sneezing, and it backs up into the sinus or respiratory tract. So what begins as the relatively simple runny nose of hay fever can end up as chronic, painful sinusitis or a stubborn, bone-dry cough – or both. Then you need a decongestant.

Nasal decongestant sprays and drops shrink swollen membranes in the nose and provide temporary relief of hay fever. If decongestants are relied on heavily, however, a rebound phenomenon occurs: after a couple of weeks, when the spray or drops are discontinued, the membranes swell again and congestion is worse than ever. Oral decongestants have their own drawbacks – they're adrenalin-like, and can make people hyper. So if you're a high-strung, nervous type, they're the last thing you need.

As you can see, once a hay fever sufferer boards the drug merry-go-round, it's sometimes hard to jump off. But herbs, exercise and vitamin C can all help to clear up the congestion and misery of hay fever – without the unpleasant side effects of antihistamines and decongestants.

Certain herbs act as decongestants, clearing clogged mucus. A tea of fenugreek, anise or horehound, or a concoction of garlic oil in water, made into a tea, can clear up congestion in twenty minutes. The vapours of eucalyptus also work wonders: put leaves into a large pot of boiling water and boil for five minutes. Then turn off the heat and, with a towel draped over your head, breathe in the vapours.

Many hay fever sufferers have found that vigorous exercise – running, walking or bicycling – helps to clear the nose, too.

Vitamin C acts as a natural antihistamine, reducing the swelling and inflammation that causes discomfort in nasal and sinus tissues. And, of course, it helps tremendously to avoid whatever triggers your hay fever.

Putting drugs in their place

For the pregnant woman or nursing mother, drugs for allergy symptoms must be used with special caution, and never for relief of minor allergic symptoms. In a review article for *Annals of Allergy*, Dr Wallace R. Pratt says that present knowledge of the safety of drugs used during pregnancy or breastfeeding is incomplete. Doctors know that some drugs – including iodides commonly found in expectorants – cause problems in the developing foetus when taken during pregnancy. Other information suggests that epinephrine, brompheniramine, promethazine, diphenhydramine, hydroxyzine and phenylpropanolamine also present some risks to the foetus. While epinephrine should not be withheld in the event of a life-threatening attack, Dr Pratt emphasizes that the limited and uncertain safety of many drugs during pregnancy and breastfeeding calls for prudence in prescribing allergy drugs for expectant and nursing mothers (*Annals of Allergy*, November 1981).

While most of the precautions demanded by allergy drugs apply to classic conditions such as asthma, hives and hay fever, use of drugs for *any* allergic symptoms should not be pursued casually, whether you're pregnant or not.

Because of the potential risks of drug therapy, it behoves doctors to take two things into consideration when prescribing allergy medication:

1. *Does the allergy persist in spite of earnest attempts to avoid the offending food or inhalants?* We'd be the last to deny a life-giving drug to an asthmatic. But at the same time, the individual (or parent) should make every effort to control allergic asthma non-medically – getting rid of the dog, installing an air filter, controlling diet, breathing correctly, learning to relax – to prevent emergencies from arising.

'Certainly, the answer is to find the cause rather than just take pills,' says Dr Falliers. 'If you get a headache every time you eat a certain type of fruit, instead of running for aspirin, try to find out: Is it the fruit? Is it the way it was sprayed?'

2. *Is the risk of not taking the drug higher than the risk of*

potential side effects? Intermittent use of bronchodilators in asthma that's acute, chronic and resistant to all other forms of therapy is preferred over the risk of permanent lung damage from uncontrolled asthma. And, of course, if an individual lapses into anaphylactic shock – loss of consciousness, extreme drop in blood pressure and respiratory arrest with the threat of death – drugs may be the only way to prevent these problems.

'Drugs require the proper attitude,' says Dr Falliers. 'Some families are totally dependent on drugs. Their houses look like a pharmacy, and they take one drug after another. Others are so afraid of drugs they don't take their medicine even when they really need it.'

It all boils down to one excellent piece of advice: do all you can to control your allergies before you turn to drugs.

'Not waiting until the damage is done, but preventing it – that will be the secret of success for allergy treatment,' says Dr Falliers. 'And if it will put us allergists out of a job, that's just fine.'

CHAPTER 11

IMMUNOTHERAPY: A MATTER OF CHOICE

Seventy years ago, a British doctor named Leonard Noon discovered that periodic injections of watered-down grass pollen relieved some people's hay fever. And that's how allergy injections were born.

The whole idea does seem contradictory – to gain relief by administering the very stuff that makes you miserable. Apparently, however, steady doses of allergy extract exhaust allergic antibodies, building up an individual's tolerance to allergy triggers. Immunotherapy for allergy – sometimes called desensitization or hyposensitization – can be thought of as vaccination against allergy. And, in effect, allergy injections do operate on the same basic principle as immunization against measles or the flu, which stimulates immunity to disease by injections of a live virus.

The standard course

The standard immunotherapy routine is relatively simple – perhaps you have already been through it. After several allergy tests (discussed in Chapter 9), you return to the doctor for weekly or bi-weekly injections, before or during the allergy season, or year round if necessary. Therapy begins with a small dose and is increased with each injection until you reach a protective dose, which may be continued indefinitely, sometimes for several years. Under certain circumstances, the procedure may be stepped up to daily injections, or even several per day. If, for instance, the pollen season is only three or four months away when a grass allergy is discovered, you may be put through the rush programme. If you're highly allergic to bees or other venomous insects, your doctor may want to build you up to a protective dose in as little time as possible. (Eight weeks is the minimum, though.) Doctors have also successfully desensitized people who require antibiotics against allergy to penicillin.

Ultimately, the same number of injections is needed whether you go the leisurely route or the stepped-up programme. And the potential for adverse reactions is about the same. (Oh, yes – there's always that chance.) Occasionally some people experience a little swelling and itching at the site of the injection for a day or so. If larger or more persistent swellings develop, with heat and discomfort, the dose must be reduced. Of course, that may make the therapy less effective. Anaphylactic reactions are rare, but they do occur, and for that reason some doctors say you should never be left alone for the first hour after an allergy injection (although delayed reactions have been known to occur after one hour). And one study showed that in one out of four adverse reactions, human error – giving the wrong extract or the wrong amount – was to blame (*Annals of Allergy*, April 1982).

The optimal dose, as it's called, is one that's too small to trigger a bad reaction, yet large enough to relieve your symptoms. Occasionally, treatment will fail to bring relief simply because the extract sat on the shelf too long or wasn't stored properly, thereby losing potency.

Aside from the general lack of appeal of enduring countless needles, standard immunotherapy has some limitations. Needless to say, if the skin tests upon which the therapy is based are inaccurate – which they sometimes are – the therapy can't possibly work. In other words, if the scratch test indicates that you're allergic to dust, but moulds are really your problem, injections with dust extract won't help.

Even when skin tests are correct, injections have been developed for just a few select airborne allergens. Because grass pollens tend to cross-react with one another, treatment with one grass pollen will very often reduce reactions to any grass pollen. But people who are allergic to dust aren't always so lucky – they're exposed to an almost limitless variety of dust ingredients, some of which injections probably don't contain. Immunotherapy for cat and dog dander has not proved effective in most cases. Most allergists generally recommend getting rid of the animals instead. And standard allergy injections simply don't exist for food allergies; poison ivy; bites by flies, fleas and mosquitoes; hives; eczema; allergic contact dermatitis; or migraine headaches.

Fortunately, standard immunotherapy does seem to give fairly good protection against one of the most dreaded allergies – reactions to stinging-insect venom. But because of the rather frequent incidence of systemic reaction, venom immunotherapy is generally reserved for people who are considered to be at risk for serious reactions. This includes anyone who has had anything more than a large local reaction and who reacts to a skin test, as well as people who become asthmatic after stings and adults who react with hives.

Even for those allergies for which it works, immunotherapy is rarely the *only* form of treatment necessary. Often, drugs such as bronchodilators and antihistamines are still used to achieve more complete relief. And, of course, drugs are frequently the mainstay of medical treatment for those allergies for which no immunotherapy has been developed.

Neutralization therapy – a promising alternative

Frustrated with the limitations of traditional immunotherapy, a few doctors (most of them known as clinical ecologists) are trying to revive a system of allergy testing and immunotherapy developed several years ago and collectively known as serial dilution titration and neutralization therapy. This variation of standard immunotherapy still involves lots of time in a doctor's surgery, considerable expense and allergy injections. In some ways, however, it may make up for a few of the shortcomings of traditional immunotherapy.

Serial dilution testing, as we discussed in Chapter 9, Allergy tests: what they can and cannot tell, is done on the skin (although a few doctors use drops of the test extracts which can be placed under the tongue in people who are not fond of needles). Doctors test for several common allergens, plus any others to which the individual seems to be particularly sensitive. In that respect, the test is similar to standard tests. However, the individual is not necessarily tested with one absolute amount of each test extract, but possibly with a series of up to fifteen or twenty increasing dilutions, one every ten minutes or so. The size of any weal and the nature of symptoms are noted. Doctors experienced with serial testing use the dose which does not produce symptoms – the 'endpoint' – as a guideline for choosing the optimal dose for this therapy. Again, the dose that is too small to produce a reaction yet large enough to prevent reactions is considered optimal. Doctors feel that, in this way, they can get a better picture of not only what a person is allergic to, but also how he or she reacts as an individual. What's more, they claim that the treatment dose can be used to neutralize, or turn off, a reaction. The therapeutic dose usually turns out to be much smaller than that employed in standard immunotherapy, and takes only one or two testing sessions to achieve. That compares with a period of about six months of such experimentation to reach maintenance doses in standard therapy. Once the correct treatment dose is arrived at, doctors using neutralization claim that some people gain immediate relief.

One big difference between the two therapies is that some doctors using neutralization send patients home with premixed doses of extract to help them tolerate foods and inhalants to which they are allergic. That's rare with standard therapy except for carrying emergency vials of adrenaline to be used in case of a severe bee sting reaction or other serious symptoms.

Another major difference is that neutralization is used to treat sensitivities to car exhaust, tobacco smoke, formaldehyde and other hard-to-avoid chemicals, although shots for those do not work nearly as well as injections for conventional allergens.

'People always ask us for injections against air pollution,' says Constantine J. Falliers, a traditional allergist and editor of the *Journal of Asthma*. 'Well, we have no such thing.'

Many doctors using neutralization feel that, unlike conventional therapy, it can be successfully used to treat food allergy, holding out hope to the many people who are allergic to wheat, yeast or other ubiquitous dietary items.

Both standard immunotherapy and neutralization seem to work in approximately eight out of ten people on whom the particular method is used, and both are relatively safe – they're used without reservation on the young, the old, the pregnant – and even in people who are suffering a cold or the flu. For the individual who's endured years of standard immunotherapy without relief of symptoms, neutralization certainly holds promise.

Is this really what you want?

When you get right down to it, though, needles usually hurt. Doctors' surgeries can be boring. Visits are time consuming. So no one relishes the prospect of going for allergy injections of either kind: both methods cost a great deal in terms of anxiety, discomfort, time and money. In terms of both effectiveness and comfort, the self-help, 'take charge' approach to personal allergy control can minimize the need for either standard immunotherapy *or* neutralization. Don't hesitate to enlist your doctor's help in finding out exactly what you're allergic to. After that, you owe it to yourself to methodically manipulate your diet and environment – as outlined throughout this book – to make your world as allergy safe as possible. That approach – with or without allergy injections – will no doubt require a considerable investment of thought and effort at first, possibly followed by a series of smaller maintenance measures. But in terms of total, pain-free relief, you can only come out ahead.

PART IV

Building Up Your Defences

CHAPTER 12

NUTRITION FOR ALLERGY CONTROL

Nutrition and allergy interact in a lot of ways. First, many allergic people may have trouble meeting all their nutritional requirements. Food allergies may force some to eliminate foods that customarily supply a large portion of their daily needs for particular vitamins or minerals. People who can't drink milk or eat dairy products, for instance, may get too little calcium. People who are allergic to citrus fruits may not be getting enough vitamin C. A few astute doctors and dietitians are also discovering that, because of the drain on the body created by allergies, people with allergic problems may have special needs for more of certain vitamins and minerals – and that those nutrients may even help to *control* allergy.

But the amounts of a vitamin or mineral that are needed to deal with allergic problems are often so high that a person needs to rely on supplements. People with food allergies, however, need to choose supplements as carefully as they choose their food, to avoid dyes or other ingredients that may trigger reactions.

At the time of writing, only a few people have taken a serious look at the interlocking aspects of nutrition and allergy. Those who have, however, say that proper nutrition – the right nutrients, in the right form and in large enough amounts – makes quite a difference in allergy control. Lyn Dart, a registered dietitian and supervisor of the nutrition department of the Environmental Health Center in Dallas, told us, 'We've been working with nutrition for about two years. Without it, we weren't as effective.'

Vitamin C to the rescue

The need for vitamin C seems to be greater in some allergic people,' Ms Dart told us. 'For many people, large doses of vitamin C – up to eight grams taken orally, divided over three or four hours – will break a reaction.

'That's a lot of vitamin C in anyone's book,' she commented. 'But it's at that point that the reaction or the symptoms subside.'

To determine the approximate amount of vitamin C required to break an allergic reaction in an individual, Ms Dart works gradually. First she tries three grams, then another gram, until the symptoms subside. (Ms Dart cautions that because such large doses of ascorbic acid can cause stomach or intestinal upsets, people should use the ascorbate forms of vitamin C instead.)

'The average dose to break a reaction is five to eight grams,' says Ms Dart. 'It's hard to say how the vitamin works – whether it's because of its antioxidant capabilities [which prevent cell damage], the fact that it boosts the immune system or the vitamin's antihistamine action. But we use it on a regular basis.'

Mows down hay fever

For hay fever, at least, the way vitamin C works is quite clear: it acts as a *natural* antihistamine, helping to relieve the red, watery eyes, runny nose and congestion provoked by histamine. Researchers in the department of obstetrics and gynaecology at Methodist Hospital in Brooklyn studied 400 people, and found that with higher blood levels of vitamin C, histamine was lower – and vice versa. When eleven people with low vitamin C/high histamine levels were given daily supplements of 1,000 milligrams [one gram] of vitamin C, their hay fever symptoms improved within three days (*Journal of Nutrition*, April 1980).

Dr Stuart Freyer, an ear-nose-and-throat specialist in Bennington, Vermont, prescribes vitamin C for hay fever and gives his patients relatively high amounts of the nutrient. 'Five grams or more is typical,' he told us.

Incidentally, Dr Freyer advises anyone taking that much C to take calcium, too.

'High levels of vitamin C may bind with calcium and pull it out of the bones. It's then flushed out in the urine when the body discards any excess vitamin C,' he explains. 'Vitamin C may also combine with calcium in the diet to interfere with absorption.

'There should be no problem with calcium deficiency if a person uses vitamin C in the calcium ascorbate form rather than its simple ascorbic acid form, or if the ascorbic acid is supplemented with adequate amounts of calcium,' he assured us. 'I usually recommend that my patients take 400 to 600 milligrams of dolomite calcium a day during hay fever season.'

Bioflavonoids and B Vitamins boost Vitamin C

To get the most out of your vitamin C during hay fever season, take it with citrus bioflavonoids. Studies done on animals have shown that citrus bioflavonoids may favourably alter the body's metabolism of vitamin C, raising the concentration of the nutrient in certain tissues and enhancing its availability to the body (*American Journal of Clinical Nutrition*, August 1979).

Brian Leibovitz, a nutritional consultant in Portland, Oregon, has found citrus bioflavonoids to be the answer to many a hay fever victim's prayers.

One hay fever sufferer in particular weathered every summer indoors, knowing that only the first frost would free him from his air conditioned prison, killing the ragweed that disabled him. Meanwhile, he took prescription antihistamines – eight a day. Yet he still suffered. Leibovitz recommended a nutritional programme that included six grams of citrus bioflavonoids a day. A few weeks later, during the height of hay fever season, the young man no longer required drugs to control his hay fever symptoms.

'More than once, I've had hay fever patients who did not respond to vitamin C recover when given citrus bioflavonoids,' Leibovitz told us.

Dr Freyer also has found that vitamin C works better when accompanied by B-complex vitamins, especially pantothenic acid.

'I recommend 200 to 500 milligrams of pantothenic acid, plus another 50 milligrams of B complex,' he says. 'Sometimes, when a patient has impaired absorption – and many people with allergies do – I also give pancreatic enzymes. These help to break down the foods so vitamins can be absorbed better.'

Asthma yields to vitamins and magnesium

Asthma is sometimes a consequence of uncontrolled hay fever – and can also respond quite well to bioflavonoids, says Leibovitz. 'In fact, the standard treatment for asthma, a drug called cromolyn sodium, is nothing more than a synthetic bioflavonoidlike molecule.'

And, as with hay fever, vitamin C is a tremendous boon to asthmatics. In one study, asthmatics who took 1,000 milligrams [one gram] of vitamin C a day had less than one-fourth as many asthma attacks as those receiving an inactive, fake pill. When they stopped taking vitamin C, however, they once again suffered the same number of asthma episodes as the untreated people (*Tropical and Geographical Medicine*, vol. 32, no. 2, 1980). The protective role of vitamin C in asthmatics is also discussed in Chapter 10, Allergy drugs and their alternatives.

Some exciting new research shows that magnesium may also help ease breathing difficulties of asthma. Zack H. Haddad, professor of allergy and immunology at the University of Southern California School of Medicine, evaluated thirty children with allergic asthma. Twenty of the children were then supplemented with a half-litre to a litre a day of magnesium-rich mineral water (such as Aviant). The other ten children continued as usual, with no extra source of magnesium. After three months, the blood levels of magnesium rose in the children who drank the magnesium-rich water, and they could breathe more freely (*Annals of Allergy*, abstract no. 19, April 1982).

Calcium and iron are often neglected

Aside from the special need for calcium created by vitamin C supplements, calcium is of special concern for people with milk allergies or lactose intolerance.

'We see low calcium levels across the board in people on allergy-restricted diets, in all age groups,' says Lyn Dart of her work with food allergy patients.

Nondairy foods do contain reasonable amounts of calcium. The thing is, you'd have to eat 3 lb of broccoli, or 1¼ lb of almonds – or comparable quantities of similar foods – to meet the Recommended Dietary Allowance (RDA) for calcium of 800 milligrams.

'So we rely on supplements of calcium gluconate or other calcium complexes if an individual can tolerate that,' says Ms Dart.

'Iron is the next nutrient deficiency that shows up frequently in people (especially women) on Rotary Diets or other food allergy diets,' Ms Dart continued. 'It's difficult enough for them to meet the daily requirement of 18 milligrams. Even on an unrestricted diet, a woman has to be very careful to meet the daily quota. With food allergies, women have to try extra hard. In fact, it's almost impossible.

'So we have to supplement with iron, in the form of either fumarate, citrate, gluconate or sulphate,' she told us. 'But I don't like to give iron alone. I recommend a combination of iron, vitamin C, vitamins B_6 and B_{12}, folic acid and manganese (often marked "hematinic" iron on the label).

'Selenium is another nutrient that many of our allergic patients are low in,' Ms Dart told us. 'I think that's because the immune systems in these people are highly taxed, so the nutrients that are depleted are those that are hard at work in the immune system – selenium and vitamin C.'

Ms Dart also mentioned that vitamins A, C and B_6, thiamine, and niacin seem to run consistently low in allergic people.

Eczema improves with zinc

Zinc is a key nutrient in skin health. When combined with vitamins A, D and E, plus essential fatty acids, zinc can help speed healing of eczema, one of the most common forms of allergy. Dr Jonathan V. Wright, of Kent, Washington, has used zinc-centred therapy successfully in over forty people.

Basically, zinc therapy begins at 50 milligrams, three times a day, combined with 1,000 milligrams of vitamin C twice a day. During acute flareup a tablespoon of cod liver oil (containing vitamins A, D and E) is added. After the eczema begins to subside, therapy is reduced to 25 milligrams of zinc a day, 1,000 milligrams of vitamin C a day, and daily cod liver oil in winter.

Zinc therapy takes from three weeks to six months to take effect, depending on the stubbornness of the rash. To speed healing, Dr Wright recommends the addition of essential fatty acids, which are found in vegetable oils such as safflower, sunflower, sesame and others. 'Very recently, research work has uncovered the zinc-essential fatty acid connection – showing zinc to be crucial to the transformation of some of the nutritionally derived essential fatty acids to their active form,' explains Dr Wright.

How to find hypoallergenic supplements

It would be nice if all the nutritional needs created by allergies could be met by diet alone. A few calculations, however, quickly show that you would have to eat over a dozen oranges to acquire enough vitamin C needed to break an allergic reaction. And you'd have to eat about seven cups of Brussels sprouts to get enough vitamin C to shield you against an asthma spell. And you'd need to consume over 16 fl oz/450 ml of grapefruit sections to get the amount of bioflavonoids recommended to relieve hay fever. Obviously, supplements are a convenient alternative.

'I believe in supplementation,' says clinical nutritionist Dart. 'We use it widely to treat people with allergies.'

Natural or synthetic?

Brewer's yeast, wheat and soya are often the basis for nutritional supplements, especially in natural products. Synthetic vitamins, on the other hand, often contain dyes and flavourings to make the pills more appealing or easier to identify. But whether you choose natural or synthetic isn't a matter of personal preference – it depends on what you're allergic to.

'Many people with allergies automatically lean towards natural vitamin products without sugar or colouring,' says Iris R. Bell. 'But one of the paradoxes of allergies is that some people may actually do better with synthetic vitamins.'

Lyn Dart explained that paradox a bit further. 'The brewer's yeast, wheat and soya that are added to natural vitamins are great for a non-allergic person. But if you're allergic to any of those ingredients, they are a problem.'

'Wheat and yeast are major sources of B vitamins,' reiterated Dr Bell. 'But many people sensitive to those foods do better with synthetic B vitamins or B vitamins based on nonallergenic foods such as rice.

'Because many people are allergic to corn,' continued Dr Bell, 'some vitamin companies are eliminating cornstarch, a common filler.' Vitamin C made from sago palm, for instance, is now available. (See 'Nutritional supplements' in the Appendix for names of suppliers.)

Powdered products, in fact, are generally better tolerated than tablets, according to Lyn Dart. Tablets have more inactive ingredients – such as binders and coatings – multiplying potential allergens. 'We give many people their supplements in powdered form,' she told us.

As for dyes, Dr Bell remarked that some companies now sell clear, uncoloured gelatine capsules for people who need to omit dyes from their diet.

'Still, some people can't tolerate even the clear gelatine capsules – they may be made from beef, pork or other allergenic food,' says Dr Bell. 'They can usually tolerate their contents, though, so they should empty the capsule, take the contents and discard the capsule itself.'

People who are allergic to wheat must be wary of vitamin E from wheat germ oil, and they may have to use synthetic forms of vitamin E. Similarly, people who are allergic to fish may react unfavourably to vitamins A or D from fish oil. And people who are allergic to soya beans may not be able to tolerate lecithin.

Before you buy any supplements, you should automatically check labels for wheat, soya, yeast, corn or any other ingredient to which you are allergic.

Junk food is not on this menu

Even if you take supplements, a sound diet of wisely selected, nutritious food is critical to successful allergy control. First of all, if your diet is in any way limited because of food allergies, there's simply no room remaining for nutrient-poor foods. Secondly, snacks and other processed or convenience foods are more likely to quarter hidden offenders than straightforward, wholesome fare. More broadly, however, allergies of any kind demand all the goodness and nutrition you can muster from your diet so that you bolster total health. It's much like proper car maintenance: the best tune-up in the world won't make your car run well if you're still pumping low-grade petrol.

Dr Robert W. Boxer, an allergist in Chicago, told us, 'I give everyone who walks into this office a list of foods to avoid – coffee (including decaffeinated), soft drinks, beverages with chemical additives and preservatives, chocolate, sweets, biscuits, cake, pastries, refined sugar (beet or cane), bleached white flour and some brands of ice cream. I tell them, "I don't think these

---

QUESTIONS ABOUT BEE POLLEN AND HONEY

From time to time, people ask us about the reputed potential of bee pollen and honey for reducing hay fever or other allergy symptoms. So we checked into them.

As it turns out, there is no scientific evidence of any kind demonstrating the ability of bee pollen to relieve allergies. Even if it works as well as some individuals claim, though, the risks clearly outweigh the potential benefit. Raw bee pollen may contain impurities such as insect hair, insect parts, mites, bacteria, fungi and pesticides – all potentially allergenic. And the pollen itself is a common asthma and hay fever trigger. Researchers at the Mayo Clinic and the Medical College of Wisconsin, in fact, report that three people developed severe allergic reactions after taking a single tablespoon or less of bee pollen.

So while bee pollen is a wonderful food for bees, it's not so wonderful for people with allergies – especially those with any kind of pollen allergy.

Modern folklore also says that people with asthma or hay fever will suffer less during the pollen season if they eat local honey containing the pollen to which they are allergic. By taking one teaspoon to one tablespoon of local honey a day, some people swear that they get through the season with little or no symptoms. Presumably, the pollen immunizes them. However, there has been no medical research to back up those claims.

As far as hay fever goes, you're much better off seeking relief from the safe, documented nutritional means highlighted in this chapter.

---

foods are good for you. They have no nutritional value – or very little – and they may hurt you. So, in my opinion, you should stay away from them. Your allergies will bother you less. You'll have more resistance to toxins in your environment."

'I tell that to every patient, and I've been doing it for many years,' says Dr Boxer. 'I don't expect them to stay off junk food totally, because they won't be able to. But to the extent that they can, they should.'

One way to cut down on nutritionally poor food is to stop eating snacks or desserts that you don't really want. Casual and almost constant nibbling – reaching for a food just for the sake of something to do – does more harm than an occasional full-scale binge.

You may find that cutting down on junk foods comes easily and naturally. For people who are serious about controlling their allergies, good nutrition appears to be one more solid stepping stone to total relief.

CHAPTER 13

MIND OVER ALLERGY

The pain suffered in a personal tug-of-war with allergy is like the pain of any struggle – partly physical and partly psychological. Anxiety, depression and fatigue may be direct results of an allergic reaction somewhere in the body. Or they may result from the many aggravations of dealing with a chronic allergy: sticking to a restricted diet. Vigilance against airborne allergy triggers. The fear that no matter how careful you are, you'll get zapped anyway. The sense of alienation from your non-allergic spouse, family or co-workers. Resentment over your bad luck. And above all, the desire to lead a normal life again.

Those are the 'effects of the effect', as one highly allergic person put it. And easing the psychological and emotional effects of being allergic goes a long way towards successful, drug-free relief from the allergies themselves. In the case of asthma, for instance, one doctor observed that people who have uncontrolled apprehension – panic over breathing problems, fear of recurring symptoms and so on – tend to over-use steroids and other asthma medication. And they're more likely to be frequently hospitalized for their condition, adds Jerald F. Dirks, Psy. D, former chief of clinical psychology at the National Jewish Hospital and Research Centre and the National Asthma Centre in Denver.

Beating the allergy blues

Actually, a little anxiety over allergy is useful – it motivates an individual to do something about the problem, rather than just roll up his or her sleeve for an injection or swallow a pill. Too much anxiety, on the other hand, can lead to an unhealthy preoccupation with the illness, to the point where you begin to neglect the other important aspects of life – family and friends, career goals, travel plans, hobbies. In the case of food allergies in particular, over-anxiety can lead to what one doctor calls 'food neurosis' – an all-consuming obsession with what you can and cannot eat, and paranoia about eating away from home.

'Allergic people can easily slip into the me versus them attitude if they're not careful,' says Iris R. Bell, a psychiatrist in San Francisco. 'Many people begin to look at their environment as their enemy. Soon, they feel that everything they eat or breathe might make them sick. And it's a very difficult position *not* to get yourself into, because it's true that certain things *can* make you sick,' she acknowledges.

'But too much worry over allergies can make allergies worse,' Dr Bell continued. 'That may explain why some people feel worse when they first begin to pay attention to their diet or environment. One theory is that they develop what psychologists call a "conditioned response". After one or more symptom-causing encounters with an identified allergen, they may break out from simply looking at chocolate, or start to feel sick when someone nearby reaches for a cigarette.'

The secret to avoid 'worrying yourself sick' is to learn to cope with allergies realistically, rather than to let yourself slip into the role of a lonely exile. And coping is easier if you avoid focusing on being a 'patient'. Granted, you may feel like a patient if you have to record every mouthful of food you eat or if you're following a Rotary Diet. Nonetheless, says Dr Bell, you should try your best to shift away from the mindset of 'I'm sick' – towards 'I'm getting well'.

'Some people say, "I'm sick today, and until I'm well I can't do this or that," ' continued Dr Bell. 'That attitude can lead to a terrible cycle in which you never do anything, and then you feel worse about yourself because you aren't doing anything you enjoy.'

In other words, allergies can exact quite a toll in terms of damage to self-image – but only if you let them.

'I don't expect people to deny that they're sick,' says Dr Bell. 'But on the other hand, I've seen people who focused so much on being allergic that it became their whole identity – and a way to avoid life's stresses.'

Unstressing your life

The impact of stress on health is undeniable. Stress is not a disease, however, but a normal element in the weather of life. It's like rain. With too little, life is barren. With too much, you get flooded.

For people with allergies, the stress clouds hang a bit thicker and lower than usual. Along with the usual stresses of everyday life – temperamental children, money worries, job hassles – people with allergies have additional concerns. Changing your habits or diet to side-step allergy triggers is fraught with stress. Plus there's the strain sometimes created by trying to get other people to accommodate you.

'The other people you live with may resent being asked to go outside to spray their hair, or having to remember not to polish their shoes around you,' says Dr Bell.

All that stress may have a direct effect on the immune system, aggravating allergic reactions.

'Any period of stress may weaken the immune system so that you react more easily to foods or chemicals,' explained Dr Bell. 'But if you have yourself in better control of stress, when something does happen – when you encounter an allergy trigger – your symptoms won't get as bad.' In other words, managing stress helps you weather allergic encounters.

Relaxation

'An important approach I use to alleviate stress is some form of relaxation therapy,' says Dr Bell. 'There are a variety of approaches. One is imagery, in which I tell people to imagine themselves in a safe environment whenever they find themselves exposed to a threatening food or chemical. That takes advantage of what the mind can do for the body; a message is sent from the brain to the rest of the body, putting you in a stronger biological state.

'The relaxation method you choose is not all that important, as long as it works for the individual,' she adds. 'All achieve the same basic goal – reducing stress.' They do that, she explained, by putting your body in a state that is the exact opposite of how it operates when you feel tense and under stress. (A specific relaxation technique to control asthma is described in Chapter 10, Allergy drugs and their alternatives.)

Positive thinking

We spoke to a young man who has been highly allergic to many things from early childhood on. He has learned to suppress allergic reactions at the first inkling of symptoms by concentrating very, very hard and saying to himself, 'I will not react'. He calls it 'willing the allergy away'. And it works! There's nothing magical about it, either. Robert W. Boxer, an allergist in Chicago, told us, 'It's well established that, just as the body can affect the mind, the mind can affect the body. You can actually lower your body's levels of chemical mediators [histamine and other allergy-provoking substances] by your mental attitude – how you look at things and how you handle stress.'

'It comes down to a matter of how much control you have,' says Dr Bell. 'Some people are extremely good at using their minds to control their bodies. For them these techniques are ideal. Most of us fall into a range – we can be at our best if we're relaxing in some way, *plus* watching our diet and perhaps doing one or two other things.

'For most people, I see stress control as an additional aid. If you slide off your diet, it will help you recover. Or you may not slip quite as much or quite as fast.'

Exercise can calm you down – and cheer you up

Regular exercise may be an additional way to defuse stress in your life – and reduce your allergy symptoms at the same time. A study by Shae Graham Kosch, of the Department of Community Health and Family Medicine, University of Florida, and an associate at the Southern Academy of Clinical Nutrition, compared anxiety levels and overall health of two groups of people. Those in the first group either jogged fifteen minutes a day or walked briskly for thirty minutes a day. People in the second group did nothing more strenuous than play golf, garden or participate in other activities considered to be relatively low in exertion. The people who exercised regularly reported less anxiety and fewer medical symptoms than those who did not exercise. 'These findings imply that exercise . . . [is] capable of exerting a powerful influence on adaptations to [stress],' conclude the researchers (*Stress*, Spring, 1982).

There are definite reasons why exercise reduces anxiety:

'A hallmark of anxiety is the excessive, prolonged and useless secretion of adrenaline [a powerful hormone],' says Dr Jerome Marmorstein, from Santa Barbara, California. 'Use of exercise to improve conditions – even just walking – is the only natural release for that. It even helps to reduce the adrenalin buildup in the first place,' he says. 'Exercise is a balance factor. It promotes conservation of energy and an overall reduction of chronic anxiety. You feel better mentally and experience a sense of emotional well-being.'

So if allergies have you feeling depressed, exercise can give you a psychological lift. 'Just minor, non-vigorous exercise like walking can produce measurable, beneficial psychological changes,' says Dr Ronald Lawrence, a California psychiatrist-neurologist.

A journal helps keep allergies in proper perspective

Some people, of course, have so many allergies or are so highly sensitive that in spite of all their efforts to 'buck up', they still have days – or weeks – when they feel sorry for themselves. For them Dr Bell has found that keeping a personal journal can help put things in perspective.

'Keeping a journal can be very helpful and supportive, like a sympathetic friend with whom you can talk everything out. I've used it myself,' says Dr Bell, who has some allergies. 'By a journal, I don't mean a documentation of every symptom you have, although certainly symptoms are part of it. But by writing down how you're feeling amidst the events that are swirling around you, you have something to which to return later, to look at yourself when you were last feeling down, when it seems there was no sky above. Then read the next entries and see how you got out of it. And notice how quickly you got better. Because during a depressed period, you may feel like you're always sick, when in fact reactions may last only a few hours or less.

'You can also refer to your journal when you can't remember the last time you felt well,' adds Dr Bell. 'It corrects the kind of negative thinking that depressed people fall into, the all-or-nothing view of things. It reminds you that you felt good once, and you'll feel good again.'

Whatever psychological resources you choose – imagery, meditation, exercise, a journal – all help you enjoy life in spite of your allergies. You may even find yourself laughing at some of the absurd problems created by allergies.

'When a person begins to look at everything as a threat to their health, they lose their sense of humour. And a sense of humour is very important,' says Dr Bell. 'I really believe in laughter as a way of treatment.'

CHAPTER 14

WHAT TO DO IN AN ALLERGIC EMERGENCY

If you're like most allergic people, chances are good that you'll never have a life-threatening reaction. Even then, there's only one chance in a million that the reaction will be fatal – and those odds are less than that if you know how to handle it.

As with choking or heart failure, a severe allergic reaction calls for immediate first aid. The first ten or fifteen minutes are the most critical. (The very most you can hope for is an hour – then it might be too late.) But that 'grace period' still doesn't give you much time to locate and reach a doctor. So it's imperative that you learn to recognize an allergic emergency and know exactly what to do about it.

Know the warning signals

As the term implies, an allergic emergency is a reaction that can be fatal. The most common life-threatening reaction is anaphylaxis – an explosive bodywide response to an allergic encounter. The individual first becomes weak, pale, anxious, dizzy, has hoarseness or difficult breathing – then usually collapses. That may be followed by any of various symptoms, involving four major organ systems:

– gastrointestinal tract: nausea, vomiting, stomach cramps, bloating and diarrhoea;
– skin: intense flushing, itching, hives and swelling (especially swelling at the site of an insect sting);
– heart and blood vessels: rapid heartbeat and low blood pressure (this is itself also known as anaphylactic shock); and
– respiratory tract: sudden runny nose, swollen vocal cords, uncontrollable coughing, wheezing, bronchospasm and constricted airways (caused by internal swelling).

The basis of all anaphylactic symptoms is an overwhelming surge of histamine and other allergy-provoking substances (for example, newly recognized leucotrienes) from mast cells and basophils, the allergen-sensitive tissues discussed in Chapter 1, What is an allergy?

Of those symptoms, however, the biggest threat to life is constricted airways, which can cause death within minutes if not opened. The second is low blood pressure, or shock.

Penicillin is the most common cause of anaphylaxis and accounts for about three out of four fatal reactions. It's followed by – in order of incidence – venomous insect stings, radiographic dye (a diagnostic medium), aspirin and related drugs, and foods such as eggs, nuts or seafood.

Less common than anaphylaxis but equally threatening is laryngeal oedema (swelling of the windpipe or throat). It may occur alone or as part of anaphylaxis. A severe, uncontrollable form of asthma called status asthmaticus is also considered an emergency.

The symptoms of a serious asthma attack are:

– an attack that fails to improve or is increasing in severity after several hours, or that does not respond to routine drugs;
– wheezing that is first loud and then stops, accompanied by extremely laboured and difficult breathing;
– fatigue and weakness;
– irregular heartbeat, or a pulse higher than 140 beats per minute (or higher than 160 in children under age six); and
– obvious bulging of the neck muscles, expanded chest cage, sweating and noticeable deepening of the notch over the breastbone.

Be prepared – it can save your life

Emergency kits of allergy drugs, sold through chemists, are prescribed to people who have at any time experienced life-threatening reactions or who have a history of very severe symptoms. If you fall into either of those categories, you should own an allergy kit or an automatic-injectable adrenalin kit. One kit should be carried in your handbag, briefcase or car, and another should be kept at home. If you begin to react and have any reason to feel you're headed towards a severe, uncontrollable reaction, you should be prepared to take emergency action immediately.

Say you inadvertently eat nuts, to which you are extremely allergic, and you begin to feel very sick. The first order of business is to reverse all the alarming changes your body is going through. So every emergency kit contains a vial of adrenalin. That's a synthetic form of epinephrine, the hormone that plays a key role in keeping all body systems running on an even keel. A single shot of adrenalin pushes blood pressure back to normal and reduces swelling (which keeps your airways open and helps you breathe). It's the quickest and most effective way to neutralize a severe reaction. Adrenalin calls for medical directions; your doctor should teach you how to give yourself an injection and supervise a practice shot. The procedure is easy to learn, since adrenalin is simply injected into the fatty tissues under the skin, and not into a hard-to-pinpoint muscle, vein or artery.

The adrenalin in your emergency kit should be checked once a month to be sure the solution is not discoloured or out-of-date, which would indicate a decrease in potency. The drug deteriorates in sunlight, so don't store the kit on the dashboard of your car or in front of a window.

Adrenalin is also available in an aerosol form, which you can inhale to restore normal breathing. Although not a substitute for injected adrenalin, the aerosol may help to relieve laryngeal oedema or asthma more quickly. Test spray your aerosol adrenalin periodically to be sure that the valve opening is free of dust. If it's clogged, clean it with soapy water.

Kits are also usually equipped with antihistamine tablets to further counteract the flood of antihistamine that is to blame for much of an allergic reaction. Find out exactly how much antihistamine you should take, to save valuable time in an emergency. If you've been prescribed asthma medication, be prepared to take that, too. As much as we advocate drug-free means for day-to-day control of allergies, you shouldn't hesitate to use whatever first-aid measures are necessary in a life-threatening situation. The possible side effects of a single dose of these drugs is a minor concern compared with the certain consequences of not taking them.

Tourniquets are also included in many allergy first-aid kits. Applied near a sting, a tourniquet will slow the circulation and absorption of venom. The problem is that a tourniquet also stops the circulation of blood. While routine use of tourniquets is discouraged by most doctors, many allergists say that if a highly sensitive person is stung by an insect, a tourniquet is justified – *if* it's applied immediately after the sting occurs and on an arm or a leg only. Even then, a tourniquet is merely a stopgap measure to block the spread of venom until a doctor can be reached.

If no tourniquet is available, you can make do with a strip of cloth, thick cord, belt, dog leash or other similar device. Tie the tourniquet two to four inches above the sting (towards the trunk of the body). Do not tie the tourniquet so tightly that circulation is cut off. You should be able to slip your fingers under the band. And be sure to loosen the tourniquet every five minutes.

If the sting was inflicted by an insect with a stinger, scrape the stinger out of the skin with your fingernail or a dull knife. Do not grasp or try to pull the stinger out – that would only squeeze more venom into the wound. (For more information on reactions to insect stings, see Chapter 6, What to do about insect allergies.)

Place a cold pack or ice wrapped in cloth on the sting area to reduce total swelling.

After taking these first-aid steps, you should call an ambulance or have someone drive you to the nearest hospital casulty department. There you will be given further medication and oxygen, if necessary, to bring the reaction under complete control.

During any severe allergic reaction, you should lie down on your side or with your head turned to the side to avoid choking if you are sick. Even if you don't feel nauseated, though, you'll be more comfortable if you can stretch out.

Obviously, there's always the possibility that you may not be able to take emergency action yourself. If you can't breathe or you pass out, someone near you will have to take over. Your spouse or other family member should be as familiar as you are with the location and use of emergency medications. If you aren't breathing and no medication is on hand, the person with you should call for emergency aid and know how to give mouth-to-mouth resuscitation to open your airways.

The name and phone number of your doctor should be posted near every phone in your home, along with the number of your ambulance service and the location of the nearest hospital.

Anyone with serious allergies should also wear a bracelet or tag or carry a drug information card identifying items to which the individualis allergic. The information will save precious time and prevent medical personnel from mistakenly treating you for other causes of collapse, such as stroke or heart failure.

There are those rare occasions, of course, when an individual reacts to an allergy injection received in a doctor's surgery as part of routine therapy. For that reason, your doctor probably won't send you merrily on your way as soon as you've had your injection. No one should be left unattended for the first thirty minutes, at the very least, after having an allergy shot. Some doctors, in fact, prefer to play it safe and keep you an hour. And any doctor giving allergy shots should be prepared to give adrenalin, open an airway and if necessary give oxygen to a person who unexpectedly reacts in the office. You shouldn't hesitate to ask if your doctor has all the necessary medication and equipment on hand. That's especially true if your pediatrician, ear-nose-and-throat doctor or G.P. customarily gives you your allergy injections. A caring doctor isn't likely to take offence at your concern. After all, doctors want to avoid trouble just as much as you do.

PART V

Allergic Reactions from A to V

ALLERGIC REACTIONS FROM A–V

Allergy can disguise itself in any of dozens of different ways. Yet once you know how to *recognize* allergy – and what to do about it – you stand an excellent chance of feeling well again.

That's what this section is for – to help you identify all the masks of allergy. The common problems of sneezing, wheezing, itching and digestive upsets are discussed here in full, of course. But while allergies most often affect the nose, lungs, skin and stomach, doctors are learning that there's no reason to assume that allergies ignore the rest of the body. Thanks to the insight of several pioneering doctors mentioned in the following pages, people are learning that the same allergy that's causing their asthma, hay fever, eczema or hives may be spilling over to other parts of their body, producing seemingly unrelated discomforts. The truth is that *many* stubborn or unexplained health problems, from high blood pressure to overweight, may be caused or aggravated by allergy.

For instance, say you have eczema but you also get nagging headaches frequently. Good detective work of the type described in the earlier chapters of this book reveals that both milk and enzyme-containing laundry detergents contribute to your skin trouble. You eliminate them and within a few weeks your eczema clears up considerably – but not completely. Reading the entry on headaches (a problem not usually thought of as a symptom of allergy), it occurs to you that you may also be allergic to citrus fruit. So you avoid oranges, lemon and all other forms of citrus. Both the eczema and headaches disappear completely.

You may not have eczema or headaches, of course. That's just an example of how the information in this section can be used to help anyone with sensitivities to food, inhalants or other allergens find more complete and lasting relief from *all* their symptoms. And in a way, the people who benefit most from allergy detective work are those with less clear-cut forms of allergy – fatigue, muscle aches, ringing in the ears and the like. They've probably consulted half a dozen or more doctors but have found no explanation or effective treatment. And when people have a health problem that defies diagnosis, they react in one of two ways. Some imagine the worst and convince themselves that they have cancer or some other terrifying disease. Others worry that they're just imagining their aches and pains and that they've turned into hypochondriacs. And still other people try to tough it out the best they can. But all tend to grow more depressed and frustrated by the day, their lives ruled by nagging, mysterious complaints. And that's too bad. Because so many people might find complete relief from chronic health problems by using a guide like this to figure out how allergies are affecting their condition.

Like most people, you're probably so accustomed to thinking of allergies in terms of sneezing, wheezing and itching that you'll be surprised to learn that allergies can show up as so many different ailments. Few other allergy books even mention those health problems or discuss them in the depth that we present here. We hope you and your family will find this section as useful and interesting as the rest of the book. Since avoidance is usually the cure, the more you learn about your individual – and very unique – form of allergy, the better your chances for a complete recovery. As one doctor told us, 'People become very smart when they're ill.'

Of course, allergy isn't the only possible cause of many of these conditions. Many can be caused or aggravated by infection or other disease. It's wise to get a medical checkup in order to rule out other causes, especially in infants and children or anyone who is chronically ill.

Yet even if you find that some of your health problems are not allergies, you'll soon see that treating them will build up your defences and make treatment of allergy all the more successful.

Acne

Most causes of acne have nothing to do with allergies. However, there's one type of acne – acne cosmetica – that doctors blame on use of makeup, creams and moisturizers. People most often affected by this type of acne are women in their early twenties and thirties, many of whom have never had acne before in their lives. In those people, 'makeup is the culprit unless proven otherwise,' says Susan Elliott, a professor in the department of dermatology at the University of California at San Francisco. Foundations, blushers and powders tend to be comedogenic (acne-forming), she told us. Those labelled 'non-comedogenic' are okay.

Creams and moisturizers, used to prevent drying and aging of the skin, may also contribute to acne formation in allergic people. Not only can the extra oil plug pores, but fragrances, lanolin, cocoa butter and other ingredients are common allergic triggers. (Table 21 in Chapter 7 gives a more extensive list of allergy-triggering cosmetic ingredients.)

If you feel you need a moisturizer (and most women do, at least in winter), choose a bland product. Look for non-greasy, light-textured, unscented creams and lotions with as few ingredients as possible. Dermatologists to whom we spoke recommended Vaseline Dermatology Formula, Nutraderm, and Nivea lotion, all available at chemists.

When you wash your face, be thorough to remove as much oil and bacteria as you can. But be gentle. Acne-prone skin is sensitive. Use a mild cleansing bar, free of potentially allergenic fragrances, dyes and preservatives. And be sure to rinse your face thoroughly afterwards. Soap residue left on the skin can block pores and encourage acne.

Astringents wipe away surface oil, but don't really decrease deepdown oil production. In fact, one doctor says that an astringent may actually stimulate oil production if it contains irritants (fragrances, dyes or preservatives) to which the individual is sensitive. So for acne sufferers, astringents are dispensable.

And how about diet in general? Why can some people eat whatever they want to and never break out, while others are forced to give up foods they crave? *Individual susceptibility*. It's a combination of allergies, heredity, hormones and sensitivity to bacteria in sebaceous glands. If that combination hasn't worked out in your favour, cut down on chocolate, other sweets, cola drinks, soft drinks, beer, wine and alcohol, and fatty foods.

For a more extensive discussion of allergic skin problems, turn to Chapter 7, Contact (skin) allergies.

Aggression

When Gary Mark Gilmore was asked why he impulsively and deliberately shot a motel manager in cold blood in 1976, all he could say was, 'I just felt like it. I felt like I was watching someone else do it.' In fact, Gilmore barely remembered the incident.

Could Gary Gilmore's aggressive behaviour have been an allergic reaction?

Quite possibly. Kenneth E. Moyer, professor of psychology at Carnegie-Mellon University, has seen many situations in which aggressive and sometimes violent behaviour occurred after an individual ate specific foods to which he or she was allergic. And Dr Moyer isn't the only researcher to link aggression with allergies.

'Aggression as an allergic response is a well-documented phenomenon that has been known to researchers since early in this century,' says Dr Moyer in an article entitled 'The Physiology of Violence, Allergy and Aggression' (*Psychology Today*, July 1975). Dr Moyer suggests that aggressive behaviour is triggered when the brain swells in response to allergens, just as the skin often becomes irritated on contact with an allergen.

'When this swelling occurs in an area of the brain that contains the nerve connections controlling aggression, the results can be immediate and dramatic,' Dr Moyer continued. The individual usually becomes impulsive, combative, unruly, perverse and quarrelsome – a lot like Gary Gilmore, in fact. Behaviour that an individual would otherwise control takes on a momentum of its own.

Not everyone with allergies is aggressive, obviously. In those who are, says Dr Moyer, the intensity of the symptoms varies from mild irritability, in which the person is a little more easily annoyed than usual, to a psychotic aggressive reaction. He cites a typical case: one ten-year-old girl experienced a prolonged asthma attack when exposed to alcohol. Several times during the reaction, she became extremely belligerent and tried to bite her mother, whom she did not even recognize.

The variety of allergens that can produce aggressive behaviour ranges from pollens and drugs to many foods, of which milk, chocolate, cola, corn and eggs are some of the most common, according to Dr Moyer.

There is no easy way to test for allergy-triggered aggression, says Dr Moyer. 'The only definitive way to show that aggression and allergy are interrelated is to eliminate a suspected irritant from a person's environment. If the symptoms disappear, the irritant is reintroduced to see if it provokes the expected aggressive behaviour.'

Unfortunately, Mr Gilmore is no longer around to benefit from allergy research. But if you have a tendency towards aggression and extreme edginess, controlling allergies may help you keep your cool.

Because aggressive symptoms often overlap with hyperactive behaviour and learning disabilities in children, or lead to criminal behaviour in adolescents, we suggest that parents read the entries *Criminal behaviour*, *Hyperactivity* and *Learning disorders*.

Alcoholism

If you've ever craved a chocolate bar, you know how an alcoholic feels about his or her next drink. That preoccupation with alcohol, along with the compulsion to continue drinking once he or she's started, is what separates an alcoholic from a social drinker. Alcoholics also tend to drink large amounts every day, and to start early in the day. Others drink in binges. Either way, an alcoholic responds to alcohol quite differently from the way most of us do.

Why some people become alcoholics and others do not is one of the unsolved mysteries of medicine. Heredity takes its share of the blame – although some of the biggest drinkers have parents who are strict teetotalers, and some abstainers have parents who are alcoholics.

A compulsive addiction to alcohol in many ways mimics the addiction to allergic foods that we described in Chapter 1, What is an allergy? In other words, in spite of their attraction to alcoholic beverages, problem drinkers may actually be allergic to the stuff. They may either be allergic to the alcohol itself, or to the grains, corn, fruits, yeast or sugar from which alcoholic beverages are made. (See Table 11 in Chapter 3 for specific ingredients of various alcoholic beverages.)

And alcoholics do tend to have more food allergies than other people. A research team at Deaconess Hospital in St Louis, Missouri, tested seventy-five drinkers for allergy to seventy foods. Compared with non-drinkers, alcoholics were nearly twice as susceptible to food allergies (*Modern Medicine*, October 15–30 1978).

Alcohol may also aggravate food allergies indirectly by interfering with the complete digestion of food proteins in the stomach, leading to bowel troubles, gas and diarrhoea, among other discomforts.

We're not saying that alcoholism is always caused by allergy. After all, alcoholism is a complex problem. But if you've reached a point where you know you're drinking too much, too often, understanding your compulsion could be the first step towards controlling it. If you are indeed allergic to foods from which alcohol is made, eliminating them could help you beat the problem once and for all. (See Chapter 3, Finding your no-allergy diet.)

Incidentally, doctors have noticed that people who drink a lot seem to suffer more than their share of stubborn skin problems. If you drink heavily and have a skin rash that you can't get rid of, it might clear up if you stay away from alcohol.

Because depression and anxiety can lead to alcoholism, people with drinking problems should also read the entries on those topics in this section.

Anorexia-bulimia syndrome

Anorexics are a strange breed of dieter. No matter how thin they become, they still feel fat. They literally starve themselves down to nothing, all the while insisting that they 'should really lose a few more pounds'.

When anorexics do give in to hunger, they don't just nibble. They binge compulsively (called bulimia), craving and eating up to several pounds of food. Then, to cancel out their guilty feelings of indulgence and to relieve the bloating the food produces, they force themselves to vomit or purge themselves with laxatives, diuretics and diet pills.

A frightening number of people between ten and thirty years of age, most of them women, have this distorted attitude towards food and body image known as anorexia-bulimia. It's the flip side of obesity. And doctors don't know for certain what causes it – or what to do about it. Because most psychiatrists blame anorexia-bulimia on deep feelings of anxiety, depression and poor self-image, counselling and antidepressant drugs are standard treatment. Sometimes those help, but sometimes they don't. About 65 per cent of the women continue their self-destructive habits, and about half of them eventually die from malnutrition, infection or other kinds of physical breakdown. Anorexia-bulimia is far from a harmless weight loss scheme.

'It's a very tragic illness in that anorexics are usually highly intelligent, creative people,' says Bernard Raxlen, a psychiatrist and director of the Graduate Center for Family Studies in Ridgefield, Connecticut.

Reforming an anorexic-bulimic is about as difficult as reforming an alcoholic, though.

'The compulsive eating and purging is emotionally soothing,' says Dr Raxlen. 'It relieves not only hunger but distressing thoughts and emotions. Normal eating is not enough to dispel that tension, but binge eating is – even though it is accompanied by a constant fear of not being able to stop.'

The binge-and-purge cycle is the sort of addictive behaviour that's typical of unsuspected food allergy (discussed in Chapter 1, What is an allergy?). Acting on that observation, Dr Raxlen and a colleague, Dr Leonard Galland, tested eight women with anorexia-bulimia for allergies and gastrointestinal problems, among other possible health problems. All the women showed serious abnormalities of some kind or another. Drs Raxlen and Galland then designed an experimental treatment programme that, in addition to psychological therapy, included:

- a Rotary Diet for food allergies;
- immunotherapy injections for foods, chemicals and other inhalants;
- a yeast-free diet with aggressive treatment of abdominal candidiasis (yeast infestation of the small bowel); and

– digestive aids, including pancreative enzymes, betaine hydrochloride and *Lactobacillus acidophilus* (a beneficial bacteria commonly found in yoghurt).

While the treatment did not produce dramatic results, three of the women seemed to do much better on the programme, says Dr Raxlen.

The binge-and-purge cycle of anorexia-bulimia may be a bizarre twist in the basic workings of food cravings and allergy. Hopefully, Dr Raxlen's research will stimulate more doctors to investigate food allergy as a possible cause of distorted eating habits in people (usually women) with anorexia-bulimia.

Anxiety

Few people need to have anxiety described for them. It's that combination of uneasiness and apprehension you feel when you face uncertainty: a new job, a move to a new community, a second marriage, seeing your first child off to college and so forth.

Some degree of anxiety seems to be an unavoidable part of the human condition, given all the uncertainties of life. Certain periods of life – adolescence and middle age – are particularly fraught with anxiety.

To balance out anxiety, we turn to activities we enjoy: time with our friends; participating in hobbies, games or sports; listening to music or reading books. When the causes of anxiety are real, those antidotes usually work pretty well.

But when anxiety is chronic and free-floating – that is, not traceable to any specific cause – those antidotes don't work. Instead, one experiences an increasing sense of panic. Or the feeling that everything inside is wound up tight. You force yourself to take deep breaths, but that doesn't calm you down. Perhaps you fly off the handle at the least little thing, then a wave of depression sweeps in. You tend to burst into tears frequently – or feel like you're going to. In many people, anxiety is accompanied by headaches, stomach troubles or other physical complaints.

When an anxious person goes to a doctor with his or her problem, he or she's apt to be given a tranquillizer. Or referred to a psychologist, who spends a lot of time investigating past experiences and relationships with other people. Sometimes that works. But sometimes it doesn't, and the person still ends up with a prescription for tranquillizers.

In a case like that, anxiety is a puzzle – with one of the pieces missing. That piece may an allergy. Working on the possibility that anxiety and allergy are sometimes linked, certain doctors have solved the puzzle of their patients' 'baseless' anxiety. Ronald Finn and H. Newman Cohen, of the Royal Southern Hospital in the Department of Medicine at the University of Liverpool, worked with six people who suffered anxiety and other mental symptoms. All had failed to improve after extensive examination and prolonged medical treatment. The researchers found that coffee and tea were responsible for much of the patients' anxiety and other psychological problems.

'The symptoms produced by excessive coffee are probably due to caffeine,' say Drs Finn and Cohen. 'The symptoms, which may mimic an anxiety state, include irritability, palpitations, headache and gastrointestinal disturbances.

'Although these reactions to coffee have been well documented,' say the researchers, 'it is clear that the diagnosis is often overlooked.'

The implications are clear: if you've been overly anxious for no good reason and drink coffee every day (most coffee drinkers do), you'd be smart to give up the brew for a few weeks. Of course, that also means giving up tea, cola, chocolate and over-the-counter pain-killers, which contain either caffeine or caffeinelike compounds. It may take several days for you to completely recover from caffeine, but if that's the cause of your apprehension, you'll notice a dramatic drop in anxiety levels.

While Drs Finn and Cohen single out caffeine, they also feel that almost any food to which one is allergic may be the unrecognized cause of baseless anxiety.

'Unlike conventional allergic reactions, such as a skin rash, the patient is usually unaware of the food to which he is sensitive and may even be unaware that his symptoms might be due to food intolerance,' say Drs Finn and Cohen. 'The offending agent is often a favourite food which is taken daily, usually in large quantities' (*Lancet*, 25 February 1978).

Food may not be the only possible offender. Marshall Mandell, an allergist in Norwalk, Connecticut who has done extensive work in the field of allergy, tells of a twenty-five-year-old woman who suffered from anxiety, along with fatigue, depression, menstrual discomfort and conventional allergic problems such as hives and nasal symptoms. Medical treatment had been no help, and she'd been advised to seek psychiatric help. Instead, she went to Dr Mandell, who checked into the possibility that her problems were caused by allergy to foods and chemicals.

'I learned that she reacted to freshly manufactured plastics and rubber articles, hair sprays, paints, furniture oils, fumes from gas stoves, car exhaust, chlordane insecticide and a number of foods,' says Dr Mandell. 'When she cleaned up her home environment by removing all offending household products, had her gas stove removed and the inlet pipe that supplied her house sealed off at the meter so that no gas entered her home, and went on to a Rotary Diet that eliminated all of the food to which she had reacted, her symptoms began to subside and in less than a month all of her complaints cleared up' (*Dr Mandell's 5-Day Allergy Relief System*, Thomas Y. Crowell, 1979).

You may not have to take as many steps as that woman did to clear up your anxiety. But all of the avoidance methods mentioned by Dr Mandell – plus several other helpful tips – are covered in detail in earlier chapters. They can be used to identify and eliminate allergic causes of anxiety in people who've gone the whole route of medical and psychological evaluation and are still burdened with free-floating anxiety. In particular, Chapter 3, Finding your no-allergy diet, and Chapter 4, Clearing the air, can help you to control food and inhalant allergies, including allergy to caffeine or chemicals, two of the most common causes of anxiety.

Because anxiety is so often accompanied by headaches, stomach troubles and depression, many readers will find the entries on those topics, later in this section, very helpful.

Arthritis

Arthritis is a handicap. Swollen, tender, inflamed joints limit motion. The simplest tasks – writing a letter, opening a car door, walking across the room – become a chore.

The two most common forms of arthritis are osteoarthritis and rheumatoid arthritis. Osteoarthritis affects the joints that receive the most wear and tear: knees, big toes, fingers, lower spine. The cartilage that covers the end of the bones disintegrates, and the bones themselves wear away.

In most cases of rheumatoid arthritis, joints are inflamed and may eventually become deformed. Rheumatoid arthritis is regarded by some as an autoimmune disease – the body produces antibodies against its own cells and tissues. In short, the body behaves as though it's allergic to itself. In addition to the joint changes in rheumatoid arthritis, the adjacent bones, muscles and skin waste away – explaining the muscle aches that so often accompany arthritis.

Regardless of the variety, treatment of arthritis consists mostly of relieving pain and maintaining motion. Mercifully, arthritis pain tends to come and go, granting its victims periods of relief.

Research by Theron Randolph, a Chicago allergist, suggests that some cases of osteoarthritis may improve when food and environmental allergens are avoided. To illustrate his claim, Dr Randolph tells of a thirty-year-old pianist and violinist who had been well until she moved into an all gas-equipped house. At the same time, she began to switch from natural-fibre clothing to synthetics. She then did some travelling, during which she was exposed to heavy traffic fumes.

At that point she became so incapacitated by muscle aches and joint pains that she had to give up playing both the violin and piano.

Dr Randolph found that the woman was allergic to corn, tomato, peas, beets and beet sugar, lamb, rice, wheat, milk and beef. Those foods produced varying degrees of fatigue, stiffness and joint pain, all of which disappeared when the foods were avoided. When she returned home she found that her arthritis flared up again, but that she felt better when she was outside. She replaced her gas stove and heating system with electric appliances and made her bedroom into a pollution-free oasis. She then reintroduced suspicious items one at a time. Polyester bedsheets and several other plastic and synthetic items seem to trigger her discomfort.

'At the present time, [the woman] is free of muscle and joint pain,' reports Dr Randolph. 'But there remains some impaired motion in the left wrist, due to the destruction of tissue caused when her illness was uncontrolled. She also gets a mild increase in arthritic symptoms before her monthly period, after housekeeping, when the pine trees in her yard are putting out new growth and when she is working in the yard.

'However, there is simply no comparison between the minor problems she has now and the crippled patient whom we admitted to the hospital a few years ago,' says Dr Randolph (*An Alternative Approach to Allergies*, Lippincott and Crowell, 1979).

Rheumatoid arthritis, too, may be helped. While following a diet that excluded certain foods to which they were allergic, twenty out of twenty-two English patients suffering from rheumatoid arthritis found that their symptoms were relieved. On the average, it took ten days of being on the diet for the patients to begin feeling better.

The foods to which one or more of the people were sensitive included grain, milk, seeds and nuts, beef, cheese, eggs, chicken, fish, potato, onion and liver. When they later tried to eat these foods, nineteen of the people found that their arthritis worsened – sometimes in as little as two hours (*Clinical Allergy*, vol. 10, no. 4, 1980).

Furthermore, speaking at a meeting of the American College of Allergists in January 1981, I. T. Chao, of Brooklyn, New York, said, 'Food incompatibility, although unrecognized, is a common cause of many forms of chronic arthritis'. (*Annals of Allergy*, August 1981).

One family of foods, the nightshades, seems to be particularly troublesome for some arthritics. Tomatoes, white potatoes, aubergines, peppers and tobacco contain mild toxins such as solanine, which don't bother most people. But to the 5 or 10 per cent of the population who are sensitive to those toxins, nightshades seem to trigger arthritic flareups.

According to Norman F. Childers, a retired professor of horticulture at Rutgers University in New Jersey, many arthritics who avoid the nightshades find dramatic relief from joint tenderness, pain and stiffness. While not an allergy per se, nightshade sensitivity is managed like an allergy – by avoiding all traces of those foods, plus tobacco. And like other allergy diets, the no-nightshade approach requires careful planning.

'You find tomatoes, white potatoes and peppers in a wide variety of dishes, and they must all be avoided to give the diet a chance to work,' says Dr Childers. 'Even paprika on fish can cause a reaction in sensitive people,' he says. Seasonings containing paprika and other red peppers are widely used in processed foods. (Black pepper is not related to the nightshades and can be eaten on this diet.)

We can't go so far as to say that control of allergies will reverse the degeneration that's responsible for arthritis – the disease tends to progress no matter what you do, especially if it's reached the stage where your joints are deformed. And arthritis is one of those conditions where no one therapy – environmental or medical – works for everyone. But those reports seem to indicate that some people with milder forms of arthritis can experience much-welcomed relief of pain, swelling and stiffness after changing their diet or home environment.

Asthma

Imagine what it would be like to try to breathe with a 300-lb gorilla sitting on your chest. That'll give you an idea of the panic and helplessness an asthmatic experiences during an attack. If you have asthma yourself, you know just what we mean.

Fortunately, asthma isn't always that bad. Some days you just wheeze – your airways whistle and rattle as you breathe ever so cautiously. You cough – not a healthy, productive cough but a dry, nagging cough. Exercise seems to be entirely out of the question.

If you could peer inside your chest, you'd discover what's behind that struggle for air. The muscular fibres around the bronchial tubes, or airways, tighten up or twitch at the least provocation – cold air, air pollution, over-exertion. Or they act up after an encounter with something to which you're allergic – pollen, dust, moulds spores, pet dander, food or a drug.

At the same time, the linings of the lungs react by becoming swollen and inflamed. And the lungs produce a sticky mucus that no amount of coughing will force out. All that swelling and tightening blocks the free flow of air.

That's asthma. Asthma is the most common chronic disease of childhood. Some asthmatics grow out of the disease, just as some teenagers grow out of acne. For others, the years of wheezing and fatigue go on and on. Either way, it's a long wait.

What can you do to get the gorilla off your chest?

No doubt you've already learned a few basic defence tactics – farming out the dog, purging the house of dust and mould, shunning whatever foods give you trouble. For some people, such avoidance tactics alone will take care of the brunt of the problem.

'In children, particularly, I find that taking care of the environment – dust control, mould control, pet control – may be more than 50 per cent of the secret of allergy relief,' says Constantine J. Falliers, an allergist in Denver, Colorado and editor of the *Journal of Asthma*. 'And I've seen many people who have just stayed away from food dyes and preservatives, and all their symptoms suddenly disappeared.'

One of the dyes Dr Falliers is referring to is tartrazine, E102, a common problem for asthmatics who may also be sensitive to aspirin, a notorious asthma trigger. Fortunately, foods containing the dye are required to say so on the label.

Other asthma triggers, however, are ever-present but less obvious. The biggest offenders are pollen, pollution and unexpected pets in other people's homes – to say nothing of tobacco smoke, an asthma trigger in the sense that it irritates already sensitive airways. So you need to take the offensive – by stopping asthma before it starts, and knowing how to thwart an attack at the earliest warning signal.

Air filters are a basic defence against asthma. Doctors we spoke to told us that the best models are the High Efficiency Particulate Air (HEPA) filters, which have been known to relieve asthma symptoms within ten to thirty minutes. A study at a summer camp for asthmatic children in West Virginia found that the use of HEPA filters in the bunkhouses significantly reduced the number and severity of asthma episodes (*West Virginia Medical Journal*, July 1977).

At home, air filters are just as effective.

'I nearly always prescribe air filtration,' says Robert W. Boxer, an allergist in Chicago. 'I feel that it's helpful. I've seen patients for whom adding an air filter to their asthma therapy has helped their asthma immensely.'

Still, you can't always live in a well-filtered bubble. Some airborne asthma triggers are bound to slip through, gumming up your lungs with mucus and strangling your airways.

To unstick your breathing equipment, drink plenty of fluids. Water and other beverages act as natural expectorants, keeping mucus thin and coughable, says Doris J. Rapp, author of *Allergies and Your Family* (Sterling Publishing, 1981). She recommends drinking one-half to one cup of liquid *every* waking hour, if at all possible. Just be sure you don't drink *cold* beverages – the chill can shock sensitive airways into spasms. And be careful to avoid drinks that contain cola or food dyes, common asthma triggers.

Taking your beverages hot helps even more. A warm drink acts as a natural bronchodilator, or airway relaxer, as it glides past respiratory passages. Drinking soup or herb tea when you feel an attack coming on will do fine.

'Sometimes a warm liquid relaxes the bronchial tubes and you may not even need to use your bronchodilator spray,' says Dr Falliers. 'We've had kids in the hospital for treatment, and when they can't breathe, we try to get them to drink something warm, maybe just water or something with a little more flavour, like hot apple cider. They relax, control the panic and start breathing quietly again.'

Controlling panic is a big part of controlling asthma. If you know you're an asthmatic and begin to sense an attack coming on, you may tend to panic and fight for air. That tightens your chest further. For children, the anxiety is heightened if they see Mum or Dad panic, too. If your child has asthma, you can help by simply trying to appear calm and confident, no matter how frantic you may actually feel. The sight of a reassuring adult in itself may help the youngster.

'Some children relax the minute they see their doctor enter the room, even before they're given any medication,' says Dr Rapp.

Relaxation, in fact, is such a useful shield against asthma that many doctors are teaching child and adult asthmatics variations of the relaxation technique, described in the box, How to relax away an asthma attack, in Chapter 10. Because it loosens tightened muscles surrounding airways, relaxation is a form of protection that can be used whenever an asthmatic feels an attack coming on.

In a subconscious effort not to tax temperamental lungs, asthmatics tend to take short, shallow breaths. Doctors call it 'stingy breathing'. By filling and emptying only the top portion of the lungs, however, asthmatics don't pull in enough oxygen. During an attack they get even less.

'The average asthmatic is breathing at only 60 or 70 per cent of capacity,' Dr Falliers told us. 'And during an asthma attack, that can drop to 20 per cent.' In the throes of an asthma attack, you may actually turn blue for lack of oxygen.

'But if you're having an asthma attack, you don't think about breathing physiology and oxygen metabolism,' says Dr Falliers. 'You just think of how to get your next breath.' By learning to breathe deeply and efficiently, you can increase the amount of oxygen you take in, so an attack isn't nearly as disabling. (See the box, Basic deep-breathing exercise for asthma, in Chapter 10.)

Exercise can also help. Interestingly, school teachers who have asthmatic children in their classes are often confused about exercise. One child has a doctor who says, 'This child has asthma, so he can't take gym.' Another child's doctor says, 'This child has asthma and should be encouraged to exercise.'

Who's right?

'They're both right,' says Dr Falliers. 'Until the asthma has been treated, a child should be excused from exercise. But as treatment progresses, the child should be encouraged to develop and improve his or her fitness.'

That's because improving overall fitness can help keep asthma under control.

'If you're not fit – if you haven't exercised in six months – and then you start exercising, your heart will beat very fast,' explains Dr Falliers. 'But if you're physically fit, your heart will beat more slowly. And a slower heartbeat means better absorption of oxygen from the lungs. Being fit is like having your carburettor properly adjusted: you run and breathe more smoothly.'

Of course, exercise can also help keep your weight down, which is also beneficial for asthmatics.

'If you have two inches of excess fat around your diaphragm, it's going to make it harder for you to breathe,' says Dr Falliers. 'For a person with asthma – or any kind of breathing problem – being overweight is like wearing a very tight garment. You don't have enough room for your muscles to expand the lungs.'

The type of exercise you choose will make quite a difference in how well you tolerate exercise. Activities that involve brief spurts of action, separated by rests, are much less apt to trigger asthma attacks than sports that call for continuous exertion. An asthmatic who goes in for baseball or golf, for example, is not as likely to start wheezing and coughing as one who plays basketball or runs the mile. Swimming, too is ideal for asthmatics, provided that rest is taken at proper intervals.

'So often, it's not the exercise that triggers asthma, but fast breathing of cold air,' says Dr Falliers. 'Cold air irritates sensitive airways. If you breathe through your nose, instead of your mouth, the air will be warmed, and you may not react.'

A light, cotton face mask may also help to protect against cold, dry air – or pollen and air pollution, for that matter. Scientists at the National Asthma Center in Denver observed the effectiveness of face masks on ten boys and girls, all asthmatic. After exercising for six minutes, the youngsters experienced much less asthma than usual – or none at all. The researchers concluded that a 'simple face mask may be an inexpensive [drug-free] alternative for alleviation of exercise-induced asthma' – especially in runners and skiers with asthma. (*Journal of the American Medical Association*, 14 November 1980.)

Similar research at Yale University also showed the protection offered by face masks against exercise-induced asthma. In both air conditioned and refrigerated rooms, asthmatics with face masks fared better than those without masks – probably due to the rewarming of air inside the mask, said the researchers, adding, 'We have shown that under [these] circumstances . . . the use of a mask offers a simple, inexpensive and effective form of [protection]'. (*Annals of Allergy*, January 1981.)

Wearing a scarf pulled up over your mouth before going outdoors in winter achieves the same effect.

During the nineteenth century, it was noticed that sailors with scurvy stopped wheezing when they ate citrus fruit. Modern research shows that vitamin C may help to widen air passages during exercise or exertion. In one study, volunteers who customarily suffered asthma after exercise were given 500 milligrams of vitamin C before an exercise test. Their tolerance of exercise was doubled (*Journal of the American Medical Association*, 13 February 1981).

Vitamin C also seems to help asthmatics whether they tolerate exercise or not. In another study, asthmatics who took 1,000 milligrams of vitamin C a day had less than 25 per cent as many asthma attacks as those receiving an inactive dummy pill. When they stopped taking vitamin C, however, they once again suffered the same number of attacks as the untreated people (*Tropical and Geographical Medicine*, vol. 32, no. 2, 1980).

So breathe easier. By definition, asthma is a reversible condition. And relief depends largely on factors that you can control.

'Proper education of the public and the right health attitude – not waiting until the damage is done, but preventing it – will be the secret of success in controlling asthma,' says Dr Falliers. 'And if that puts us allergists out of a job, that's just fine!'

Bedwetting

Most bedwetters grow out of the problem after age three. But some don't. And when physical causes such as a urinary tract defect or a chronic infection have been ruled out, the situation becomes emotionally trying for parents and child alike. In fact, 99 per cent of these children continue to wet the bed indefinitely, in spite of strategies such as denying them fluids in the evening or strapping moisture-sensitive buzzers to the mattress.

In the 1920s and 1930s, a few doctors discovered that some bedwetters lost urinary control after they ate particular foods, but had perfect control when they avoided them. Unfortunately for millions of bedwetting children since then, those observations went largely unnoticed for decades. Then in 1957, a scientific study once again showed that avoiding certain foods meant no more bedwetting for many youngsters.

A closer look at those children showed they had 'oedematous' (fluid-filled) bladder tissues, much like the swollen nasal tissues in a person with hay fever. A swollen bladder is a smaller bladder; it can't stretch to hold the amount of urine it should. And if the sphincter muscle controlling flow out of the bladder is also swollen, the problem is compounded: the muscle tires more easily and cannot close tightly enough to hold back urine, especially when the person is asleep and relaxed. The result is overnight 'accidents'. When food allergens are avoided, the swelling subsides and the bladder can hold urine during sleep.

'Control of food allergy is effective in curbing bedwetting in four out of five patients,' says Dr James C. Breneman, chairman of the Food Allergy Committee of The American College of

Allergists. He bases that assertion on a study of 400 bedwetters whose loss of urinary control could not be explained by physical problems other than allergy. Cow's milk was the most common offender, followed by wheat, egg, corn, chocolate and pork (*Basics of Food Allergy*, Charles C. Thomas, 1978).

Dr Breneman suggests keeping a detailed diary of diet and night-time accidents to help identify foods at fault in bedwetting. Chapter 3, Finding your no-allergy diet, gives detailed instructions on how to accurately track down and avoid problem foods.

Blood-sugar problems (diabetes and hypoglycemia)

The fundamental problem of diabetes is a disruption in the way the body uses carbohydrates – the starches and sugars in the food we eat that turn into blood sugar, or glucose. Too little insulin – the hormone that regulates glucose – is secreted. As a result, glucose piles up in the bloodstream, never reaching the muscles and other cells that require it.

Hypoglycemia, on the other hand, is marked by periods of low blood sugar. The most common symptom is fatigue – a 'burned out' feeling – especially in the morning or late afternoon. Headaches, particularly the migraine type, are also common. This type of hypoglycemia is medically known as 'functional' or 'reactive', to distinguish it from the type of hypoglycemia that results from a disease.

To test for either diabetes or hypoglycemia, doctors usually give a glucose-tolerance test. After you drink a flavoured solution of sugar and water, the lab technician takes periodic samples of your blood over a period of six hours to measure your glucose levels. If glucose soars too high or plummets too low, you presumably have a blood-sugar problem that calls for adjustment of your carbohydrate intake.

Treatments for functional hypoglycemia and diabetes are essentially the same: a diet which evenly distributes moderate amounts of carbohydrates over six meals. And the diet emphasizes high-protein foods – chicken, turkey, eggs, milk, cheese and so forth. Sugar, alcohol, coffee, tea and cola beverages are forbidden because they raise blood sugar levels by overstimulating the release of insulin.

A small group of doctors feel that this diet may be ineffective, and that food allergy plays an unrecognized role in blood-sugar problems.

'The typical assumption is that diabetes is a disease of carbohydrate metabolism, but we believe that it is a result of carbohydrate metabolism *being interfered with*,' says Dr Thomas L. Stone, of Rolling Meadows, Illinois. 'And allergy is just one of many things that can disturb carbohydrate metabolism. Yet the so-called diabetic diet contains the *very* foods that can raise blood glucose if you're allergic to them – milk, eggs, chicken.

'Our approach to diabetes is somewhat different. I measure people's blood glucose after *individual* food tests. They avoid a food for four or five days, then eat it and I measure blood glucose thirty minutes to an hour later. In some people, blood sugar reaches as much as 375 (considered very high). When the foods that raise glucose are removed from the diet, the need for insulin goes down. We have yet to see someone who fails to improve with this approach.

'As for hypoglycemia, there is a lot of confusion because most doctors rely on the conventional glucose-tolerance test to diagnose it,' continues Dr Stone. 'The glucose-tolerance test evaluates your blood sugar's reaction to one food only – corn sugar – when in fact many foods can cause or aggravate blood-sugar problems. But reactions from those other foods won't show up on the glucose-tolerance test. Not only is the test faulty; so is the diet. Many of the patients with hypoglycemia would get dramatically better within three months on a standard high-protein diet, but their symptoms would tend to return, even if they conscientiously stuck to the diet. So I felt a different approach was needed.

'As with diabetes, I measured glucose levels after individual food tests,' says Dr Stone. 'As a result, each person has a unique set of foods he or she can and cannot eat to control their blood sugar. No one leaves here on the same diet.

'I don't want to imply that blood-sugar problems are simple. They're not. The body is very complicated,' says Dr Stone. 'Blood sugar is only one aspect of a total problem, and allergy is just one thing that can disturb carbohydrate metabolism. But

I've treated thousands of people with this approach. Even people who are quite sick get better in a couple of weeks.'

Bruises

A bruise is a purple splotch on the skin caused by broken and bleeding blood vessels underneath the surface. Bruises usually result from unexpected clashes with sharp corners or from other forceful encounters.

Some people bruise at a loving tap, though. Or they frequently wake up with unexplained bruises. Their bruises seem to appear for no reason. Spontaneous bruises are no serious threat to health, yet they're embarrassing – and puzzling.

Could a bruise be a blood vessel's way of reacting to an allergen? Very possibly, says Dr William J. Rea, a cardiovascular surgeon in Dallas, Texas. For one thing, blood vessels are fifteen times more sensitive to certain environmental chemicals such as formaldehyde and pesticides than are other tissues of the body. And in the course of treating several people for phlebitis (inflammation of the blood vessels, usually in the leg), Dr Rea noticed two things. All of the people with phlebitis were spontaneous bruisers, and when they were admitted to a chemical-free 'environmental control unit' of his hospital, their phlebitis cleared up *and* they no longer bruised as easily (*Annals of Allergy*, November 1981). So Dr Rea proposes that in some people, bruising is part of a reaction to chemicals coursing through their blood vessels.

'I've seen at least a hundred bruises that were caused by environmental allergy,' Dr Rea told us.

For guidelines on how to purify the air of chemicals, see Chapter 4, Clearing the air.

See also *Phlebitis*.

Canker sores

Canker sores are those fiery ulcers that seem to flare up willy-nilly in the inside of your mouth.

Are canker sores really so impromptu? Or do they have a predictable, controllable cause?

A doctor in Dublin, Ireland, thinks that, for allergic people, canker sores tend to be a result of food allergy. Dr C.W.M. Wilson noticed that of a group of sixty-one people with hay fever, over half had a long record of canker sores. In one out of five of those people, specific foods were clearly to blame. (The most common offenders were milk, eggs, cabbage, turnips, parsnips, pork, wheat germ, tea and coffee.)

Dr Wilson feels that in allergic people, the tissues in the mouth serve as a barometer of allergic stimulation. The burning and tangy sensations that precede a canker sore signal that they've eaten a food to which they are allergic.

'These sensations probably correspond to similar sensations in the skin associated with allergic eczema,' says Dr Wilson. Incidentally, half of the canker sore sufferers also had gas, diarrhoea and other abdominal discomforts, plus fatigue – common symptoms of food allergy (*Annals of Allergy*, May, 1980).

Other doctors tell of a particularly stubborn case of painful, depressing canker sores that responded to food allergy treatment. Ever since birth, a thirteen-year-old girl had never been free of canker sores for more than three weeks at a time. She'd been given almost every drug in the book, to no avail. During an elimination diet to identify food allergies, she reacted to potato, coffee and chocolate. (Potatoes rarely cause allergy, but the girl had been eating raw potatoes daily all her life, thus potentiating an allergic reaction.)

'After withdrawal of these foods, the canker sores healed and she has been completely free of ulcers for four months,' report Drs Ronald Finn and H. Newman Cohen, of the Royal Southern Hospital in the Department of Medicine, at the University of Liverpool (*Lancet*, 25 February 1978).

The foods blamed for canker sores in these two studies are by no means the only possible offenders. The most common food allergens – and the means to identify them – are listed at length in Chapter 3, Finding your no-allergy diet.

Car sickness

Most people think car sickness is just one variety of motion sickness – the nausea and dizziness that attack some travellers on aeroplanes, buses and cars. A few people with car sickness, however, may be reacting to car exhaust fumes, moulds and dust in the car air conditioner or the odour of new vinyl upholstery. All those triggers can make an allergic traveller feel nauseated and sometimes dizzy or headachy.

But even if they don't feel outright nausea, people with allergy induced car sickness can become irritable and easily annoyed by delays or other drivers' mistakes. And there are a host of other possible symptoms. They may feel dopey and under-react to traffic situations. Perceptions may dull and reflexes slow down. Vision may blur. The driver may underestimate the time and distance needed to stop, or even fall asleep at the wheel.

If you get sick, tired or irritable on car trips, take less heavily travelled routes to avoid breathing heavily polluted air. Above all, don't drive in the wake of a bus or diesel truck if you can possibly avoid it.

When you stop to fill up, close the window while the service station attendant fills the tank. At self-service stations, wear a handkerchief over your nose and mouth to block out fumes while you fill your tank. (Be sure to remove the handkerchief when you approach the cashier, so he won't mistake you for a robber!)

As we mentioned in Chapter 4, Clearing the air, allergic people should have their car air conditioners cleaned regularly before and during the hot weather season to eliminate mould and dust. As for sensitivity to vinyl car interiors and upholstery, you'll be less likely to get sick if you buy a car that's at least two years old. As vinyl ages, it gives off less odour.

Much of the fatigue that's blamed on 'highway hypnosis' may actually be due to car-related allergies. Following these precautions will not only help you arrive at your destination feeling well, but will also cut down your chances of a traffic accident along the way.

Coeliac disease

People with coeliac disease react to gluten – a nutritious protein in wheat and other grains – as if it were poison. Gluten damages their intestines so badly that they cannot absorb food, vitamins or minerals. They suffer abdominal cramps, gas, diarrhoea, malnutrition and weight loss. The disease is so debilitating that children with it grow slowly – if at all.

Coeliac disease isn't an allergy. But it's related to allergy in that many cases are provoked early in infancy by an allergic reaction to cow's milk. The damaged intestines then reject not only wheat and milk, but sometimes other foods as well. And coeliac disease is treated much like an allergy – by careful avoidance of gluten-containing grains.

The four offenders in coeliac disease are wheat, rye, barley and oats (although some coeliacs can eat oats safely). Their close botanical relative, rice, and distant cousins, corn and millet, have such low levels of gluten that most coeliacs can tolerate them, especially after several months of totally avoiding all sources of gluten.

But even when eating high-gluten grains, some coeliacs do not get as severely ill as others. A study in Britain tested the effects of barley, rye, rice and corn in a group of coeliacs. As expected, rice and corn did no harm. With barley and rye, the damage varied from one person to another, even though everyone ate the same amounts. Evidently, coeliacs vary in how much damage their intestines suffer when they eat gluten (*Quarterly Journal of Medicine*, January 1978).

Standard treatment for coeliac disease begins with a high-protein, gluten-free diet of skimmed milk, egg whites, lean meat, fish, liver and protein-rich vegetables such as peas and beans. Starchier foods such as fruit, vegetables and low-gluten grains come later, after the digestive system has healed enough to be able to handle them.

But because gluten can show up where you least expect it, you need to stop and think before you put *anything* in your mouth. For example, a woman in Toronto was doing very poorly despite a strict gluten-free diet. Doctors finally discovered that the woman, a Catholic, was receiving daily Communion – and that the wafers were made of wheat flour. Within two days of taking Communion without wafers, she no longer had abdominal cramps, bloating or diarrhoea (*Lancet*, 8 November 1975).

'It's not unusual for a person to adhere strictly to the diet but to be unaware that the Communion wafer or stick of gum may be an unsuspected source of gluten,' says Joyce Gryboski, a pediatrician at Yale University School of Medicine (*American Journal of Diseases of Children*, February 1981).

Chapter 3, Finding your no-allergy diet, gives tips on how to avoid hidden sources of gluten, especially when you're shopping for bread and baked goods. If you prefer to bake your own, the box Cooking without wheat (in Chapter 3) gives directions on how to substitute rice flour, potato starch and other gluten-free starches in recipes that call for wheat flour.

Until you heal, you will probably need to take a B-complex vitamin and other nutritional supplements to replace nutrients lost either through poor absorption or from avoiding grain and other B-vitamin-rich foods.

After you've done well on the high-protein, low-gluten diet for six months, you can work towards a regular diet by adding one food at a time. It may take a year or two for the intestinal damage to heal completely. Some coeliacs can eventually eat wheat and other sources of gluten, especially if they begin with rice or corn. A few lucky ones – mostly children – are able to eat gluten indefinitely without symptoms. But the basic tendency for gluten intolerance will remain, so it's best to eat only small amounts of gluten-containing foods occasionally rather than making them a major part of your daily diet.

Some people, however, may not improve until milk or egg has also been removed from the diet. One doctor noticed that out of 120 people with coeliac disease, ten did not improve on a gluten-free diet until milk protein was avoided. Two other coeliacs failed to get better until egg was avoided (*Progress in Gastroenterology*, vol. 1, 1968).

Other doctors report the case of a woman who was careful to follow a strict gluten-free diet, yet failed to improve. They noticed that her symptoms were the worst when she ate egg, chicken or tuna. But when those foods – along with gluten – were removed from her diet, she made a full recovery, say Drs Alfred L. Baker and Irwin H. Rosenberg, of Chicago, Illinois. The doctors emphasize that while coeliac disease due to foods other than gluten is unusual, it does occur (*Annals of Internal Medicine*, October 1978).

Coeliac disease seems to be somewhat preventable. The first step is for women to breastfeed their babies, especially if coeliac disease or allergies run in their family – or if they're Irish. (Irish people or their descendents are genetically more susceptible to the problem.) A study done a few years ago shows that coeliacs are more likely to have asthma, hay fever and eczema than non-coeliacs. While no one understands the full significance of the coeliac-allergy connection, it could indicate that since breastfeeding protects against allergies, it may guard against coeliac disease, too. Also, by delaying exposure to cow's milk until the baby has developed the proper enzymes to handle it, breastfeeding also prevents the intestinal damage that sets the stage for coeliac disease.

And don't be too hasty to add cereal and other solid foods to the baby's diet. Wait until the infant is at least four to six months old, and then add each grain, one at a time, in small amounts. Begin with rice, millet and other low-gluten grains.

'Delayed introduction of gluten to the diet in infancy may prevent . . . gluten intolerance and lead to a drop in the number of people who get coeliac disease,' say doctors in Britain.

Other doctors report that as more mothers breastfeed – and breastfeed longer – the incidence of coeliac disease seems to be dropping. 'We believe that the incidence of coeliac disease in childhood is falling and that this is directly related to changes in infant feeding practices occurring in the mid-1970s,' they conclude (*Lancet*, 20–27 December 1980).

It's nice to hear that even some of the most mysterious health problems are within our control – if we know what to do about them.

See also *Colic*; *Colitis*; *Diarrhoea*; *Indigestion, bloating and abdominal pain*; and *Schizophrenia*.

Cerebral palsy

Cerebral palsy can produce any one of a number of physical problems – poor co-ordination, muscle spasms, poor balance or an unsteady walk. Some defect or injury in the brain is to blame, perhaps caused by an infection or mishap shortly after birth. But allergy might make the problem worse.

A twenty-seven-year-old man with cerebral palsy went to a doctor because of constant colds, sore throats and other respiratory problems. He suspected he might be allergic to something. Tests showed he was. But exposure to various allergens provoked both his respiratory symptoms and his palsy.

Marshall Mandell, an allergist in Norwalk, Connecticut, who treated the man, reports thirty other people whose cerebral palsy improved considerably after discovery and treatment of unsuspected allergies.

'The study strongly suggests evaluation of unsuspected allergy [would be worthwhile] in the one million cerebral palsy victims in this country,' says Dr Mandell. 'Their chronic symptoms can be reduced and the quality of their lives greatly improved'. (*Annals of Allergy*, abstract no. 28, August 1981.)

Dr Mandell is also investigating the influence of allergies in Tourette's syndrome and multiple sclerosis, two other central nervous system disorders.

Colic, infant

For the first four or five months of life, babies do little more than eat, sleep and cry. If the crying goes beyond occasional fussiness to hours of constant shrieking, parents become frustrated. And if a clean nappy, a warm breast or bottle and lots of cuddling fail to silence the baby's cries, parents become frightened – and probably ask their doctor for help. In most cases, the doctor says the baby has colic. In other words, large amounts of gas are building up in the baby's intestines, causing lots of discomfort and the constant crying.

Allergy to milk is the most common cause of colic. In bottle-fed infants, the treatment is simple and obvious: change from a milk-based formula to a soya-based or other type of milk-free formula.

But occasionally, even a breastfed infant will get colic.

'The colicky breast-fed infant is also allergic to milk,' says Del Stigler, a pediatrician and allergist in Denver. 'Not to the mother's milk, though, but to the cow's milk the mother is drinking. Particles of cow's milk reach the infant through the breast milk and cause colic. Take the mother off cow's milk and the baby will be well in two or three days.'

Many parents have been delighted to discover that a milk-free diet for Mum wipes out colic for baby. In a study by Swedish doctors, eighteen mothers of colicky babies were put on a milk-free diet. 'Colic promptly disappeared in thirteen of the infants,' say the researchers. 'We conclude that infantile colic in breastfed infants can be caused by cow's milk consumption by the mother, and we suggest a diet free of cow's milk for the mother'. (*Lancet*, 26 August 1978.)

Any hard-to-digest foods that a nursing mother eats or drinks are also apt to pass through her breast milk to the baby and cause colic. So in addition to suggesting a milk-free diet to nursing mothers, many pediatricians recommend that they avoid 'gassy' foods such as beans, beer, broccoli, brussels sprouts, cabbage, carbonated beverages, champagne, lentils and mushrooms, plus any spices that seem to cause irritability in the breastfed baby.

If colic persists, the next step is to eliminate cereals or any other solid foods that the baby is eating. Most foods require several enzymes for digestion. A young baby's body needs time to develop all the enzymes required to digest more complex food. If you give a baby solid food before his stomach and intestines are equipped to handle it, he'll get gas. After a couple of months of freedom from colic, you can reintroduce solid foods – one at a time and several days apart – to test the baby's tolerance.

Doctors sometimes also suggest that parents of a colicky baby temporarily withhold the baby's vitamin supplements, to see if sugars or additives in those products could be the problem. (The Appendix gives purchasing sources for less allergenic supplements.)

For additional information on how to deal with allergy to milk and other foods, see Chapter 3, Finding your no-allergy diet.

Colitis

Colitis – what a doctor would sedately call an 'inflamed colon' – is more like a fiery nightmare. Diarrhoea so constant the bathroom seems like a prison cell. Stools that are bloody and full of mucus. Abdominal cramps. Fever. Pale, sweaty skin. What's worse, an attack can hit at any time, so that a colitis sufferer *always* has to have a bathroom nearby. Not exactly a fun way to plan your life.

The traditional view is that peace of mind will produce peace in the colon – stress and anxiety are considered major causes of an attack (some psychiatrists even claim they're at the root of the problem). But trying to avoid stress is a never-ending and not always successful effort. There are temporary ceasefires, but the colon remains a battle zone.

Because the colon is the section of the intestine where food fibre absorbs water to create a stool, diet is another logical focus of treatment. The only problem is that nobody can agree which diet is right. 'More fibre!' cry some doctors. 'Less fibre!' recommend others. 'A straight answer!' pleads the colitis victim.

Well, although fibre may not be the solution, it could be that the diet-therapy doctors are on the right track. As with many other gastrointestinal complaints, *milk allergy* is a common cause of colitis. Less frequently, colitis is caused by allergy to wheat, corn, eggs, chocolate, meats or nuts. In a very few cases, water or antibiotic drugs are the cause.

'As the first line of treatment [of colitis], all food or drug allergens are removed from the diet,' says Dr James C. Breneman, chairman of the Food Allergy Committee of the American College of Allergists. Dr Breneman feels that allergy therapy should be given a fair chance in the treatment of colitis before drugs or surgery are used – as they often are. An allergy-free diet, in many cases, may be the *only* treatment necessary, says Dr Breneman. In his words, 'It's better to remove the milk than to remove the colon.'

Sometimes colitis gets so bad that ulcers form in the intestine. Then, too, food allergy can be at fault.

'I've found that in susceptible people allergic reaction to commonly eaten foods is the direct cause of ulcerative colitis,' says Barbara Solomon, a doctor in Baltimore, Maryland. Dr Solomon tests all her patients for food allergies. She finds that people with ulcerative colitis are always allergic to milk products and grains that contain gluten: wheat, oats, barley, rye and corn. When her patients eliminate those foods (and sometimes other foods as well), the disease improves greatly. But not always.

'Food allergy isn't the only cause of ulcerative colitis,' Dr

Solomon told us. 'Sometimes a patient doesn't get well until I take him off tap water and have him drink only distilled water. Tap water is full of chemicals, and one of them could be causing the problem.'

Robert Rogers, a doctor in Melbourne, Florida, also treats ulcerative colitis as a food allergy. The first patient he cured of the disease was himself.

'I developed ulcerative colitis early in my medical school career,' he told us. 'I had bleeding from the bowel, a lot of profuse diarrhoea and terrible cramps. It was very debilitating. I got books out and read about it and the professors told me about it.

'But the only treatment was drugs. Drugs to slow down the feacal stream, drugs to take the cramps away, drugs to coat the bowel, drugs to tranquillize me. But while I was taking all these drugs, I was feeding the disease with the foods I was allergic to,' says Dr Rogers. 'Eventually I discovered on my own that all forms of dairy products and chocolate and caffeinated beverages were my enemy. If I don't eat those foods, I don't have ulcerative colitis.'

Guidelines for tracking down allergy to milk and other foods or water are given in Chapter 3, Finding your no-allergy diet, and for dealing with antibiotic allergy in Chapter 5, Don't overlook drugs as a cause.

Constipation

If constipation is accompanied by fatigue, headaches, abdominal pain or colitis, there's a good chance that food allergy is at least partly to blame – especially if eating high-fibre foods like bran, exercising a few days a week and keeping a fairly standard daily routine don't help.

'Constipation is an important symptom of food allergy,' says Dr Frederic Speer in his book *Food Allergy* (PSG Publishing, 1978). Most people know that milk is an extremely common cause of constipation, says Dr Speer, although many mistakenly believe that it's only boiled milk or cheese that causes trouble. But milk in any form, as well as other foods, can cause constipation.

'Several doctors have noted that normal bowel control is

often promptly achieved in many allergic children when a food to which the child is allergic is eliminated from the diet,' says Dr William G. Crook, a pediatric allergist in Jackson, Tennessee. 'Milk and chocolate are especially common offenders,' he adds.

Dr Crook says that allergy can cause constipation by triggering spasms in the circular muscles of the bowel, interfering with the normal elimination of stools. And once the waste disposal mechanism is disturbed, stools can back up in the lower colon and rectum. That in turn stretches the bowel muscles so out of shape that they lose their strength and elasticity, making it harder to expel waste material.

See Chapter 3, Finding your no-allergy diet, for more information on how to control allergy to milk and other common causes of food-induced constipation.

Criminal behaviour

Crime and violence are increasing, especially among young people. Yet despite the best intentions of rehabilitation workers, counselling and attempts at reform are often futile. Some people seem destined to stay in trouble with the law all their lives.

A few doctors and scientists now take the view that much crime, particularly violent crime, is caused by some biological malfunction of the criminal's brain – sometimes triggered by food allergies and chemical exposure. Not that sociological factors do not play a role. But biological factors such as allergy have been ignored too long, say these researchers.

In a speech to the California Commission on the Prevention of Crime and Violence, Bernard Rimland said that because traditional approaches to rehabilitation of criminals haven't been very successful, it's time to examine the influence and correction of other factors, specifically:

– food allergies,
– food additives,
– excess sugar intake,
– pesticides and herbicides inadvertently added to food and water,
– fumes from industrial and other environmental sources and
– alcohol use.

Interestingly enough, many of those same factors have been found to be responsible for allergy-induced hyperactivity, learning problems and aggression, which are often directly related to criminal behaviour.

Dr Rimland described the brain as a 'soggy computer' – a compact information and control centre that's 85 per cent water by weight. Doctors already know that if an individual takes in too much of a toxic metal like lead, or too little of an essential nutrient like thiamine, something will go wrong. By the same token, if a person eats a food or breathes a substance which is basically harmless but to which he or she happens to be allergic – wheat, pollen, aspirin or whatever – the brain will act up. The result can be distortions of judgement and control that can easily lead to antisocial and criminal behaviour.

'It's well known that allergies may cause such symptoms as hay fever, asthma and hives,' says Dr Rimland. 'Since it is so widely recognized that the nasal membranes, the lungs and the skin can be affected by a food or other substances to which some individuals are intolerant, [it's not surprising that] the brain, the most intricate and biochemically complicated organ in the body, could also be affected by allergies.

'Individuals who have cerebral [brain] allergies to wheat, beef, milk, corn and other common foods are likely to experience chronic problems such as headaches, feelings of unreality and lack of control over their behaviour, sometimes resulting in violence or, surprisingly, specific compulsions such as to steal or commit arson,' says Dr Rimland. 'Individuals who are allergic to or who cannot tolerate substances [which they eat or encounter less frequently] such as oysters, walnuts or formaldehyde, may experience unexpected and uncontrolled episodes of aberrant behaviour with intervening periods of trouble-free behaviour.

'The "brain allergy" concept has important implications for correcting criminal behaviour through diet,' says Dr Rimland.

As it happens, many of the dietary changes designed to improve criminal behaviour have involved the elimination of non-nutritive items such as sugar and food additives. Alexander Schauss, a noted criminologist, reports the following sequence of events at a military prison in Seattle. On 1 November 1978, white flour was replaced with whole wheat. On 3 February 1979, sugar was eliminated – including all pastries, cakes, ice cream and soft drinks. Records subsequently showed that after the menu changes, discipline problems among the inmates were down 12 per cent from the same period a year before (*Diet, Crime and Delinquency*, Parker House, 1980).

But removing *any* incriminated allergens can correct criminal behaviour. Dr Doris J. Rapp, an allergist in Buffalo, New York, tells of one unco-operative young man who had a history of stealing. During the nine months that Dr Rapp treated his allergies, the stealing stopped. When therapy was discontinued (at his mother's request), stealing resumed. Three other patients in Dr Rapp's care had a recurrence of stealing when allergy treatment was discontinued (*Journal of Learning Disabilities*, November 1979).

'One wonders how many children and adults have been drugged and placed in institutions because of violent behaviour related to adverse food reactions,' says Schauss.

Because 90 per cent of delinquents have reading difficulties and other learning problems, we suggest that parents of troublesome children also read the entry on *Learning disorders* later in this section. The entries on *Aggression* and *Hyperactivity* may also be helpful.

Deafness

Does your family repeatedly ask you to turn down the volume on the TV or radio?
Do you frequently have to ask people to repeat what they've said?
Do people seem to mumble a lot lately?
Do you have trouble understanding what's being said from the pulpit or stage?
Do you lose the thread of conversation at the dinner table or at family gatherings?
Are you afraid that you're going deaf?

If so, don't write it off as old age. If you smoke cigarettes or have allergies to foods or inhalants, your hearing loss could be reversible.

Cigarette smoking seems to hasten deafness. A doctor in Cairo studied the effect of smoking on hearing loss in 150 smokers and 150 non-smokers. 'Average hearing loss in smokers was significantly higher than in non-smokers,' says Amal S. Ibrahim.

Cigarette smoke has a number of damaging effects on the delicate structures that make up the inner ear, and all of these effects contribute to hearing loss. One of them is an allergic reaction in the mucous membranes of the eustachian tube and the middle ear, says Dr Ibrahim.

'Allergy to tobacco smoke may cause eustachian [tube] blockages, symptoms of sinus trouble and postnasal drip,' says Dr Ibrahim (*World Smoking and Health*, Summer, 1982).

In a similar way, allergies to foods and inhalants can also impair hearing.

'Nasal allergy from pollen or . . . airborne inhalants or dusts can also cause oedema [fluid retention] in the eustachian tubes, middle ear or cochlea [hearing structures], resulting in impaired hearing,' says Albert Rowe, Jr, co-author of the book *Food Allergy* (Charles C. Thomas, 1972).

If you lose your hearing, you live in a vacuum. So no effort should be spared to restore it – and that includes an investigation of allergy.

Incidentally, people who take high doses of aspirin daily for years – such as people with rheumatoid arthritis – may lose their hearing as a side effect of the drug. Hearing returns when aspirin dosage is reduced or discontinued.

See also *Ear inflammation and hearing loss*; *Ménière's syndrome* and *Tinnitus*.

Depression

We all have an occasional blue mood. A day when we don't feel like doing much or seeing anyone. But when problems you usually overcome with relative ease assume a gloomy, out-of-proportion importance; when you can't shake off the feeling that nothing you do ever goes right; when it gets to the point where you *never* feel like doing anything – you may be genuinely depressed. No small matter, considering that severe depression is responsible for many suicides.

But even mild depression is nothing to ignore, especially if you can't tie your melancholy to a specific cause, such as an illness or death in the family, loss of your job or a divorce.

Depression can lead to marital discord, inefficiency on the job, alcohol abuse or retirement woes. To say nothing of the fact that depression takes all the enjoyment out of life.

Few medical problems are as difficult to diagnose or treat as depression. But if you're depressed and have other allergic problems – such as asthma, hay fever, hives or eczema – there's a reasonably good chance your depression is at least partially related to allergy, especially if other causes have been ruled out.

The role of adverse reactions to foods and environmental chemicals in depression was first noted in 1950, says Theron Randolph, a Chicago doctor who has been the forerunner of the environmental approach to illness. And the late Albert H. Rowe, and his son Albert Rowe, Jr (also pioneers in food allergy research), said in 1972 that symptoms of food allergy may include depression, lack of energy and ambition, lethargy and an inability to think or concentrate (*Food Allergy*, Charles C. Thomas, 1972).

Dr Randolph tells of two typical cases in which treatment of allergies put an end to lifelong depression.

One college-age woman, named Meryl, had suffered depression and various health problems all her life. One summer she visited relatives in the country and during that time contacted a nutritionist who was familiar with clinical ecology.

'The combination of relatively pure air and a partial diagnosis of her food problem worked wonders,' says Dr Randolph. ' "I discovered what it was like to feel good," she later said. For the next six months she remained on a Rotary Diet and avoided some incriminated foods. But on Christmas Day, at a family party, she began cheating on her diet and continued to slip downhill all week. She was very distraught and severely depressed.'

After going back for treatment, she felt well again. Tests revealed she was highly allergic to corn, cod, red snapper, eggs, avocado, cauliflower – all of which produced varying degrees of depression, crying, panic, anger and a 'spacy' feeling.

'In Meryl's case,' says Dr Randolph, 'there was a clear link between her reactions and her eating habits.'

Connie, an attractive woman in her early thirties, seemed to be someone who has everything a person needs to be happy: a loving spouse, a beautiful home, a good education and a rewarding job. Yet she was so depressed she felt like killing herself.

Connie had been sick nearly all her life with severe asthma and stomachaches. In college, she began to slip into a chronic malaise. On some days, she couldn't get out of bed, couldn't concentrate and could barely stay awake.

'To combat these problems,' says Dr Randolph, 'she relied on junk food. She would drink cola beverages or eat chocolate and sweets whenever she had to cram for a test.' A psychiatrist blamed Connie's depression on pressure to achieve during her childhood. In fact, however, her parents hadn't pressured her at all.

'As bad as all her symptoms were,' says Dr Randolph, 'Connie's condition took a sharp turn for the worse when her new home was sprayed with powerful pesticides, inside and out. Winter came, and the gas-fired heater was turned on. Soon afterwards she started to feel so weak that she could not get out of bed. She was depressed to the point of dwelling on suicide. Her husband would come home each day to find her crying uncontrollably.'

But after being hospitalized, diagnosed and treated for food allergies and chemical sensitivity, Connie became completely well.

'The food Connie was most allergic to was beef,' says Dr Randolph. 'After eating a portion of beef during allergy testing, she wandered the halls of the hospital, crying aimlessly. The next day she said that she felt as though she "had been run over by a bulldozer".

'All of her many symptoms were reproduced in several weeks of food testing,' says Dr Randolph. What's more, tests showed she was highly sensitive to various chemicals – explaining why she got so much worse after her house was sprayed with pesticides and the gas heater was started up.

Dr Randolph ends the story by saying that Connie has made excellent progress by controlling her food and chemical difficulties (even though it's not always easy to avoid exposure to natural gas). Despite occasional setbacks, Connie's mental state has been for the most part cheerful (*Allergies: Your Hidden Enemy*, 1983).

How does an individual distinguish between depression that calls for psychological counselling and depression caused by allergy? Keeping a journal can help – writing down what you do, where you go, chemicals you think you are exposed to, what you eat and, of course, how you feel. Compare your good days to your bad days (or your good weeks to your bad weeks, as the case may be) to help identify possible allergic causes. (Women who are still menstruating should factor their monthly periods, since hormonal cycles can have a direct bearing on one's mood.) Then use the techniques described in Chapters 2 to 8 of this book to help you steer clear of the depression triggers.

'Treatment of the allergy will, in most cases, "cure" the depression,' says Abraham Hoffer, a psychiatrist in Victoria. British Columbia, Canada. 'I have seen this in several hundred patients over the past six years'. (*Journal of Orthomolecular Psychiatry*, vol. 9, no. 3, 1980.)

Because dealing with any kind of allergies (asthma, hay fever, skin problems or whatever) can get you down even if your depression is not directly triggered by foods or inhalants, we suggest you also read Chapter 13, Mind over allergy. And because depression often coexists with anxiety, fatigue, overweight or alcohol abuse, many readers may find the entries on these topics helpful.

Diarrhoea

Diarrhoea is one of the most common symptoms of food allergy, especially in children. In allergic people, the bowel tends to react to certain foods as though they were laxatives, unpredictably flushing out loose stools throughout the day.

But being caught offguard is only part of the problem. Prolonged diarrhoea – lasting more than a week – leaves the body dangerously weak and dehydrated from loss of fluid and minerals like potassium. With too little water and nutrients, your muscles and nerves don't work. In children, diarrhoea is especially risky – their bodies are too small to deal with drastic losses of water and minerals. As a result, uncontrolled diarrhoea can leave children as limp as a ragdoll. Or they can have convulsions.

Diarrhoea has several possible causes other than allergy. But if your doctor has ruled out infection or disease, you should consider food allergy. In children, milk is to blame for one out of three cases of diarrhoea caused by food allergy. For them, diarrhoea is nature's way of rejecting a food that it regards as harmful.

'Because cow's milk is not a natural food for an infant, the body often tries to reject it with allergic reactivity, especially when a family tendency to allergy exists,' says Dr Albert Rowe, Jr, co-author of the book *Food Allergy* (Charles C. Thomas, 1972). Dr Rowe mentions one study which found that out of 140 children allergic to cow's milk, 24 per cent – about one out of four – had diarrhoea.

In infants, breast milk nearly always relieves allergy to cow's milk, especially if the nursing mother also avoids cow's milk. When the child gets older, he or she may eventually be able to tolerate milk. It may take six months, or it may take twelve years. Trial and error is the only way to tell.

After milk, fruit and sugar are frequent causes of allergic diarrhoea. Apparently, some people cannot tolerate fructose, the sugar found in honey and sweet fruits such as plums, apples and grapes. In still others, any kind of sugar causes diarrhoea. Two Swedish doctors report the cases of four people who had suffered diarrhoea, abdominal pain and bloating for up to six weeks at a time. Between these episodes, they had milder discomfort. 'All had noticed an aggravation of symptoms whenever they had eaten fruits, or food containing appreciable amounts of cane sugar,' say the researchers. 'All patients were free from symptoms on a fructose-free diet'. (*Acta Medica Scandinavica*, vol. 203, no. 1–2, 1978.)

And based on a study of several young children with diarrhoea, doctors at Adelaide Children's Hospital in South Australia suggest that children with chronic diarrhoea should eat a sucrose-free diet for at least two months. If sugar is the problem, the diarrhoea will go away (*Lancet*, 7 August 1982).

In still other children, both milk and sugar must be avoided in order for diarrhoea to let up. One group of pediatricians studied seventy-five children (all younger than one year) treated for diarrhoea and other related problems. After several days on a milk-free, soya-based diet formula, some of the children were gradually given cow's milk again, while the others received a soya formula free of milk and sugar. The children drinking cow's milk continued to have diarrhoea indefinitely, while the children on milk-free and sugar-free formula got better fairly soon (*Lancet*, 26 January 1980).

Occasionally, wheat and other cereals will cause diarrhoea. Instructions for avoiding milk, sugar, cereals and other common causes of food allergy appear in Chapter 3, Finding your no-allergy diet. To test for any of those foods, the diet must be tried for at least one week and often longer, since it takes several days after food is eaten for it to be completely eliminated from the body.

Sometimes food causes diarrhoea during the pollen season, but not during the rest of the year. For example, a child may be able to drink milk or eat cereal all year round with no diarrhoea, but will suffer several weeks of loose bowels when trees and grasses are pollinating in spring or summer.

Parents of children with diarrhoea should not hesitate to see a doctor, because of the immediate threat to health and the possibility of infection or disease.

See also *Colic* and *Indigestion, bloating and abdominal pain.* (Because eczema is also a common symptom of milk allergy, the entry *Skin inflammation (atopic dermatitis and eczema)* may be of help to some people.)

Dizzy spells

A woman from Denver whom I met on a plane told me that she had had dizzy spells off and on for a couple of years. She'd be walking down the street, for example, when suddenly her head would start to spin. She'd begun to worry that she might have a brain tumour. But a thorough neurological exam, including a brain scan, failed to detect one.

An allergist eventually discovered that the woman was allergic to yeasts and moulds in foods – cheese, wine, mushrooms and so forth – and that they were the cause of her dizzy spells.

The woman told me that she still eats an occasional piece of cheese or drinks some wine at parties, but not very often and not very much. The biggest relief, she said, comes from knowing that she doesn't have a brain tumour or some other life-threatening illness.

Dizzy spells can be pretty scary. So when a controllable cause is uncovered, doctor and patient alike are relieved. Allergy, however, is rarely suspected. And allergic causes *are* rare – but they exist. Dizziness from allergy to foods or inhalants results when they cause fluid retention in the inner ear that throws equilibrium off balance. You feel faint, or have the sense that you're going to fall.

The allergen can be anything from an easy-to-avoid food to a hard-to-avoid chemical. Marshall Mandell, an allergist in Norwalk, Connecticut, tells of a ten-year-old girl who became quite dizzy when leaving the kitchen to walk to school every morning. (The kitchen had a gas stove.) She also became dizzy and nauseous in school every time freshly printed papers were passed around in class or when she was in the same room with a mimeograph machine. When Dr Mandell tested her for allergy to ethanol (a petroleum product in gas and copying fluid) and other environmental substances, the girl became very ill.

At Dr Mandell's suggestion, the girl's parents then replaced all gas appliances in the home with electric models and discarded any household cleaning materials that contained petroleum byproducts.

'This environmental change was of considerable benefit,' says Dr Mandell. '[The girl's] morning dizziness disappeared along with her fatigue' (*Dr Mandell's 5-Day Allergy Relief System*, Thomas Y. Crowell, 1979).

If you suffer unexplained dizzy spells, an allergy investigation could give you some helpful answers. Chapter 3, Finding your no-allergy diet, and Chapter 4, Clearing the air, outline how to go about identifying allergy to food or chemicals.

Because dizzy spells are often accompanied by nausea or headaches, you could also find it helpful to read the entries on those topics in this section.

Ear inflammation and hearing loss

Inflammation inside the ear – frequent cause of earaches and periodic hearing loss – is often the result of an allergic reaction in the nose or throat. Airborne allergens – pollen, dust and the like – are the most common offenders, and the problem shows up most frequently in children with hay fever or asthma. But adults can be affected, too.

in the nose or throat. Airborne allergens – pollen, dust and the like – are the most common offenders, and the problem shows up most frequently in children with hay fever or asthma. But adults can be affected, too.

In one study, eight people with hay fever developed ear trouble after breathing ragweed or timothy grass pollen, common allergens to which they were allergic. (Their hay fever flared up at the same time.) But when they breathed pine pollen – to which none of them were allergic – their ears were fine.

In another study eleven out of twenty-five people with hay fever had ear trouble after exposure to rye grass pollen (*Wellcome Trends*, March 1982).

Ear inflammation can also be caused by sinusitis, infections, enlarged tonsils or adenoids, nasal polyps or congenital defects. But, in any of those conditions, allergy can *aggravate* ear inflammation.

Decongestants and antihistamines can temporarily clear up an allergic ear inflammation. But unless *all* allergic factors are recognized and avoided, the problem may persist – and eventually cause permanent hearing loss. In fact, uncontrolled ear inflammation is the most common cause of deafness in children. (To help control your exposure to airborne allergens, see Chapter 4, Clearing the air.)

If ear inflammation is caused by an infection, your doctor may prescribe antibiotic ear drops. But if you're allergic to antibiotics, the problem is likely to persist – or get a lot worse. A study in Britain found that out of forty adults who had ear inflammation for longer than a year, fourteen were allergic to one or more antibiotics in the ear drops they were using. Neomycin, framycetin, gentamycin and ciolquinol – four commonly used antibiotics – were to blame. The doctors reporting these cases recommend that people with persistent ear inflammation should be tested for possible allergy to antibiotics (*Journal of the Royal Society of Medicine*, vol. 75, 1982).

Medicated ear drops can also cause contact allergy on the outer ear. So can earrings, spectacle stems and perfumes. (See Chapter 5, Don't overlook drugs as a cause, for more on allergies to drugs and Chapter 7, Contact (skin) allergies, for more on allergies to jewellery, cosmetics and other contact items.)

See also *Asthma*; *Hay fever*; *Nasal polyps*; *Sinusitis* and *Tinnitus*.

Fatigue

Feeling tired all the time without knowing why can be very frustrating. You can't blame your washed-out feeling on heavy work demands or other stress. No infection, diabetes or thyroid problem is present. And with no medical reason to explain your fatigue, your doctor is apt to write you off as bored or depressed – probably skipping over the possibility of allergy unless you bring it up. If allergy is indeed the cause – as it sometimes is – controlling it can put an end to the stagnation you feel.

Because allergic fatigue is usually a combination of mental and physical tiredness, one doctor has adopted the term 'brain-fag' to describe the dullness and lack of ambition that sometimes result from allergy. Brain-fag is unrelieved by rest or sleep, and is frequently worse in the morning.

Dr Theron Randolph, of Chicago, describes a young man who had classic allergic fatigue, or brain-fag. The man wanted to become a doctor, but he was so tired in college that he couldn't study, concentrate or complete his work. He was also nervous, tense and frustrated. Even after sleeping eight or nine hours, he would wake up tired.

When tested for allergies, it was found that two glasses of milk brought on extreme fatigue in the young man. He had to lie down until he could return home. On another occasion, he ate eggs and got a headache shortly afterwards. Dr Randolph removed milk and eggs (which he had been eating daily) from the man's diet, along with beef and peanuts, which other tests incriminated.

After just two weeks on the diet, the young man felt much less tired. Eventually, he was able to eat the foods to which he'd been allergic, but only on a four-day Rotary Diet (as described in Chapter 3, Finding your no-allergy diet). The man's grades improved, and Dr Randolph reports that today he is a practising physician.

One symptom of allergic fatigue is loss of memory. Allergy-induced dullness can turn a 'walking encyclopedia' into a computer with a short-circuited memory bank. You can't remember where you put your keys, you can't recall phone numbers you dial every day, you forget names and dates – and you begin to feel that you're getting senile before your time.

Dr Randolph believes that many people have allergy-based fatigue, but that in most cases it goes undiagnosed.

'They've "graduated" to this condition through a number of previous levels of physical and mental distress,' says Dr Randolph. 'They usually have thick medical files, filled with long lists of complaints, many of them seemingly mental in origin. In truth, their problems are basically physical in origin (responses to foods or chemicals), but no one realizes this. To their doctors, their family and sometimes even themselves, they are classic "hypochondriacs" and attention seekers' (*Allergies: Your Hidden Enemy*, Thorsons, 1983).

Because children are, as a rule, energetic, fatigue in youngsters causes special concern.

'In my experience, allergy is the most common cause of otherwise unexplained fatigue in children,' says Dr William G. Crook, a pediatric allergist in Jackson, Tennessee. 'I've been thrilled by the number of pale, drowsy, tired, listless children whose entire outlook on life has changed when hidden food allergens were removed from the diet,' he adds.

'Although food is the usual cause of allergic fatigue, pollens and other allergens may also cause fatigue,' continued Dr Crook (*Pediatric Clinics of North America*, February 1975).

Adults can hope for the same rejuvenation. Once you uncover the cause (or causes) of fatigue and learn how to steer clear of them, you'll feel like a machine that just had a tuneup (and hopefully perform like one).

Start with your diet. Ironically, many of the foods that people rely on to give them 'go' – sweets, pastries, soda or coffee – contain the very culprits that may be wearing them down: wheat, milk, sugar, chocolate or caffeine. (Food allergy is discussed at length in Chapter 3, Finding your no-allergy diet.)

While foods are by far the most common cause of allergy-based fatigue, chemicals can squelch your drive, too. Dr Randolph tells of a teacher who came to him complaining that she was so exhausted she couldn't seem to rouse herself to do anything, Dr Randolph tested her and treated her for a few food allergies, but she was still tired. He then investigated her home and classroom. The classroom was the source of the trouble.

'The janitor cheerfully showed me the plethora of chemicals used to clean the premises and to spray for insects on a regular basis,' says Dr Randolph. 'I suggested to [the woman] that this environment was helping to perpetuate her [fatigue] and that she seek another job, which she did.' And that was the end of her fatigue (*Allergies: Your Hidden Enemy*, Thorsons, 1983).

Chances are you won't have to quit your job to regain your energy. Chapter 4, Clearing the air, describes simple but effective measures you can take, at home and at work, to reduce your exposure to airborne allergens, thereby eliminating the possible causes of allergy-induced fatigue.

Incidentally, drowsiness and fatigue are the predominant side effects of antihistamines, drugs routinely prescribed for hay fever, skin rashes and other common forms of allergy. So if you're taking antihistamines, there's a distinct possibility that they're contributing to your exhaustion. To learn how to reduce allergic reactions without sacrificing your energy, read Chapter 10, Allergy drugs and their alternatives.

A WHOLE-BODY APPROACH TO FATIGUE

While you work on controlling your allergies, pay special attention to nutrition and personal habits. Hard-to-explain fatigue may have more than one contributing factor, allergy being only one. For total relief of fatigue, consider the following (all of which have been shown to contribute to fatigue).

- **Lack of regular exercise. Twenty minutes, three times a week, help to keep your battery charged.**
- **Overuse of coffee or alcohol. Every 'up' is followed by a 'down'.**
- **Deficiency of one or more vitamins. The B vitamins folate, pantothenate and B_{12} are vital to high energy levels.**
- **Deficiency of one or more minerals. Potassium, magnesium, calcium and iron boost stamina.**
- **Boredom. Lack of interest equals lack of ambition.**
- **Stress. Your body uses up a lot of energy to fight money worries, family conflicts and impossible deadlines.**
- **A 'perfectionist' attitude. Setting unrealistic standards for yourself practically guarantees a sense of underachievement.**

Stamina and self-esteem go hand in hand. Once you overcome fatigue, your whole approach to life will improve. And if you happen to have other allergies, such as asthma, hay fever or eczema, overcoming fatigue will give you the energy you need to help manage those problems, too.

Because unexplained fatigue can have multiple causes, please read the accompanying box, A whole-body approach to fatigue.

See also *Anxiety*; *Depression*; *Hypoglycemia*; and *Migraine and other headaches*.

Gallbladder problems

You've probably never given your gallbladder a thought – unless it's given you trouble. A holding tank for the digestive fluid known as bile, the gallbladder is located just below the liver. And in certain people, it's subject to attacks of inflammation. Sometimes an attack causes nothing more than indigestion. More than likely, however, gallbladder attacks bring periods of pain and tenderness that are almost unimaginable to anyone who hasn't experienced them.

Mild or severe, gallbladder attacks tend to repeat themselves. If the inflammation doesn't quieten down, the gallbladder must be surgically removed, or else it will eventually rupture. If gallstones develop, surgery is almost a certainty.

Heavy meals and fatty foods receive most of the blame for those merciless attacks. But many frustrated gallbladder sufferers have found that while eating light meals and fat-free food helps a little, their gallbladder still kicks up on them.

Dr James C. Breneman, chairman of the Food Allergy Committee of the American College of Allergists, has found that in many people, gallbladder attacks are brought on or aggravated by food allergy. He kept track of a group of gallbladder patients, all of whom had had stones and some of whom had even had their gallbladders removed but still had pain.

The foods that caused those patients' gallbladder problems were, in order of frequency, egg, pork, onion, fowl, milk, coffee, orange, corn, beans and nuts – all common allergens. As long as those people didn't eat anything to which they were allergic, says Dr Breneman, they had no more pain.

Dr Breneman explains the role of food allergy in gallbladder disease by saying, 'The ingestion of the food allergen creates oedema [fluid retention] in the bile ducts, and the drainage of bile from the gallbladder is impaired. This inadequately drained area is prone to infections. These infected areas then form the [breeding place] for . . . stone formation. When the food allergen is removed from the diet, there is no oedema . . . so the patient is symptom-free.' (*Basics of Food Allergy*, Charles C. Thomas, 1978.)

Dr Breneman's treatment begins with one week of eating only what he considers to be 'low-allergy-risk' foods: beef, rye, soya, rice, cherries, peaches, apricots, beets, spinach and plain water. If allergy is the cause, symptoms should begin to disappear in three to five days on this 'elimination diet'. Then the individual starts to add other foods, one at a time, to test tolerance. Presumably, the gallbladder will let them know loud and clear if and when they eat something to which they are allergic. The list of common food allergens in Table 1 in Chapter 3 serves as a guide for testing possible food allergens.

Occasionally, an individual may be allergic to one of those first nine 'low allergy' foods mentioned by Dr Breneman, in which case a doctor-monitored five-day fast can help to sort out the offending foods.

Dr Breneman and a few other doctors recommend the elimination diet for gallbladder problems because skin tests for food allergy aren't reliable and blood tests are quite expensive.

One woman who followed Dr Breneman's approach found she was allergic to eggs, milk, yoghurt and cheese – foods that she'd been eating practically every day for years. But when she got rid of those foods, she got rid of her gallbladder problems, too.

'My diet *is* restricted,' she told us. 'But I'm willing to do anything if it means no more gallbladder attacks. They're just awful!'

Complete guidelines for testing for food allergies are given in Chapter 3, Finding your no-allergy diet.

Hay fever

Hay fever is like a cold without germs. When you breathe something you're allergic to, histamine and other allergy-producing chemicals are released and the membranes of your nose and respiratory tract immediately become inflamed, swollen and soggy. The results? A runny nose. Itchy, watery, puffy, tired eyes. Constant bouts of uncontrollable sneezing. Sometimes this discomfort can leave you so irritable, headachy and tired that you don't feel like doing much of anything. At night, sneezing fits interrupt your sleep. And you share your misery with about 3 million other Britons.

Hay fever (doctors call it allergic rhinitis) is more than a nuisance, however. Uncontrolled, it can lead to migraine headaches, sinus infection or hearing loss. You can't just let it take its course.

Antihistamine drugs alleviate hay fever – but they leave most people too groggy to think straight. In small children and older people, antihistamines have the opposite effect, leaving people restless and unable to sleep. And after a while, antihistamines lose their effectiveness – you need to take more and more to get the same level of relief. Nasal decongestants have similar drawbacks, as we discussed at length in Chapter 10, Allergy drugs and their alternatives. Clearly, drugs aren't the solution.

Vitamins, herbs and exercise can help

Vitamin C, however, acts as a *natural* antihistamine, counteracting the tide of histamine that causes your rose to swell, ache and run. According to doctors we spoke to, the average dose of vitamin C needed to break a bout of hay fever is about five grams a day – ranging from four to eight grams (individual doses), depending on the individual.

Bioflavonoids – compounds found in the white pulp of oranges, grapefruits and other fruits and vegetables – boost vitamin C's ability to relieve hay fever symptoms. Studies show that citrus bioflavonoids seem to favourably alter the way our bodies use vitamin C, concentrating the nutrient in certain tissues and making it more absorbable (*American Journal of Clinical Nutrition*, August 1979). Bioflavonoid tablets – up to six grams a day – are the most convenient way to get the amounts needed to break a reaction.

For those days – or nights – when your nose is so stuffy that you feel like it's been embalmed with rubber cement, there are several ways to get your head unstuck. One of them is pantothenic acid, a B vitamin. Sandra Stewart, former assistant director of the Out-Patient Department of Children's Hospital in Columbus, Ohio, decided to try it when she found she couldn't tolerate antihistamines.

'I took a 100 milligram tablet at night,' she says. 'And I found my nasal stuffiness would clear in less than fifteen minutes. I could breathe again. And I [no longer woke up] at four or five in the morning with a cough and mucus secretions. So pantothenic acid appears to have an antimucus-secreting effect on me personally.' And, she adds, many of her patients report that it helps to relieve their nasal congestion, too (*Annals of Allergy*, July 1982).

Hot broth also speeds up the flow of mucus, especially if the broth contains fiery foods or herbs such as onion, garlic, cayenne pepper or horseradish.

The vapours of eucalyptus leaves (available in many health food stores) also help to clear the head quickly. Place a few leaves in a large pot of boiling water for five minutes. Turn off the heat. With a towel draped over your head, breathe in the vapours. (Be careful not to get too close to the steam – you could scald your face.)

Exercise, too, promotes free breathing. Many hay fever sufferers find that running, walking, bicycling or other vigorous exercise relieves their stuffiness. Evening jaunts are best if you exercise outdoors – the pollen levels are lowest then. Pollen counts also tend to be lower after it rains and near lakes, ponds or other large bodies of water. Indoors, fifteen or twenty minutes of rope skipping or dancercise may do the trick.

Take a permanent holiday from hay fever

To a great extent, relief also depends on how well you can avoid airborne allergens. In fact, the first thing most allergy doctors usually tell their hay fever patients is: 'Avoid whatever bothers you.' But that advice is only useful if you're also told exactly *how* to avoid the problem.

You *can* install an air filter in your bedroom, however. Giving yourself eight solid hours of breathable air every night goes a long way towards round-the-clock relief. For some people, flicking on an air filter has been known to relieve hay fever misery in as little as ten minutes. (Brands and purchasing sources of doctor-recommended air filters are listed in the Appendix.)

Another way to 'filter' pollen is to rinse your hair and change your clothes and shoes the minute you come in from working or playing outdoors. This helps to shed pollen grains that would tend to stir up symptoms if allowed to stay on your clothes.

Reducing your exposure to other common hay fever triggers – such as dust and moulds – can be just as simple. For instance, switching from a conventional bag-type vacuum cleaner to a more efficient and thorough water-trap vacuum cleaner will help you to get *all* the dust out of a room. And hooking up a dehumidifier (the kind you can buy in any department store) in the basement or bathroom cuts down on growth of moulds and mildew.

The odours of aerosol air fresheners and other household cleaning products can also aggravate your hay fever. Substituting simple, less noxious cleaning agents for complex chemical products cuts down on indoor air pollution and can leave you breathing more freely after just a day or two. (A list of safe cleaners appears in Table 15 in Chapter 4.)

All in all, there are over seventy practical and effective ways to purify the air you breathe, discussed in Chapter 4, Clearing the air. You can follow as few or as many recommendations as you see fit, depending on what sets off your hay fever. Most people, however, notice a big improvement after making just a few of the basic changes we suggest.

One last suggestion: if you smoke, try to quit. Smoking irritates the respiratory tract and will only aggravate your already beleaguered nose and airways. In fact, Stuart Freyer, an ear-nose-and-throat specialist in Bennington, Vermont, told us, 'Smoking is madness for anyone who suffers from hay fever.'

You'll find other recommendations for dealing with hay fever in Chapter 4, Clearing the air; Chapter 10, Allergy drugs and their alternatives; and Chapter 11, Immunotherapy – a matter of choice.

Heart spasms

A 'skipped' heartbeat is scary. What makes irregular, fluttering heartbeats (or arrhythmias) *even more* frightening is that they are usually accompanied by shortness of breath, crushing or pounding chest pain and a general sense of disorientation. In short, you feel as though you're going to die. Fortunately, arrhythmias aren't usually fatal. But they are undeniable signals that something is wrong.

One cardiovascular surgeon has found that some heart irregularities may be triggered by overexposure to chemicals to which a person is highly allergic. Dr William J. Rea, a clinical associate professor at University of Texas Southwestern Medical School, describes twelve people who had no artery-clogging plaque (the main symptom of heart disease), but who suffered arrhythmias or chest pains (or both) when exposed to one or more chemicals commonly found in the home or workplace – natural gas, cigarette smoke, chlorine, perfume, floor cleaners, formaldehyde and pesticides. When placed in a setting free of all traces of chemical fumes, all heart symptoms cleared in ten out of the twelve individuals (*Annals of Allergy*, April 1978).

One particularly frightening type of arrhythmia is a heart spasm. It feels as though you're being hit in the chest with a two-by-four. In fact, some medical researchers now believe that spasms trigger some heart attacks, irrespective of any buildup of plaque in the coronary arteries. Dr Rea's research indicates that, in some individuals, heart spasms may be a response to allergens by the muscles around the heart's blood vessels. We spoke with a nurse in Dallas, a patient of Dr Rea's who experienced heart spasms as a direct result of exposure to inhalant allergens. Her story is a dramatic example of the effectiveness of his approach.

'One day I had some very sharp chest pains,' she told us. 'I got very lightheaded and dizzy. The doctor I work for sent me right over to the hospital, where tests showed I had a "malfunction of the heart of unknown cause", as the doctors put it. They gave me some nitroglycerin.

'Some months later, I was driving home from work when my heart raced and then seemed to stop. I passed out. When I came to, I had real sharp chest pains. I put two nitroglycerin under my tongue and drove home. My husband took me to the hospital and I was admitted to the coronary care unit.

'The EKG showed some changes, which they diagnosed as a heart attack. Then they did an arteriogram [a series of X-rays of the heart], which showed spasms in the heart's main blood vessel.

'However, they overlooked the fact that I was allergic to the iodine in the arteriogram dye, even though the information was on my chart. I guess the doctor who ordered the arteriogram didn't believe in allergy to medications. Anyway, he recommended heart surgery.'

But the nurse suspected that the iodine had something to do with the spasms during the arteriogram. At that point, Dr Rea was called in. 'The first thing Dr Rea said was, "Before we talk about surgery, let's talk about your allergies,"' she told us.

Tests showed that besides allergy to iodine, she was also allergic to pollen and other inhalants and to nine foods, as well as being highly sensitive to chemicals. As a nurse, she used various antiseptics and disinfectants in her daily work. No one had ever considered that fumes from the scrubbing solutions had anything to do with her heart spasms.

After a long and laborious process, Dr Rea formulated immunization injections for her allergies to pollen and other inhalants, and her reactions to chemicals such as scents and fragrances.

Dr Rea comments, 'When I first saw this woman, I thought she was having one continuous heart attack. But we've finally pulled her out of it. She's having fewer spasms, and she's much better now.'

In addition to receiving her injections, the woman has learned certain techniques to avoid the odours and fumes which give her trouble. In supermarkets, for instance, she bypasses the aisles with scented candles, laundry soaps and household cleaners – or she holds her breath as she quickly passes through those sections. She also carries a pocket-size negative ion generator with her, and is very careful to avoid foods to which she is allergic.

Although this case is highly unusual, Dr Rea feels that it fits in well with current medical understanding of the role of spasms in heart disease. He believes that in certain cases, coronary artery spasms are the blood vessel's reaction to not only foods and chemicals, but to anything in the environment to which the individual is highly sensitive. He also thinks that reducing exposure to allergens in such people – especially massive exposure to chemicals in the home, work-place or shopping areas – takes a huge burden off the heart and fosters rapid recovery.

'Susceptibilities gradually subside and the patient is able to return to functioning in the outside world,' says Dr Rea. 'However, a home oasis must always be preserved' (*Annals of Allergy*, April 1978).

(A 'home oasis' is a separate room that has been cleared of all possible sources of chemicals and other allergic offenders, sometimes with the help of an air filter. See Chapter 4, Clearing the air, for full details.)

High blood pressure (hypertension)

Blood pressure is affected by seventeen known variables. Smoking, over-weight, salt consumption, stress, use of oral contraceptives, exposure to lead and cadmium – these, among other factors, are all possible causes of hypertension. To that list we may eventually add allergy.

A few years ago, Dr Lloyd Rosenvold, of Hope, Idaho, noticed that some of his patients developed high blood pressure from allergy to certain foods. Another doctor, George Fricke, of Sacramento, California, studied a group of twelve hypertensive people – some with blood pressure as high as 210/140 – in whom elimination of allergic foods brought blood pressure down to normal. And in a study of food allergies and migraine, Dr Ellen Grant, a neurologist in London, discovered that when a group of fifteen hypertensive people avoided migraine-producing foods, their blood pressure also returned to normal (*Lancet*, 5 May 1979).

Surprising findings? Not really. High blood pressure is more than a simple matter of getting too much salt in the diet. After all, we all know someone who salts his or her food heavily and has normal blood pressure. Whether blood pressure rises or not seems to be a matter of individual sensitivity to many factors, some of which doctors haven't yet identified clearly. Allergy, it seems, is one of those factors, and its presence could help to explain why certain foods or habits raise blood pressure in some people but not others.

Hives

Hives – those ugly red or pale bumps that seem to pop up out of nowhere – are truly the scourge of any self-respecting skin. Science has even given hives a creepy-sounding name: urticaria. Actually, it's not the skin itself that's reacting to allergens, but tiny blood vessels *in* the skin, which release histamine and other substances that cause the skin to swell, burn and itch.

One out of five people has hives at one time or another, and an episode can last six weeks. Some people even get hives again and again. To top it off, hives are one of the most unpredictable of allergic reactions: one young woman we know is so susceptible that she broke out in hives just being *interviewed* about her allergies.

That brings us to the psychological side of hives – which has been quite overrated. While you are more apt to break out when you're worried or distraught, most people get hives in response to something they eat, breathe or touch.

Drugs such as penicillin and aspirin are the most common cause of allergic hives. If you're a victim of chronic hives, you should read Chapter 5, Don't overlook drugs as a cause. In 5 to 10 per cent of all people with hives, diet aggravates or triggers the problem. The most common causes of food-induced hives are nuts, fish, eggs, seafood, strawberries, yeast, salicylates (aspirin-related compounds in certain foods), azo dyes (such as E102, or tartrazine) and benzoic acid or other benzoates (common preservatives in fruit products and fruit drinks).

As a matter of fact, researchers have noted that nearly half of all people with chronic, hard-to-diagnose hives are allergic to aspirin and other salicylates, and, to a lesser degree, to tartrazine and benzoates. So if you're bothered by hives, it may be worthwhile to eliminate those substances from your diet and see if the problem subsides. A researcher in the Netherlands did just that with forty-seven of his patients, and the results were terrific. Sixty-seven per cent of the people with chronic, unexplained hives had a prompt and permanent cure. Even more surprisingly, half the people with heat-induced hives – usually a thorny problem – were cured. Going off the diet and eating one of the offending substances invariably triggered a rapid and immediate outbreak of hives – confirming the diagnosis (*Dermatology*, vol. 54, no. 5, 1977).

Two other common additives that are beginning to show up as causes of hives are BHA and BHT (butylated hydroxyanisole and butylated hydroxytoluene). In one instance, a thirty-two-year-old pediatrician suffered from hives for three years before allergy specialists finally isolated BHA and BHT as the cause (*Annals of Allergy*, February 1979).

Potato chips, breakfast cereals, canned pudding, doughnuts and pork sausages are just a few of the foods likely to contain BHA and BHT. Reading labels helps to avoid those and other additives, as does cutting down on processed foods.

Detailed instructions for completely eliminating any of the foods that cause hives are outlined in Chapter 3, Finding your no-allergy diet. (Incidentally, it's a little-known fact that benzoic acid occurs naturally in peas and bananas. If you're trying to avoid benzoates, avoid those two foods.)

As bad as hives are, people with hives are luckier than people with other allergic reactions – hives have a tendency to disappear for good. People with food-induced hives are often able to return to their regular diet after as little as six months of dietary control.

Infants who develop hives when new or solid foods are first introduced may later tolerate those foods if they are withdrawn and reintroduced after the child is twelve months old. By that time, their intestinal enzymes will have matured enough to break down food molecules so that they are no longer allergenic, says Dr John R. T. Reeves, of the University of California, San Francisco, School of Medicine.

People who get hives from the cold should also read the entry on allergy to cold temperatures in Chapter 8, Other unexpected allergies. And because hives tend to be aggravated by emotional distress, we suggest readers review Chapter 13, Mind over allergy, for tips on how to cope with stress.

Hyperactivity

Hyperactivity is the everyday term for what medical books refer to as 'attention deficit disorder with hyperactivity'. While there are over 100 possible symptoms of hyperactivity, children with the problem are generally restless, impulsive and agitated. Their attention spans are often so short that they turn from one task to another without completing any. They frequently swing from quiet withdrawal to sudden rage with little or no provocation. They run wild, throw things, whine and pick on siblings.

In short, a hyperactive child is the ultimate 'problem child'. Babysitters are scarce. Parents are at the end of their rope. At school, hyperactive children can't sit through class, so they're often labelled troublemakers. They do poorly at schoolwork – despite normal or even above-normal intelligence. Teachers give up.

Hyperactive kids themselves don't feel very good about their behaviour, either. They can't control their actions, no matter how much they want to. *And they do want to.*

Not every hyperactive child is the reincarnation of Attila the Hun, of course. Hyperactive behaviour varies from occasional outbursts to nonstop 'parent abuse'. And to some degree, hyperactivity may be in the eye of the beholder. What's hyperactive to Grandma may be simply normal spunkiness to a more patient adult.

How do you know, then, whether or not *your* child is active or *hyper*active? If your child's moodiness and tantrums interfere with schoolwork, alienate all of his or her playmates and disrupt the household, you may be living with a hyperactive. And it's time to do something about it, for your sake as well as the child's.

The best treatment

For years, the only known treatment for hyperactive behaviour was daily doses of Ritalin, an amphetaminelike drug that suppresses hyperactivity. Many parents, of course, were uneasy about putting their children on a drug. But short of calling in an exorcist, parents were given no other choice. Even then, Ritalin worked in only 50 per cent of the children for whom it was prescribed. And while behaviour improved, concentration and learning skills did not.

Ten years ago, real hope emerged. The late Dr Benjamin Feingold, an allergist and pediatrician in San Francisco, proposed that hyperactive behaviour is caused primarily by food additives. (He also suspected aspirin-related compounds known as salicylates, found in various fruits.) Placing a hyperactive child on a diet free of those additives and compounds, said Dr Feingold, produced a dramatic improvement in behaviour in 50 per cent of the children treated. Dr Feingold published his dietary theory and programme in two popular books, *Why Your Child Is Hyperactive* (Random House, 1975) and *The Feingold Cookbook for Hyperactive Children* (Random House, 1979).

Parents of hundreds of thousands of hyperactive children, eager for an alternative to Ritalin, put their children on the diet. And happily, many children improved. Yet in other children there was no change. Because the Feingold diet worked for some children – but not others – critics began to wonder if there was any real basis to the claims that the Feingold diet was a success. And many pediatricians flatly rejected the notion of any link between diet and hyperactivity. (Some still do.) Other pediatricians, however, believe that the Feingold diet sometimes fails because it doesn't consider *all* possible triggers. It's true that food colouring, flavouring and preservatives (such as BHA and BHT) can cause hyperactivity. But, say these doctors, so can sugar, milk, wheat – or any other food, for that matter. And they point out that hyperactive behaviour was first described in medical journals over 100 years ago – long before artificial additives became standard food ingredients.

These doctors have found that once the offending food or food ingredients are identified, diet therapy for hyperactivity works quite well – in almost all cases. One of those pediatricians is Dr William G. Crook, of Jackson, Tennessee.

'In my opinion,' says Dr Crook, 'too much of the controversy over diet and hyperactivity has revolved around the food colours, dyes and additives, rather than taking a broader look at the child's diet and considering the possibility that the hyperactivity may be related to adverse or allergic reactions to other common foods, including sugar, milk, corn, wheat, eggs, chocolate and citrus fruits.

'In my experience and in the experience of many other physicians who have placed their patients on properly designed and carefully executed elimination diets, most hyperactive allergic children will improve within five to seven days after being placed on such a diet. However, in approximately 20 per cent of my patients, the symptoms do not improve significantly until the offending food or foods are avoided for eight to fourteen days.

And occasionally, a three-week period of avoidance is required' (*Pediatrics*, August 1981.)

Whether your child responds sooner or later may depend on age. Over the years, Dr Feingold observed that younger children seemed to respond much sooner than older children and teenagers, probably because older children have been exposed to chemicals longer. Either way, parents who see their little hellions transformed into cherubic darlings in a matter of days feel their prayers have been answered at last.

Finding the cause of your child's hyperactivity

Naturally, it would be helpful if a test existed to identify the foods at fault in hyperactivity. But as we mentioned in earlier chapters, skin tests rarely detect food allergy accurately, and blood tests are very expensive. For those reasons, many pediatricians feel that elimination diets are still the best method.

Dr Doris J. Rapp, author of *Allergies and the Hyperactive Child* (Sovereign Books, 1979), has done some of the most extensive work on diet and hyperactivity. To find out if hyperactivity in a child is related to food, Dr Rapp recommends that parents put their child on 'a simple diet composed solely of fruit, vegetables and regular meats (no sausage, luncheon meats and the like) for one week, and then restore the questionable foods one each day during the second week (i.e., milk, wheat, eggs, sugar, dyes, corn and chocolate) and note the effect of each food (*Lancet*, 15 May 1982).

Incidentally, salicylate-containing foods (listed here in Table 25) may cause problems in children allergic to aspirin, a salicylate compound. But Dr Feingold told us that he had reconsidered the role of salicylates and thought that they weren't nearly as much of a problem as additives.

To help identify those children who are most likely to respond to a change of diet, Dr Rapp gives this thumbnail sketch of the child who most often experiences food-related hyperactivity: 'If they have dark eye circles, bright red ears and a glassy look when the Jekyll and Hyde behaviour develops, the answer may be a food.

'These children often have associated classical hay fever or asthma symptoms, headaches, abdominal complaints, leg aches and [other] behaviour problems.

TABLE 25

Foods Containing Natural Salicylates

Salicylate foods may be reintroduced to the diet following four to six weeks of avoidance, provided no history of aspirin allergy exists in the individual or his or her family.

Almonds	Cucumbers and pickles	Oranges
Apples, cider and cider vinegar	Currants	Peaches
	Gooseberries	Plums and prunes
Apricots	Grapes, raisins, wine and wine vinegar	Raspberries
Blackberries		Strawberries
Cherries	Mint	Tomatoes
Cloves	Nectarines	Oil of wintergreen

SOURCE: *Benjamin F. Feingold,* Why Your Child Is Hyperactive *(New York: Random House, 1975).*

'The symptoms are often triggered by the very foods they crave (sugar, peanut butter, orange juice, apple juice) or foods they detest' (*Lancet*, 15 May 1982).

The nicest thing about dietary control of hyperactivity, say doctors who use it, is that it's totally safe.

'In medical school we learn, or common sense tells us, that if a treatment will not harm and may help the patient, then it should be available to the patient and used,' says Dr Richard G. Wanderman, of Memphis, Tennessee in a letter written to a medical newspaper and supporting dietary therapy of hyperactivity. 'Is there anyone who will say that a good, nutritious diet without added chemicals, overly processed foods and poorly prepared foods will harm a patient?' (*Family Practice News*, June 1982.)

An added bonus is that even normal but active children behave better on a controlled diet. In a study of 300 elementary school children, researchers found that after two weeks on the Feingold diet, even non-hyperactive children were less easily distracted, could concentrate on work or play, and were less fidgety and demanding of attention (*Journal of Learning Disabilities*, March 1981).

The only real problem with a controlled diet is that some hyperactive children may begin to see themselves as sickly or somehow different from other children. Parents can minimize that problem by taking a positive attitude towards dietary changes and following these tips.

• Don't give a hyperactive child the impression that you find preparing special dishes to be a burden or nuisance. Instead, make 'safe' foods that the whole family can enjoy.

• Include the child in meal planning so he or she feels that his or her personal preferences count. That way, the diet will seem more like a game than punishment or therapy.

• Keep the child off cola drinks, tea, chocolate and other caffeine-containing foods. The last thing an overactive child needs is more stimulation.

• Read labels like a hawk. Be sure to watch out for unsafe ingredients in products such as toothpaste and chewing gum – or anything that goes into your child's mouth, for that matter.

• Routinely record your child's behaviour and diet, even if it is a simple matter of rating how good or bad the day's behaviour was on a scale of 1 to 10 (10 being excellent or uneventful, and 1 being the worst).

• In addition to eliminating the bad foods, increase the good. That will build up the child's resistance to colds, sore throats and ear infections. Your child will be sick less often and have a better self-image.

• Don't overreact to minor infractions. Kids can't be expected to have any more willpower than adults when it comes to sticking to a diet 100 per cent. Accept the fact that, once in a while, Johnny or Susie will sneak a soda or whatever. To help minimize these opportunities, though, keep plenty of safe foods in the cupboard and refrigerator – with enough variety available so that your child has lots to choose from. And be sure to send your child off to school with a favourite 'safe' snack or two tucked in his or her lunch box.

• Be on the alert for all forms of sugar, including corn syrup, honey, brown sugar and molasses. Doctors say that sugar in any form seems to fuel hyperactivity, no matter what else the child is allergic to. A pediatrician in Denver told us that he recommends diluting fruit juices with 50 per cent water, to help reduce a child's total sugar intake.

Set an example. Children are born mimics, and you're going to have a hard time getting a youngster to avoid sugar and additives if you routinely swig soda and snack on junk food.

(The accompanying box, Ten tips for coping with a hyperac-

TEN TIPS FOR COPING WITH A HYPERACTIVE CHILD

Barton Schmitt, a pediatrician at the University of Colorado Medical Center in Denver, gives parents of hyperactive children the following general advice:

1. *Accept your child's limitations.* Parents must accept the fact that their child is basically active and energetic – and possibly always will be. A parent should not expect to totally eliminate hyperactivity, but merely to keep it under reasonable control.

2. *Provide outlets for the child's excess energy.* Hyperactive children need daily outdoor activities such as running, sports or long walks. In bad weather, it helps to have a recreational room where the child can do what he or she wants without criticism.

3. *Keep the home environment organized.* Mealtimes, chores, bedtime and other household routines should be kept as consistent as possible to help the hyperactive child accept order.

4. *Don't allow hyperactive children to become fatigued.* When they're exhausted, the children's self-control breaks down and hyperactivity increases.

5. *Avoid taking children to formal gatherings.* Settings where hyperactivity would be extremely inappropriate and embarrassing – church, restaurants and so forth – should be avoided. Don't take the child to stores or supermarkets unless it's absolutely necessary. After a child shows adequate self-control at home, he or she can gradually be introduced to those situations.

tive child, gives additional advice on coping with hyperactive behaviour in the event the child does go off the diet.)

Adults can be hyperactive, too

Parents may find *themselves* a lot calmer after their child's been on a good diet for a few weeks. First of all, they have a less disruptive child to contend with. Second, they may have been a little hyperactive themselves and not realized it.

While most hyperactive behaviour appears in children, adults aren't immune. After all, we eat a lot of the same foods. (In fact, one of the very first people whom Dr Feingold noticed

6. *Maintain firm discipline.* Hyperactive children tolerate fewer rules than normal children. Set down a few clear, consistent, important rules, formed mainly to prevent harm to the children themselves or others. Parents should avoid constant negative comments such as 'Don't do this' and 'Stop that'.

7. *Enforce rules with non-physical punishment.* Striking or shaking the child should be avoided since they need to learn that aggression is unacceptable. Instead, send the disobedient hyperactive child to his or her bedroom or other 'time-out place' to settle down.

8. *Stretch the child's attention span and reinforce non-hyperactive behaviour.* Dr Schmitt suggests activities such as reading to the child, colouring pictures together and matching pictures, followed by games of increasing difficulty – building blocks, dominoes, card games and dice games. The child shouldn't be given too many toys – that can be distracting. And, of course, the toys should be unbreakable.

9. *Try not to reinforce the child's neighbourhood reputation as a 'bad kid'.* Refer to the child as 'a good boy (or girl) with a lot of energy'. Otherwise, problem behaviour becomes a self-fulfilling prophecy.

10. *From time to time, get away from it all.* Living with a hyperactive child 24 hours a day would make anyone a wreck. Periodic breaks help parents to tolerate hyperactive behaviour. Occasional evenings out or other time away from the child relieves pressure and helps parents to rejuvenate themselves.

SOURCE: *Adapted from 'Guidelines for Living with a Hyperactive Child,' by Barton Schmitt,* Pediatrics, *September 1977.*

reacting to food additives was a twenty-six-year-old woman.) The only difference between us adults and our children may be that we've learned to modulate our behaviour.

How can you tell if you've been a little hyperactive? Well, you probably couldn't concentrate on your work for more than five or ten minutes at a time. You didn't sleep well. You were easily irritated and always a little excited. In fact, a lot of the impatient, aggressive 'Type A' behaviour exhibited in people at high risk for heart disease and other stress-related disorders may be a reaction to foods to which they are allergic. So if you tend to be fidgety and impulsive, you should take a serious look at what you've been eating, too.

That's especially important for mothers of hyperactive children who are expecting another child. Dr Feingold told us that there's a good chance that exposure to hyperactivity-triggering foods during pregnancy plays a big role in determining whether or not the child will be hyperactive. And, as we explained in Chapter 3, Finding your no-allergy diet, breastfeeding is the best insurance you can take against food allergies of any kind.

Child or adult, however, a successful response to a change in diet reinforces good behaviour: once behaviour improves, and when an individual feels better about himself or herself, self-esteem goes up and hyperactive behaviour fades away into a bad memory. It's a real joy to see the face of a disruptive, moody child transformed into one that says, 'Colour me happy'.

We've presented specific steps for detecting and eliminating allergic foods in Chapter 3, Finding your no-allergy diet, which also includes many helpful tips for reading ingredient labels and shopping for additive-free food.

Because hyperactive behaviour often overlaps with learning problems, we suggest that you also read the entry on *Learning disorders*, which appears later in this section.

Indigestion, bloating and abdominal pain

Food allergies affect the digestive system more than any other part of the body because of the close and repeated contact of food with the stomach and intestines. Many people with food allergies suffer from sour stomach or abdominal aches and pains, especially if they're allergic to milk, eggs, wheat, corn, fruit or other frequently eaten foods. Aside from the annoying and disabling discomfort, digestive problems can be demoralizing – if your doctor doesn't know you're allergic, he or she is apt to think you're a hypochondriac. And you might start to believe it! (Incidentally, the word hypochondria comes from the Greek word for the upper abdomen.)

Indigestion is hard to define precisely. Basically, it's what happens when your food doesn't get proper treatment after it reaches the stomach. And that can cause various sorts of problems: heartburn, queasiness, or fullness and bloating.

Heartburn is simply a colourful way of describing a burning sensation (that sometimes feels like angina) underneath the sternum, the bone in the centre of the chest. Food allergy is often the cause.

A related problem is the sensation of having a lump in your throat after you eat. That is caused by a spasm in the oesophagus, and has been relieved by control of food allergy, says Dr Albert Rowe, Jr. who has treated people with food allergies for thirty years.

Abdominal bloating, or gassiness, is so characteristic of food allergy that many allergy doctors automatically suspect food intolerance in people who complain that they have to loosen their belts after meals.

Abdominal pain, on the other hand, is harder to analyse. It can be dull or sharp, and can spread over the whole trunk or focus on one spot – under the rib cage, behind the navel or in the lower abdomen. Food-induced abdominal discomfort can easily be confused with menstrual pain, stomach ulcers, diverticulosis or gallbladder disease. When other causes have been ruled out, investigation and treatment of food allergy can lead to complete relief.

Dr Rowe reports many cases of allergy-related abdominal pain. One man, for instance, had pain in the lower and middle-left abdomen every night around three or four a.m., which was relieved by avoiding foods to which he was allergic. A woman experienced pain across the upper and middle abdomen for six weeks until wheat was excluded from her diet.

If the allergy is severe, the slightest dietary infraction – often from an unsuspected source – can trigger an attack. One of Dr Rowe's patients who was allergic to eggs had a severe ache across the upper abdomen within one hour after eating candy that contained a trace of egg. The pain lasted eighteen hours.

'These abdominal symptoms are best explained by allergic inflammation and muscle spasms causing disturbances in the stomach, oesophagus and other digestive organs,' Dr Rowe points out as the co-author of the book, *Food Allergy* (Charles C. Thomas, 1972). 'Burning, bloating and belching, for which antacid tablets and liquids are used by thousands of people daily, can be controlled when the offending foods are eliminated – thus making those medications unnecessary.'

Complete guidelines for tracking down food allergies appear in Chapter 2, Are you allergic?, and Chapter 3, Finding your no-allergy diet.

Infertility

Doctors have found that some women cannot become pregnant because they are allergic to their husbands' sperm. A blood test can determine just how allergic the woman is. In some cases, if the husband uses a condom during sex for a few weeks, the allergy will subside. When unprotected sex is resumed, the woman can become pregnant. The researchers involved say that sperm allergy could be the cause of many cases of unexplained fertility.

For more on sperm allergy, see Chapter 8, Other unexpected allergies.

Insomnia

An occasional sleepless night is nothing to worry about. But nothing saps your energy like night after night of insomnia. If you frequently lie in bed for hours, unable to fall asleep – or wake up early and can't fall back to sleep – you're going to feel tired and frazzled. Short daytime naps to 'catch up' aren't always practical, and they can actually prolong the problem.

Asthma, hay fever or any other allergy-related discomforts can keep you awake, and controlling those problems will probably help you sleep better. But insomnia may also be a separate allergic reaction to a food or inhalant eaten or inhaled a few hours before bedtime. Anything to which you're allergic can give your brain unsolicited wake-up calls – or prevent you from nodding off in the first place.

If you've tried all the sleep-inducing tricks in the book and still find yourself wide awake at night – no matter how tired you are – it may be time for you to consider allergy as a cause. Chapters 2, 3 and 4 can help you identify possible allergic causes of your abnormal wakefulness.

Anyone with insomnia should also avoid coffee, tea, cola and cigarettes, which act as stimulants for most people, as well as alcohol, which disturbs sleep patterns.

See also *Anxiety*; *Depression*; *Fatigue* and *Hyperactivity*.

Irritability

Coping with an allergy can make anyone cranky. A stuffy nose or itchy skin can leave you tense and tired.

But irritability can also be a direct allergic reaction to foods, chemicals and other inhalants. Their effect on the nervous system can leave you restless, emotional, tense, sullen and tired despite having had enough sleep. Allergists call allergy-induced irritability the 'tension-fatigue syndrome'.

An irritable person may be described by others as argumentative, easily hurt, excitable, hard to please, highly-strung, hot tempered, jittery, jumpy, moody, nervous, over-sensitive or temperamental. If any of those labels apply to you, you may be allergic. An irritable, allergic child may be hostile, hyperactive and subject to fits of crying.

'Although the most frequent cause of this problem is a food, such as food colouring, sugar, milk, chocolate, eggs or corn, it is also possible that other common allergenic substances can be at fault (pollens, dust, moulds, perfume odours),' says Dr Doris J. Rapp, an allergist in Buffalo, New York.

Staying away from those allergens that spark tension can make life more pleasant for the allergic person – and everyone around him. For example, Dr Rapp tells of an eleven-year-old youngster named Sean who was irritable, clumsy, restless and hostile. Sean fought constantly with his family and schoolmates. Within one week of eating a diet free of common allergenic foods, Sean was much easier to get along with.

'As foods were re-added to his diet, it was found that . . . food colours and sugar caused irritability, hostility and violent behaviour,' says Dr Rapp. When Sean avoided those foods, he led a peaceful life. Several months later he tried to eat a normal diet. His teachers reported a dramatic return of irritable behaviour. Back on his allergy-free diet again, Sean calmed down and played happily with others.

Sean's story shows how rearranging one's diet to omit allergens can make a person less edgy and argumentative.

'The allergic tension-fatigue syndrome should be considered in *every* patient who for no obvious reason is subject to [hyperactivity], irritability, weakness or sluggishness,' says Frederic Speer, M.D., in his book *Allergy of the Nervous System* (Charles C. Thomas, 1970). 'This is especially true if other causes have been ruled out. Certainly no patient should be classified as [neurotic] until allergy has been considered.'

See also *Aggression*; *Anxiety*; *Depression*; *Fatigue* and *Hyperactivity*.

Itching

Allergic people tend to have itchy skin more than non-allergic people. But that's not too surprising; the skin is the largest organ in the body, so it's logical that it suffers a fair amount of allergic discomfort.

As with other allergic reactions, the chemical histamine is primarily at fault. Allergens prompt the release of histamine from skin cells; it irritates nearby nerve endings; they send a message to the brain that there's a problem; and the brain wires back the sensations that you feel – the discomfort, the compulsion to scratch, the *itch*.

Most allergic itching is caused by drugs, insect stings or bites, or contact with allergens such as makeup, poison ivy or nickel jewellery. It's not very often that food and inhalant allergies trigger a case of itching, although you can react to pollen that gets on your skin or from handling foods to which you're allergic.

Itching, of course, has many other causes besides allergens: rough clothing, dry skin, air conditioning or cold weather, and a number of diseases. Rule out these other possibilities before you investigate allergy.

If you're fairly certain that an allergen is the problem, you can soothe the itch by applying cool, wet compresses and avoiding the allergen. Chapter 5, Don't overlook drugs as a cause, Chapter 6, What to do about insect allergies and Chapter 7, Contact (skin) allergies, give specific advice for dealing with various causes of allergic itching.

When itching accompanies hives, eczema or hay fever, controlling those allergies will probably put an end to the itching. (See the entries on *Hay fever, Hives* and *Skin inflammation* (*atopic dermatitis and eczema*) in this section.)

If you pursue all those possibilities and *still* itch, consult Chapter 8, Other unexpected allergies. Your itching may be a one-in-a-million reaction to a substance that almost never acts as an allergen.

Kidney problems

Kidneys fail when the tiny capillaries that carry blood within the kidneys for purification become damaged (nephrosis). As the filtering process slows down, blood and proteins pass into the urine. Water backs up (a condition known as 'oedema'), and the body begins to swell.

Kidney damage affects children and young adults more than older people. Most often, it's caused by inflammation following an infection such as scarlet fever. But in a small number of people, kidney damage is tied to allergies, especially if the affected person has asthma, eczema or another form of allergy.

Douglas Sandberg, professor of pediatrics at the University of Miami School of Medicine, has encountered many children whose kidney problems were linked to allergies. These problems responded to restriction of certain foods or airborne allergens. In the book, *Food Allergies: New Perspectives* (Charles C. Thomas, 1980), he reports a number of cases.

• Out of one group of nineteen children with kidney disorders, seventeen were allergic to one or more foods. Eating those foods increased the amount of protein in their urine – a major feature of kidney malfunction. Several of the children improved significantly when their food allergies were treated.

'A Rotary Diet alone produced good results in two patients,' says Dr Sandberg. (Rotary Diets are described in Chapter 3, Finding your no-allergy diet.) In eleven other children, therapy also included allergy injections, which helped them to tolerate hidden foods such as milk, wheat and corn.

• Three children, ages thirteen to fifteen, were allergic to several foods. (All had asthma and one had eczema.) The kidneys of two of these children healed when milk was avoided.

The third continued to suffer relapses. Dr Sandberg speculates that she may have had an undetected viral infection or chemical allergy.

• A five-year-old boy had severe kidney inflammation, with abdominal pain and blood in his urine. To test him for allergies, he was put on a gluten-free Rotary Diet, with no one food eaten more often than once in four days. Individual foods were then tried. Tests showed the kidneys got worse when he ate milk, eggs and lima beans. Eventually, Dr Sandberg found that the boy was also allergic to a number of other foods and some chemicals, such as household cleaning solutions and insecticides, and that those allergens aggravated his kidney condition.

'With a management programme including a limited Rotary Diet, environmental control measures, and food and inhalant injection therapy, [his kidneys] became normal within six months and remain so,' says Dr Sandberg.

• A five-year-old girl was tested and found to be allergic to cow's milk. Blood, urine and kidney function tests showed that her kidneys got worse after she drank cow's milk and healed when it was avoided. Oedema, or water retention, also increased visibly when she drank milk and decreased when she didn't drink it.

'The patient was also . . . sensitive to other foods, as well as to some airborne allergens, and has improved on a limited diet and food and inhalant injection therapy,' says Dr Sandberg.

According to Dr Sandberg, those cases strongly suggest that food allergy is one of the many causes of kidney malfunction, and that inhalant allergies also play a role.

'It would appear that these patients have an unusual degree of sensitivity to environmental agents,' says Dr Sandberg. Allergy, he believes, may trigger a chain of events that produces different forms of kidney damage in different individuals.

Dr Sandberg's work follows in the wake of several studies by Japanese doctors who found that certain foods aggravated proteinuria (protein in the urine) in many people with kidney inflammation. In one group of thirty-six such people, foods that provoked protein loss, in order of frequency, were: milk, eggs, soya beans, pork, red beans and tuna. Invariably, a single feeding of a food was enough to provoke trouble – which disappeared when the offending food was avoided (*Clinical Ecology*, Charles C. Thomas, 1976).

Bedwetting, painful urination and a frequent urge to urinate have also been associated with food, chemical or pollen exposures, according to Doris J. Rapp, a pediatrician and allergist in Buffalo, New York.

Kidney problems are not the sort of thing you can diagnose yourself. If you have bloody or wine-coloured urine, with back pain, headaches, a rundown feeling and a slight fever, see your doctor immediately. And don't be afraid to raise the question of allergies. While certain forms of kidney trouble are associated with reactions to pollen, drugs, toxins or insect bites, reactions to foods have only recently been recognized.

See also *Bedwetting*.

Learning disorders

Children frequently complain, 'I'm allergic to school!' Parents smile at this whimsy; they know the 'allergy' for what it is. Yet, in a very real sense, children *can* be allergic to school. For if a child begins the school day with a breakfast of foods to which he or she is allergic . . . and then is exposed to airborne allergens such as classroom dust, the odour of floor wax and industrial cleaners . . . and then eats lunches and snacks laden with additives and colourings . . . well, schoolwork is bound to be affected.

The child may read below grade level, spell poorly and lag in maths skills. He or she may not understand verbal instructions. Handwriting could deteriorate to chicken-scratch. He or she may have trouble copying from the board. So he develops school phobia – headaches, stomachaches – anything to avoid the situation. All of which prevents an allergic child from realizing his full potential. Teachers are likely to say, 'He'd do better if he'd just try.'

Allan Lieberman, a South Carolina pediatrician, says, 'I'm totally convinced that a lot of learning disabilities are caused by kids' adverse reactions to multiple ecological factors – allergies – and if you reduce or neutralize their total allergic load by altering their diet and environment, most of them can be helped.'

A growing number of doctors like Dr Leiberman are finding

that non-reading and other learning problems are due to something in the diet or environment, not laziness or stubbornness.

'Allergies affect different areas of the brain in different children,' says Doris J. Rapp, a pediatrician and allergist in Buffalo, N.Y. 'For example, we've seen reading ability plummet from eighth- to fifth-grade level because of an allergic challenge. And in one particularly graphic study, we noticed handwriting changes. The children's writing became large, irregular, upside-down – there was letter reversal, even mirror-image writing.'

Learning disabilities can be caused by factors other than allergy, of course: visual or hearing problems; lead exposure; nervous system damage during birth or childhood illness; hereditary problems. But Jerome Vogel, medical director of the New York Institute for Child Development, says that over 75 per cent of the learning-disabled children seen at the Institute have allergies or food sensitivities that interfere with their behaviour and learning processes.

Besides affecting perception directly, allergies can interfere with children's learning ability by making them hyperactive. Overactive children are too busy to learn. They can't concentrate long enough to listen to the teacher's instructions, let alone carry them out. Or they simply can't sit still long enough to finish an assignment.

Since hyperactivity so often coexists with learning disabilities, the stock treatment for either is often a prescription for Ritalin, an amphetaminelike drug. But while Ritalin appears to lengthen attention span and enhance concentration in children, it does absolutely nothing for actual learning ability. What Ritalin does is turn the child into a robot: he may be able to do a few simple tasks over and over, but he can't respond to novel situations and learn new tasks. Such children soon develop a poor self-image and become convinced that they are, in fact, stupid.

Treating learning disabilities and/or hyperactivity with a drug-free therapy – mainly diet – is a better, safer way to remove the obstacles to learning. And certain foods turn out to be more common obstacles than others.

'Refined sugar leads the list of foods that such children cannot tolerate,' says Dr Vogel.

'We change a child's behaviour dramatically by lowering his or her intake of sugar,' says Patricia Hardman, director of the

Woodland Hall Academy, a school for children with hyperactivity and learning disabilities in Maitland, Florida.

'We had one child who was tested for his IQ and scored 140. Three days later, he was tested and scored 100! It turned out that Grandma had come for a visit and that morning had made the child pancakes for breakfast; of course they were smothered in store-bought, sugary syrup. Well, we waited another three days – three days without sugar – and tested him again. Sure enough, he scored 140. There's no doubt about it. Sugar makes children poor learners.

'If a child comes to school extremely depressed or complains that nothing is going right, or if he flies off the handle and can't be controlled, we ask him what he's been eating. It's almost always the case that the night before he had ice cream or soda or some other food with a lot of sugar.

'At Woodland Hall,' says Dr Hardman, 'sugar is eliminated from the diet of every child.'

Throwing out sugar often involves the elimination of many highly processed additive-laden foods – and with them go many of the most common causes of food allergy. Robert W. Boxer, an allergist in Skokie, Illinois, says, 'If every family physician and pediatrician put all of their patients with hyperactivity, learning disabilities or behavioural disorders on a sugar-free, white-flour-free, chemical-free and caffeine-free diet, I think 80 per cent of our problems would be improved.'

Of course, learning disabilities can show up as late as during secondary school or college years. But some parents notice the child is different at a very early age, even though teachers continue to pass the child along from grade to grade to avoid dealing with him or her two years in a row. But ignoring the problem only puts more distance between the child's achievements and potential. If your child is learning disabled and physical causes have been ruled out, you owe it to your child's future to consider allergies – of *any* kind.

For just as there's no *one* curriculum for each and every child, there's no *one* diet for learning improvements.

'When it comes to allergy-induced learning disabilities, we have to consider the entire world as potentially guilty,' says Gary Oberg, a pediatrician in Crystal Lake, Illinois. 'If you concentrate on only food, you may miss the boat.' (The guidelines in the accompanying box, Are your child's learning problems related to allergy?, will help you to determine if your child has allergy-related learning disabilities.)

Doctors find that when the allergens are identified and removed, the child performs better. He's calmer, pays attention longer, finishes his work, writes more clearly and is less impulsive. When he performs better, he receives praise – and self-esteem increases. That, in turn, motivates him to try harder. Allergy control gives learning ability quite an effective boost.

If your child is learning disabled, we suggest you also read the entry, *Hyperactivity*, as the two conditions often coexist.

Ménière's syndrome

The symptoms of the ear disorder called Ménière's syndrome (or Ménière's disease) are: ringing in the ears (tinnitus); extreme sensitivity to loud sounds; gradual loss of hearing; headaches; and vertigo (a spinning sensation), sometimes accompanied by nausea. Some attacks last only minutes, others continue for hours. Episodes of Ménière's can occur frequently or several weeks apart. Strangely enough, the syndrome affects mostly men between the ages of forty and sixty. In nine out of ten cases, only one ear is affected, and it can lead to total deafness in that ear.

Ménière's seems to result from fluid retention in the cochlea, the spiral-shaped organ in the inner ear that helps control hearing. Doctors don't know exactly what causes Ménière's syndrome, but, among many possibilities, allergy is one.

Ménière's resembles migraine headache in many ways, and seems to be triggered by some of the same foods. (See also *Migraine and other headaches.*) In other cases, Ménière's may be part of an allergic reaction to drugs, iodine, house dust or dog dander, according to the late Albert H. Rowe, and Albert Rowe, Jr (*Food Allergy*, Charles C. Thomas, 1972).

If allergy is in fact a contributing cause of Ménière's syndrome, it's important not only to avoid allergy triggers but also to cut down on salt and high-sodium foods. Sodium promotes water retention in all body tissues, including the inner ear, and aggravates Ménière's syndrome.

Along with allergy, other possible causes of Ménière's should

ARE YOUR CHILD'S LEARNING PROBLEMS RELATED TO ALLERGY?

This checklist was developed by the New York Institute for Child Development, based on observation of thousands of children over the past twelve years. If you answer yes to at least five of the following questions, your child may have an allergy that's interfering with the learning process.

1. **Is there any history of allergies in the family?**
2. **Is there any history of diabetes or hypoglycemia?**
3. **Was your child colicky as an infant?**
4. **Were feeding problems (such as frequent formula switching) encountered when your child was an infant?**
5. **Did your child have any difficulty when introduced to baby, junior or solid foods?**
6. **Does your child have a poor appetite?**
7. **Does your child crave sweets?**
8. **Is there any food your child craves?**
9. **Does your child eat fruits and vegetables infrequently?**
10. **Is your child unusually thirsty?**
11. **Is your child unusually sensitive to light, noise or touch?**
12. **Does your child have many colds, sore throats or ear infections?**
13. **Does your child complain frequently of headaches and dizziness?**
14. **Does your child have frequent stomachaches, constipation or diarrhoea?**
15. **Is your child a bedwetter?**
16. **Does your child have dark circles under his or her eyes?**
17. **Does your child have a pasty complexion?**
18. **Does your child suffer from eczema?**
19. **Does your child have a short attention span?**
20. **Is your child difficult to get along with?**
21. **Does your child cry easily for no reason?**
22. **Is your child depressed?**
23. **Is your child sleepy during the day?**
24. **Does your child lack energy?**
25. **Does your child feel faint if he or she eats later than usual?**

SOURCE: *The New York Institute for Child Development, Inc., 205 Lexington Avenue, New York, NY 10016.*

be investigated: viral or bacterial infection, sinus infection, hardening of the arteries or anaemia.

Readers with Ménière's syndrome may find it helpful to read the entries on *Dizzy spells* and *Tinnitus* in this section.

Menopause problems

Hormone changes can affect allergies – and vice versa. Sometimes hay fever or eczema or hives suddenly disappear when menstrual periods dwindle. Or, more rarely, allergies first appear at that time. Or unsuspected exposure to foods or airborne allergens aggravate the sweating and warm flushes that make menopause so trying for millions of women.

Menopausal sweating and flushing are routinely blamed on the drop in ovary activity that occurs naturally between age forty-five and fifty-three (give or take a few years). And for many women, that's the sole cause. But William H. Philpott, a psychiatrist from Oklahoma City, Oklahoma, feels that those symptoms won't disappear until any foods or chemicals to which the woman is allergic are avoided. Dr Philpott thinks that allergic reactions can suppress oestrogen production, particularly in menopausal women. In fact, Dr Philpott recommends that a doctor investigate and treat any allergies before prescribing oestrogen replacement.

Chapters 1 to 8 of this book can help you track down any allergies that may be aggravating menopausal symptoms. Chapters 9 to 14 can help you keep them under control.

Because depression and anxiety are often incorrectly dealt with as an expression of menopause rather than being treated in their own right, menopausal women may want to read the entries on those topics in this section.

Migraine and other headaches

One out of five people (most of them women) get migraine headaches. A single attack can last a few hours to a few days, and attacks can strike three times a year – or three times a week. All too often, nausea accompanies a migraine, earning it the nickname 'sick headache'.

If you're a person whose life has been bedevilled by migraine, you've probably been searching for a solution. And you may have suspected that a food or beverage is somehow responsible for those painful episodes. You could be on the right track.

The notion that a food in the stomach causes a pain in the head isn't new. Hippocrates, the Greek 'father of medicine', noted a connection between food and migraine. And modern research confirms his observation: a survey of 1,883 migraine sufferers in Great Britain found that *95 per cent* of the attacks suffered over a three-month period were caused by diet (*Headache*, October 1975).

Acting on this and other findings, the link between food allergy and migraine was investigated in a two-year study of thirty-three migraine sufferers by Jonathan Brostoff and co-researchers at the Department of Immunology, Middlesex Hospital Medical School in London. Both RAST tests and follow-up food tests strongly suggested that many of these people had food allergies. They were then treated with elimination diets and food rotation – and responded well.

'In the twenty-three patients who were sensitive to certain foods, elimination of those foods from the diet resulted in relief (complete in most cases) from migraine,' report the researchers. The most common migraine triggers in this study were milk, eggs, wheat, chocolate, oranges and tea.

'We have shown that food allergy is important in some [migraine sufferers],' conclude the authors. 'Patients were allergic to more than one food – usually three – and on elimination of these foods from the diet many patients became symptom-free for the first time in several years' (*Lancet*, 5 July 1980).

Ellen C. G. Grant, a neurologist at Charing Cross Hospital in London, also investigated the dietary factor in headaches in sixty migraine sufferers. The people studied had reactions to an average of ten foods each, the most common offenders being wheat, oranges, eggs, tea, coffee, chocolate, milk, beef, corn, cane sugar and yeast (much as in Dr Brostoff's study). When those foods were avoided, all the patients improved, with a dramatic drop in the number of headaches per month. Dr Grant speculates that the few patients who continued to have occasional migraines were sensitive to tobacco smoke, gas or other environmental factors (*Lancet*, 5 May 1979).

Yet another researcher, Dr Edda Hanington, of the City of

London Migraine Clinic, has noted that certain foods seem to have a distinct knack for triggering migraine. In addition to the foods noted by Drs Brostoff and Grant, Dr Hanington lists alcoholic beverages; fried, fatty food; onions; meat, especially pork; and seafood as prime offenders.

Many of those foods contain tyramines and other histamine-like substances. Some migraine researchers theorize that these substances cause the blood vessels in your head to swell, triggering a migraine. (Tyramines are also found in aged, fermented or pickled foods, such as strong cheese, red wine and pickled herring.)

Dr Hanington has also found that tartrazine (E102), a common additive in foods, beverages and medicines, can provoke migraine. So can sodium nitrite and monosodium glutamate, found in cured meats and some processed foods respectively.

Despite the work of Drs Brostoff, Grant, Hanington and others, the role of allergy in migraine remains controversial – there's some disagreement as to whether these reactions can be considered allergic in the strict sense. Regardless of the mechanism involved, however, food-induced migraine should be handled like any other food-induced reaction: by careful observation and avoidance.

To root out the cause of the migraine, Dr Hanington recommends you note everything you've eaten in the twenty-four hours prior to each attack. Or you can start by simply eliminating the most common migraine triggers.

'Without going to any extremes, every migraine sufferer should be aware of the foods which might possibly be involved. It is simple to have a trial period of, say, six weeks and exclude chocolate, cheese and alcohol, which are the most common precipitants, from the diet.

'Excluding citrus fruits and coffee may also be rewarding,' continues Dr Hanington. She adds that dietary trials are of particular value to people who suffer frequent, severe attacks but who have no inkling that the cause could be their daily cheese sandwich, chocolate bar or other customary food (*Journal of Human Nutrition*, vol. 34, no. 3, 1980).

Surprisingly enough, going *without* food can trigger migraine. In the survey of 1,883 migraine sufferers mentioned earlier, fasting for longer than five hours during the day or longer than thirteen hours overnight triggered migraine 67 per cent of the time (*Headache*, October 1975). Presumably, that's caused by the dip in blood sugar that some people experience when they go without food. (See the entry on *Blood-sugar problems (diabetes and hypoglycemia)*, earlier in this section, for more information on diet-related low blood sugar.)

Dr Donald J. Dalessio, of the Scripps Clinic and Research Foundation in La Jolla, California, offers the following guidelines for migraine sufferers.

1. No alcohol, particularly red wines and champagne.
2. No aged or strong cheese, particularly Cheddar cheese.
3. Avoid chicken livers, pickled herring, canned figs, broad beans and chocolate.
4. Use monosodium glutamate sparingly (if at all, we might add).
5. Avoid cured meats such as hot dogs, bacon, ham and salami (which all contain sodium nitrite).

In addition, Dr Dalessio warns against skipping meals or overconsumption of carbohydrates (sugar, fruit, pasta, desserts) at any single sitting, to control blood-sugar-related headache.

You may find it helpful to know that food-induced migraine tends to be dose related: some people can get away with a nibble or two of cheese, but not an entire cheese sandwich. Or they can eat one piece of chocolate, but not a handful. Or they can drink a glass of orange juice – *if* they skip their coffee or tea.

Coffee and tea, particularly in large amounts, seem to be especially bad for migraine sufferers. Researchers at the Royal Southern Hospital in Liverpool tell of a twenty-six-year-old man with a long history of migraine that did not respond to drugs. Neurological tests were normal. Yet the pain grew so severe and frequent that he had to quit his job. Further quizzing revealed that the man drank more than twenty cups of coffee a day. He was advised to give it up.

'His headaches and other symptoms promptly [disappeared],' say the researchers. 'He has remained symptomless for six months, and he has been able to set up business again' (*Lancet*, 25 February 1978).

While you may not be downing twenty cups of coffee a day, a cup or two in the morning, combined with cola drinks later on and an occasional headache tablet (many of which contain caffeine), could add up to enough caffeine to trigger a migraine.

If you can't attribute your pain to any particular food or beverage, you could be allergic to car exhaust, household cleaning fumes, tobacco smoke, perfume, paint, dust or mould. Investigating allergy to inhalants is more complicated than tracking down allergy to foods, but the guidelines in Chapter 4, Clearing the air, should help considerably.

In addition to allergy, it also appears that migraine is more likely to strike if you are under stress, having a menstrual period or taking birth control pills. Obviously a woman can't do anything about her menstrual cycle, but controlling other factors will help to ward off stubborn cases of migraine.

Non-migraine headaches may also be allergy related, in which case the approach we've described should work just as well. When a group of thirty headache patients at the Charing Cross Hospital in London were placed on a food-allergy-elimination diet, their total number of migraine attacks dropped from 187 a month to zero – and the number of regular headaches dropped from 284 to 14 (*Lancet*, 9 September 1978).

Muscle aches

Many different medical disorders can cause aching or swelling in your muscles, including bone problems, too much exercise without proper conditioning or too little exercise, says Dr William G. Crook, an allergist in Jackson, Tennessee. 'But still another cause of musculoskeletal discomfort is allergy.'

'Almost all patients with extensive food allergy complain of muscular aching,' says Frederic Speer, a professor of pediatrics at both the University of Kansas and the University of Missouri, and director of the Speer Allergy Clinic in Shawnee Mission, Kansas. 'The most commonly affected muscles are in the neck, upper back and [arms and legs].'

In fact, food allergy is a common but often overlooked explanation for 'growing pains' in children. An allergic youngster may complain that his legs ache even though his posture is good and he doesn't have flat feet,' says Dr Crook.

One of Dr Crook's patients was an eleven-year-old girl with sore neck and shoulder muscles, who also had frequent bouts of wry neck (muscle contractions along the portion of the spine that runs through the neck). Various doctors had incorrectly diagnosed her problem as everything from arthritis to rheumatic fever. Eventually, her muscle aches disappeared completely when she simply eliminated corn from her diet.

Allergy-related muscle aches can also accompany hay fever, eczema, headaches, stomach problems or other forms of allergy. You may not associate your soreness with allergy at all. Yet when allergies are brought under control, the muscle aches may disappear.

For instance, an allergy doctor reports the case of a thirty-four-year-old man who had muscular pain in his neck and shoulders for fifteen years. He also had other symptoms typical of allergy, such as post-nasal drip. Tests showed that he was allergic to several foods. After he stayed away from milk, wheat, fruit, artificial flavourings and condiments for two months, his pain went away completely.

Dust, pollen, chemicals or other airborne allergens can also cause muscle aches. If you always wake up achy in the morning, you could be allergic to mattress dust, in which case using a mattress cover and thoroughly vacuuming the mattress will help. If you feel achy after a night of partying, alcohol or cigarette smoke could be at fault. And if your muscle aches are at their worst during spring, summer and fall, pollen allergy could be to blame.

Such was the case reported by an allergy doctor of a twenty-five-year-old woman whose arms, shoulders, neck, upper back and chest were sore. She suffered all year, but ached more than ever in spring, summer and autumn. Skin tests showed that she was allergic to several grass and tree pollens. Allergy injections for pollen wiped out all her symptoms.

In people with generalized muscular aches, allergy control relieves not only muscle soreness – it relieves the worry that they're neurotic or hypochondriacs, imagining soreness that has no real cause. Relief gives them peace of body and peace of mind.

See also *Arthritis*; *Depression* and *Fatigue*.

Nasal polyps

Nasal polyps are smooth, greyish-white, gelatinelike bulbs that cling by thin stalks to the inside of the nose or sinuses. No one knows how polyps form. But they seem to crop up in people whose noses are continually congested from hay fever, especially people who suffer from a year-round allergy to dusts or other overpresent offenders. Frequent bouts with colds or the flu also tend to overactivate nasal tissues and cause polyps. So if you have uncontrolled hay fever *and* frequently get colds, you're more likely to get polyps.

'Every patient with nasal polyps should have a complete allergy study,' says Meyer B. Marks, chief of pediatric allergy at the University of Miami School of Medicine (*Annals of Allergy*, October 1982).

You can have large nasal polyps and not know it. You can't always see them yourself, even with a mirror. But you may have some clues. If your nose is continually congested and your sense of taste or smell isn't as sharp as usual, ask your doctor to check your nose for polyps.

If polyps grow so large that you can't breathe through your nose, your doctor will probably want to remove them surgically. But once you've had nasal polyps, they tend to grow back. To prevent that – or to prevent small polyps from getting larger – it's important that you keep your allergies under control. Using an air filter in your bedroom can clear up congestion and other breathing difficulties in just half an hour or so – and give you eight full hours of total relief. Vitamin C acts as a natural antihistamine clearing a clogged nose and sinuses. Regular exercise keeps nasal mucus flowing, so it can't back up and aggravate polyp-forming tissues.

Chapter 4, Clearing the air, gives details on how to effectively reduce your exposure to dusts, pollens, moulds, odours and the like. Chapter 10, Allergy drugs and their alternatives, explains the helpful role of vitamin C, exercise and other non-drug therapies for congestion. And Chapter 5, Don't overlook drugs as a cause, tells you how to avoid common but unsuspected sources of aspirin and aspirin-related additives.

See also *Asthma*; *Hay Fever* and *Sinusitis*.

Nausea

Nausea nearly always suggests food allergy. You may not vomit every time you feel nauseated – but you may feel like you're going to. And that can certainly make you less sociable and productive.

Consider the case of a thirty-two-year-old woman who had felt nauseated nearly every day of her life since childhood. The only way she could keep from vomiting in public was by taking large doses of antihistamines. Car travel was an ordeal – a two-hour trip required several pitstops.

'She became depressed, lethargic and lost her zest for life,' say the doctors who treated her. 'And her relationship with her fiancé was strained because she was becoming short-tempered and losing her sex drive because of her constant nausea.'

When the woman fainted after drinking a cup of tea, she was sent to a hospital for neurological tests. The doctors also decided to investigate the possibility of food allergies.

'On the basis of her dietary history, tea was excluded from her diet, and the vomiting and nausea ceased,' say Drs Ronald Finn and H. Newman Cohen. 'By avoiding tea she has been symptomless for five months, and is able to travel long distances by car without feeling sick'. (*Lancet*, 25 February 1978.) And oh, yes – she got married.

Most people have far less trouble than this woman did in figuring out that a particular food is making them sick. Nausea usually occurs shortly after you've eaten something that disagrees with you rather than hours later. So it's easy to notice a pattern. But if you occasionally feel nauseated for no apparent reason, you may need to keep a diet diary to trace your nausea to the offending food. Chapter 3, Finding your no-allergy diet, tells you how to keep a food diary, and outlines how to follow a safe diet after you've identified the problem food.

See also *Dizzy spells* and *Indigestion, bloating and abdominal pain*.

Overweight

If you exceed the 'ideal weight' charts by ten or twenty pounds, you really have no cause for concern as far as health goes. In fact, some studies show that people who are *under* their 'ideal weight' by that amount are at a greater risk for disease than their portly friends. But if you're *more* than twenty pounds overweight, you should probably trim down.

If you're like most people, however, you've already tried to lose weight – more than once. And most likely, you regained anything you lost. You know full well that overeating produces extra pounds, but you haven't been able to get perfect control over your food intake. Well, perhaps it's time to look at overweight and eating habits in a new way.

Think about the foods you crave, the foods that seem to go straight from your plate to your hips: cakes, pies, ice cream, chips, soda, sweets, cream, cheese and the like. They all contain either wheat, milk, eggs, corn (as corn syrup) or sugar – or some combination of those common food allergens.

'These food cravings can be due to an allergy to these foods and, once the offending foods are avoided, the craving can diminish along with the weight,' says Dr Doris J. Rapp, in her book, *Allergies and Your Family* (Sterling Publishing, 1981). In other words, food allergies can explain the compulsive eating behaviour that almost always leads to overweight.

'There is definitely a link between allergies and obesity,' says Thomas L. Stone, of Rolling Meadows, Illinois. 'When you eat certain foods – especially wheat – you get ravenously hungry and try to eat everything.'

These doctors say that an allergic person's weight loss efforts will fail unless the food allergen is identified and avoided – not merely eaten in smaller quantities.

'If you're allergic to wheat, which is a common allergen in overweight people, and you're accustomed to having the equivalent of two slices of bread and you cut down to half a slice a day, you're not going to be satisfied,' says Dr Theron Randolph, an allergist in Chicago, Illinois, 'So you'll eat more of something else to fill up.'

Another problem among people with allergies to foods is that they often experience dramatic ups and down in their weight because of water retention, and these fluctuations discourage their weight loss attempts.

'If you eat a food to which you are allergic, you can retain up to 4 per cent of your body weight,' says Dr. Stone. 'That means that if you weigh 150 pounds, you can gain 6 pounds as water within 24 hours. Food-allergy-related weight gain produces a certain puffiness.'

A Rotary Diet (in which foods are widely and carefully varied) can help people lose weight, even though the programme is not specifically designed as a weight loss diet. By breaking the cycle of eating allergenic foods every day, you will automatically eat less of those foods *and* reduce your allergy to them. It's a step *away* from compulsive eating. (Rotary Diets are described in full in Chapter 3, Finding your no-allergy diet.)

'You can abolish food cravings by taking an organized approach,' says Dr Randolph. 'I don't consider myself an "overweight expert", but I've seen this work in many people, some of whom have lost phenomenal amounts of weight.'

Phlebitis

Phlebitis is an inflammation of a vein or veins, usually in the legs, and it hurts like the dickens. In some cases, a tender, cordlike lump forms under the skin. When deeper veins are affected, a clot can form, blocking circulation and causing swelling and fluid retention. (At that point, the condition is known as thrombophlebitis.)

The pain and swelling make phlebitis very disabling. And the tendency to form clots makes it potentially life threatening – a clot that travels to the heart can cause a heart attack. Bed rest, anticoagulant drugs and sometimes surgery are standard medical treatment. Once the tendency towards phlebitis exists, however, the problem is apt to return. But for some people, a new approach may provide permanent relief.

A cardiovascular surgeon in Texas discovered that a number of his patients experienced total freedom from phlebitis when suspected allergies to environmental chemicals were diagnosed and controlled. William J. Rea, an associate professor at the University of Texas Southwestern Medical School, says the pain and swelling were so bad in these people that they couldn't even walk across a room. Anticoagulants and bed rest did no good. All were suspected of being allergic, and were divided into two groups of ten each. Those in the control group continued standard therapy, while those in the experimental group (all of whom were live-in patients in Dr Rea's allergen-free 'environmental unit' at the hospital) were tested for reactions to specific foods and chemicals. Tests revealed sensitivity to formaldehyde, phenol, chlorine, petroleum products and pesticides – all common household pollutants.

People in the experimental group were then told how to cut down their exposure to those items by making certain changes in their homes and, once their phlebitis cleared up, were sent home.

The chemical cleanup worked. Among all the people treated for chemical sensitivity, there were only two episodes of phlebitis over the next five years. In fact, not only could they all walk painlessly, but some of them could bicycle up to six miles at a clip!

In contrast, the people not treated for allergy suffered a total of 101 episodes of phlebitis and clotting, forty of which landed them back in the hospital.

Dr Rea credits the home oasis for continued relief in the treated group.

'In spite of being constantly exposed to higher pollution . . . on the job and . . . in society, it was clear that if the patients would have at least ten hours in their less-polluted oasis at home they could remain phlebitis free,' he says. 'The patients in the control group continued to be miserable and did not function well. They developed a chronically ill attitude . . . looked on life as hopeless . . . and lay around their homes and did little constructive work.'

Dr Rea is convinced that phlebitis is environmentally induced (or aggravated) in some individuals, and he speculates that irritation of blood vessels and clot formation are just two more possible manifestations of chemical sensitivity (*Annals of Allergy*, November 1981).

When that same mechanism affects the small capillaries, people may bruise easily or spontaneously. (See *Bruises*.) When the coronary arteries are affected, heart spasms may result. (See *Heart spasms*.)

Phlebitis is one problem you can't take chances with. To locate an environmentally oriented physician in your area, write to the Society for Clinical Ecology at the address given in the Appendix. Quite possibly, a doctor will recommend that you reduce exposure to chemicals in your home, in which case some useful tips appear in Chapter 4, Clearing the air.

Post-nasal drip

Do you clear your throat constantly? Think carefully. You may not even be aware that you're doing it. Throat clearing is an involuntary attempt to clear away mucus that's dripping down into your throat from the inside of your nose. Nasal or sinus congestion is the usual problem; when mucus can't flow freely out the front, it's forced to detour.

Post-nasal drip is often caused by allergies. But it can also be provoked by related irritants – such as cold weather, spicy food, odours, fumes, cigarette smoke and even anxiety and other strong emotional reactions.

Aside from steering clear of those triggers when you can, you can also exercise to clear up post-nasal drip. By stimulating mucus flow in the nose, exercise unclogs the congestion that forces secretions to trickle down the throat.

Schizophrenia

A schizophrenic doesn't have a split personality – he or she has no personality at all. Schizophrenics usually think and perceive things unrealistically. They have little social life and few outside interests. Quite often, they feel that someone or something is directing their actions. The closest a schizophrenic comes to having a 'split' personality is that he or she tends to act unpredictably, doing odd things for no rational reason.

A touch of schizophrenia may produce a great artist like Vincent van Gogh. Fully-fledged schizophrenia, on the other hand, can produce a deranged killer like Son of Sam. (Both van Gogh and David Berkowitz are considered to have been schizophrenic.) But most schizophrenics are more likely to be unexceptional people who act according to a bizarre set of rules they make up (and break) as they go along.

Psychiatrists say that schizophrenia is the most common type of psychosis. But few schizophrenics ever recover from the disorder. Drugs can help the individual to think rationally, but they produce serious side effects when used for months or years.

Schizophrenia is like cancer in that there are not only various kinds of the disease but various causes, most of which are not clearly understood. Besides genetic and psychological factors, some experts have tied schizophrenia to viruses, toxins in the air and water, and nutritional deficiencies. And one school of thought holds that allergies to foods or inhalants may be responsible in some cases.

A wheat-schizophrenia link was first suspected as a result of studies done by Dr F. C. Dohan, in Philadelphia. Dr Dohan found that when schizophrenics who had coeliac disease (an inability to absorb the gluten protein in wheat and other cereal grains) ate a gluten-free diet, their schizophrenia began to subside. They got much worse when they once again ate wheat or other gluten-containing cereals [rye, oats, rice or barley] (*American Journal of Psychiatry*, May 1979).

Later studies, by Man Singh, of Memphis, Tennessee, showed that schizophrenics improved when placed on a diet free of both wheat and milk (*Science*, January 1976). Considering that milk frequently aggravates coeliac disease, that discovery meshes well with the gluten-intolerance observation.

James R. Rice and associates report a schizophrenic who had been hospitalized for more than thirteen years, but who improved substantially on an eight-week gluten-free and milk-free diet, after which she was discharged. Another woman, hospitalized with schizophrenia for fourteen years, improved considerably on a gluten-free and milk-free diet, and lapsed back into schizophrenia when she once again ate gluten (*American Journal of Psychiatry*, November 1978).

Most recently, A. Arthur Sugerman, of Belle Mead, New Jersey, found that 80 per cent of the schizophrenics he tested were allergic to eggs (*Annals of Allergy*, March 1982).

Drinking too much caffeine, it seems, can accentuate schizophrenic behaviour. One woman, diagnosed as schizophrenic, noted that she felt very strange and paranoid if she drank more than four or five cups of coffee a day. The effect was so dramatic that she decided to do without coffee altogether, and felt much better (*Journal of Clinical Psychiatry*, September 1978).

Airborne allergens can add to the problem. William Philpott, a psychiatrist who's probably done more research on the link between allergy and emotional illness than anyone else, tells of several individuals whose schizophrenia was aggravated by fumes of natural gas, cigarette smoke, car exhaust or other pollutants.

'Approximately one-third of my patients react to various chemicals common to our environment,' says Dr Philpott. Reducing their exposure to chemicals alleviates their schizophrenia, reports Dr Philpott (*Brain Allergies: The Psycho-Nutrient Connection*, Keats Publishing, 1980).

Nearly all of us eat wheat or eggs or drink milk, though. Most adults drink coffee or other caffeine-containing beverages. And we all breathe fumes and odours. Yet few of us are schizophrenic. Evidently, those items have a disorienting effect on certain people predisposed to schizophrenia – possibly in the form of allergic reactions. You might think of allergy-induced schizophrenia as 'hives of the brain'.

Chapter 3, 'Finding your no-allergy diet', gives very detailed guidelines for avoiding wheat, milk, eggs, caffeine and other foods. Chapter 4, Clearing the air, offers similar guidelines for dealing with airborne allergens.

See also *Alcoholism*; *Anxiety* and *Depression*.

Sinusitis

Sinus trouble is one of the most common complaints treated by allergists. The basic problem is swollen, inflamed mucous membranes in the sinuses – eight hollow cavities behind your nose, cheeks and forehead. The swelling blocks the sinus openings that lead to the nose. Trapped mucus then presses against the sinus walls, so that your entire upper face and forehead feel painful and tender. And your nose is stopped up. But if you blow your nose too hard, the pressure forces mucus in the sinuses even harder against the sinus walls, inflaming the area all the more.

In allergic people, sinusitis usually affects those with chronic hay fever. It can also be caused by an infection like the type that accompanies a cold.

The first thing to do for allergic sinusitis is drain the sinuses. Applying a warm flannel to the face thins mucus and coaxes secretions out of sinus cavities. (Run the flannel under hot water to warm it, but be careful that the flannel doesn't get too hot, or you'll burn your face.) You can also breathe warm mist from a kettle of boiling water. (Don't get too close to the steam or you'll scald yourself.) Or you can drink a mug or two of steaming herb tea. Herbalists say that fenugreek is good for breaking up mucus.

Using nasal decongestant sprays or drops is not a good idea. They help reduce the swelling temporarily, but your sinuses will flare up worse than ever when you discontinue the drug. Oral decongestants aren't ideal, either – they tend to make you jumpy and irritable. Instead of drugs, try vitamin C. It acts as a natural antihistamine, shrinking swollen sinuses and reducing the hay fever reaction. (See Chapter 10, Allergy drugs and their alternatives, for more information on drug-free remedies for allergy problems.)

For complete relief of allergy-induced sinusitis, use the methods outlined in this book to avoid whatever triggers your hay fever. Doing that will prevent not only sinus pain but also permanent damage to sinuses – and uncontrolled sinusitis can lead to post-nasal drip, in which excess mucus from sinuses drips down your throat. If you don't take good care of your sinuses now, they'll bother you nonstop later on.

See also *Hay fever* and *Nasal polyps*.

Skin inflammation (atopic dermatitis and eczema)

Allergic dermatitis (skin inflammation) is one of the most common skin diseases that doctors deal with. Symptoms can include dryness, itching, redness, crustiness, blisters, watery discharges, cracking and other changes in the normal condition of the skin.

Contact dermatitis (a reaction to something touched) and irritation are the most common types of skin inflammation. Much less frequently, an individual's skin will break out after he or she has eaten something to which he or she is allergic. In that case, the skin problem is usually called 'eczema'. People with allergic dermatitis or eczema simply have hyper-reactive skin, much as people with asthma have hyper-reactive airways.

Exactly how many people have allergic skin problems is unknown because sometimes reactions are so mild that the individuals never seek medical help. But estimates say that somewhere between 1 and 3 per cent of children under age two suffer some degree of dermatitis or eczema. It's less common in adults, but by no means rare. Young or old, the affected person usually comes from a family with a strong history of allergy, or they themselves have hay fever, asthma or some other form of allergy.

To relieve discomfort and speed healing, there are over a dozen natural remedies for skin reactions, from soothing corn-starch baths to applications of zinc oxide paste (available at chemists), all of which are discussed in Chapter 7, Contact (skin) allergies. But avoiding the allergens is of utmost importance; and not only for the sake of comfort and appearance. Chronic dermatitis and eczema can cause the skin to become permanently discoloured and thickened and scratching can lead to infection and scarring.

The most common offenders in contact dermatitis include rubber and plastics, industrial chemicals, applied medications, cosmetics, clothing dyes, costume jewellery, poison ivy and other plants, detergents, insecticides and paints. Chapter 7 also goes into considerable detail to help you figure out which of those items may be the culprit (or culprits) in your case. Many helpful tips are included to help you avoid the troublemakers.

People with skin allergy need to be especially wary of topical medications, prescription or over-the-counter. In a European study of 4,000 people with skin problems, doctors discovered that one-third of all allergic contact dermatitis was caused by applied medications. Benzocaine and neomycin were the most common offenders (*Archives of Dermatology*). Table 17 in Chapter 5 gives a more extensive list of ingredients to watch out for.

Few sights are more heartbreaking than that of a baby or toddler with a stubborn skin rash. Yet in many cases, you can quickly trace the cause to soaps or lotions applied to the youngster's skin. Baby lotions often contain fragrance, lanolin and mineral oil, three of the most common causes of skin allergy.

'If a child comes in with a rash and he's being rubbed with a lotion, the cure is often as simple as substituting plain vegetable oil – sunflower, safflower or peanut – for the commercial lotion,' says Del Stigler, a pediatric allergist in Denver, Colorado. 'Even for nappy rash, I use vegetable shortening instead of medication.

'In fact,' adds Dr Stigler, 'I rarely have to prescribe a medication.'

Of course, skin can react from the inside out. Certain foods – and milk in particular – are apt to cause allergic skin reactions.

'If you have a child who has eczema, very often even a few teaspoons of milk will cause a reaction,' says Dr Stigler. 'In other children, it's dose related: they may have to drink a pint in order to react.'

To sort out and treat dietary causes of eczema, many allergists favour elimination diets over skin testing or immunotherapy. For one thing, skin tests for food are often incorrect, indicating allergy when none is present (or vice versa), even when testing is done by a highly proficient allergist or immunologist. And immunotherapy is generally ineffective against dermatitis of any kind. So your best bet is to follow the instructions for an elimination diet and food rotation, described in detail in Chapter 3, Finding your no-allergy diet.

Such methods work. In one study, twenty-one infants with allergic dermatitis were put on a strict elimination diet of soya milk, potatoes, rice, buckwheat and other hypoallergenic foods. After two to four weeks on the diet, the dermatitis healed in 33 per cent of the children and improved in another 57 per cent. When cow's milk was tested, reddening, itching and discomfort returned in 65 per cent of the children, virtually proving that milk contributed to the skin rash. Other foods that triggered dermatitis in the infants were fruit, wheat, egg and fish – all common allergens. Blood tests confirmed the diagnosis. The authors conclude by saying that the elimination diet is very useful in controlling dermatitis – and the earlier it's used, the better (*Annals of Allergy*, May 1979).

In a similar study, conducted by David J. Atherton, of the Hospital for Sick Children in London, thirty-six children were put on a soya-based diet that excluded cow's milk, eggs, beef and chicken (related food allergens) for four weeks. For the following four weeks, they ate their usual diet. For the last four weeks, they ate a control diet that included cow's milk and eggs, disguised as milk substitutes. About two-thirds of the children who completed the study improved significantly when they avoided milk, eggs, beef and chicken. Three of the children were completely cleared of eczema. The children who did not totally improve may have been allergic to still other foods, says Dr Atherton (*Lancet*, 25 February 1978).

If staying away from cow's milk and eggs doesn't help, Dr Atherton suggests a testing routine similar to the elimination diets described earlier, in Chapter 3, Finding your no-allergy diet. 'At the end of several months,' says Dr Atherton, 'each patient should have identified a list of foods to which allergy is suspected'. (*Acta Dermatovener*, suppl. 92, 1980.)

Once you have identified foods that are safe for you, be sure to eat them no more frequently than once every four days, to reduce the chances that you'll develop new food allergies. Instructions for rotating foods, along with a week's sample menu, also appear in Chapter 3.

Contact allergy and food allergy are sometimes related. Doctors at the Hitchcock Clinic in Hanover, New Hampshire, discovered five people who were extremely sensitive to *Rhus* plants – poison ivy, oak and sumac – who also reacted to raw cashew nuts. Cashews, it seems, are related to *Rhus* plants and can cause generalized skin reactions when the nuts are eaten in large quantities (*Archives of Dermatology*, December 1974).

That just goes to show that if you have skin allergy, the more you know about the condition, the better your chances of finding relief.

Since worry and stress leave you more vulnerable to an allergic outbreak, doctors generally agree that attention to the emotional aspects of skin allergy also has a bearing on relief. In other words, if you can learn to deal calmly and rationally with your allergy, you stand a better chance of enjoying clear skin. Information in Chapter 13, Mind over allergy, will help you to stay in control of the situation.

Tinnitus

Do your ears ring? Or hiss? Or roar like the ocean? Or crackle like Rice Krispies?

These are the sounds of the ear problem, tinnitus. And they're not just background noise. You can't hear every word that's spoken or enjoy radio or TV programmes without straining. In some ways, tinnitus is even worse than deafness – at least the deaf can concentrate on what they're reading and sleep without being woken up by the noises in their own head.

People with tinnitus complain of noise in one or both ears, or a different sound in each ear. In either case, the noise can become louder or softer at different times of the day. And the louder the tinnitus, the more tense and irritable you become.

Infection or injury are common causes of the problem. But it can also be a symptom of Ménière's syndrome, a hearing disorder caused by fluid retention in the ear, which in turn can be caused by allergies. And tinnitus can be a direct result of allergy-triggered inflammation of tiny blood vessels inside the ear.

As with other ear problems, allergy should be considered as a possible cause of tinnitus if:

– you have allergies of the nose, sinuses or respiratory tract (hay fever, asthma, sinusitis, nasal polyps);
– your symptoms are linked to specific foods or inhalants; or
– skin or blood tests indicate you have allergies.

Sometimes the signs of ear allergy are very subtle. One man suffered ringing in the ears and increasing deafness for eight years. The only clues to allergy were post-nasal drip and a strong dislike for milk. His doctor put him on a standard elimination diet, omitting the most common food allergens such as milk, wheat, eggs and fruit. Within two weeks, the ringing and deafness decreased; in one month noise disappeared completely and the man could hear well once again. Relief continued for two months on the diet. Individual foods were then gradually added to his diet to test for allergic symptoms. Tinnitus and loss of hearing returned only when the man drank milk or ate wheat or eggs. By avoiding those foods, his tinnitus disappeared permanently.

(Elimination diets are described in detail in Chapter 3, Finding your no-allergy diet.)

As a preventive measure, anyone who works in a noisy area should wear ear plugs or ear protectors to avoid ear damage, which can also cause tinnitus. Tinnitus can also be aggravated by too much salt in the diet, overuse of aspirin, drinking alcohol or smoking cigarettes.

See also *Deafness*; *Ear inflammation and hearing loss* and *Ménière's syndrome.*

Ulcers

Ulcers are basically white, craterlike holes that form in the glossy pink lining of the stomach or duodenum (the upper part of the small intestine, just below the stomach).

Duodenal ulcers are more common than stomach ulcers, although both can occur in the same person. Typical symptoms of ulcers are gnawing pain, 'coffee ground' vomit, black stools and weakness.

A bland diet, free of coffee, chocolate, fruit and spices, plus hourly feeding of milk and cream, was once the standard treatment for ulcers. That seemed to heal ulcers at first. But in most people, the ulcers eventually returned. Because dietary treatment failed so often, drugs and antacids are now the mainstay of ulcer therapy. But hourly milk is still prescribed for the immediate and acute stage of ulcer attacks, especially if there is bleeding.

Could milk be the *cause* of many ulcers?

Some doctors think so. Dr James C. Breneman, now chairman of the Food Allergy Committee of the American College of Allergists, first noticed a connection between ulcers and milk allergy several years ago. He was treating a man with a ten-year-old duodenal ulcer. On a hunch, Dr Breneman put the man on a typical food-allergy elimination diet – devoid of milk, wheat, eggs and other common food allergens.

'Within three days his symptoms disappeared,' says Dr Breneman. 'They did not reappear until milk was added as a test food, whereupon he was seized by abdominal pain, vomiting and weakness. After the milk was again removed, his symptoms subsided.'

The agony returned with wheat and pork, and disappeared when they were avoided.

Sixteen years later, the man was still free of all ulcer symptoms. That, says Dr Breneman, virtually proves that he was cured and not merely lapsing into one of the symptom-free periods that are typical of ulcers whether they're treated or not.

Anyone who has an ulcer and is allergic to milk will continue to suffer as long as he or she continues to drink milk, asserts Dr Breneman in his book *Basics of Food Allergy* (Charles C. Thomas, 1978).

When a bland diet does work, it's probably because people stay away from some of the foods that so frequently cause allergy: chocolate, coffee, condiments and fruit. Since those foods also tend to cause mouth ulcers, Dr Albert Rowe, Jr, co-author of the book *Food Allergy* (Charles C. Thomas, 1972), treats stomach and duodenal ulcers much as he treats mouth ulcers: by eliminating those troublesome foods, plus other common food allergens such as wheat and eggs.

But even with an allergy-control diet, an ulcer cannot be expected to heal overnight, says Dr Rowe.

'Since it usually takes two or more weeks for foods to leave the body, and a longer time for tissue changes from chronic food allergy to decrease, strict adherence to the diet is required until relief has continued for one to two months,' says Dr Rowe. 'After that, individual foods are gradually added.'

Complete instructions for diets that eliminate milk, wheat, eggs and other allergenic foods are given in Chapter 3, Finding your no-allergy diet.

As for antacids, Dr Rowe says that people find they need less as relief from food allergy occurs. 'If antacids *are* used, the unflavoured tablets and fluids should be used,' says Dr Rowe.

People with ulcers should also avoid aspirin and aspirin-containing drugs. Aspirin corrodes the stomach lining and aggravates duodenal ulcers. And since smokers are twice as likely to develop ulcers as non-smokers, avoiding cigarettes, cigars and pipes is also wise.

See also *Indigestion, bloating and abdominal pain.*

Vaginitis

The maddening itch of vaginal inflammation may be caused by three different microscopic organisms. One is the yeastlike fungus *Candida*. As you might guess, *Candida* is biologically related to moulds in cheese; yeasts in beer, wine, vinegar and bread; yeast-based B vitamins; and mushrooms.

Most of the time, *Candida* lives compatibly in the intestines and vagina along with other microorganisms that keep *Candida* in check. Under certain circumstances, though, *Candida* can overrun its fellow organisms, causing infection and inflammation (candidiasis). The vagina is especially prone to *Candida* infections for a number of reasons. Mainly, the fungus thrives in the warm, moist climate of the vagina. And *Candida* from the intestinal tract can easily find their way to the vagina from the nearby rectum, multiplying the chances for infection.

Candida infections are a special problem for people with allergies to yeasts and moulds. Their bodies react to an overgrowth of *Candida* as they would to any other yeast or mould. Nystatin and other anti-fungal medicines – in tablets or suppositories – can help kill off the fungus. But in allergic people, the itching and inflammation may not go away until all forms of fungus, dietary and internal, are kept under control.

One tactic is to adopt a low-mould diet, says a gynaecologist we spoke to from Sulphur Springs, Arkansas. 'Eating moulds or yeasts overloads the system, and the infection flares up.' (See Table 6 in Chapter 3, Finding your no-allergy diet, for lists of foods you can and cannot eat to avoid dietary sources of moulds and yeasts.)

The low-mould diet is most effective when combined with yoghurt therapy. Yoghurt contains *Lactobacillus acidophilus*, a special bacteria that suppresses *Candida*.

'*Candida* vaginitis can be controlled by applying yoghurt [live cultures] to the vagina,' we were told. 'Eating yoghurt, too, helps by controlling *Candida* growth in the intestines.'

Chemical irritants aggravate vaginitis of any kind. Women plagued by vaginal inflammation should avoid using deodorant soaps, perfumed sprays, bubble baths and coloured or perfumed toilet paper in the vaginal area. See Chapter 8, Other unexpected allergies, for more information on vaginal problems caused by allergy to condoms, spermicides and feminine hygiene sprays.

Vertigo

Vertigo is not quite the same as dizziness. With vertigo, you feel as though your head or the room is spinning; when you're dizzy, you feel unsteady, but with no spinning sensation. (You can, however, have vertigo and dizziness at the same time.) Vertigo is sometimes also accompanied by blockage in the ear, buzzing noises, nausea and vomiting.

A disease of the cochlea, the hearing mechanism in the middle ear, can cause vertigo. So can a disturbance in the balance-regulating portion of the ear known as the vestibular system. Nerve damage in the inner ear is another possible cause. But there's another cause that doctors rarely consider. Allergy.

'Vertigo can affect children or adults who have an inner ear allergy which affects their sense of balance,' says Dr Doris J. Rapp, in her book *Allergies and Your Family* (Sterling Publishing, 1981). This type of allergy can be triggered by foods, drugs, chemicals or particles like dust, pollen and moulds.

Albert Rowe, Jr, an allergist in San Francisco, tells of a sixty-year-old woman who had disturbing attacks of vertigo for twenty years, along with episodes of colitis. An elimination diet designed to control her food allergies and cure her colitis also put an end to her vertigo.

Dr Rowe also tells of a man who frequently experienced falling sensations, along with migraine headaches. Tests showed he had no central nervous system defect or other neurological problem to otherwise explain the vertigo and headaches. By avoiding some fruits, vegetables and nuts – to which he was allergic – the man rid himself of both problems.

Other doctors tell similar stories of people who overcome vertigo by avoiding such common allergens as chocolate, milk, wheat, corn or orris root (a common fragrance). If you have allergy-induced vertigo, relief will depend on finding out what bothers you and avoiding those triggers. Chapters 2 to 8 outline methods of identifying and controlling allergies.

See also *Deafness*; *Dizzy spells*; *Ear inflammation and hearing loss*; *Ménière's syndrome* and *Tinnitus*.

Miscellaneous health problems

Various allergy doctors have also noticed that the following miscellaneous symptoms are sometimes caused or aggravated by allergies:

Eyes: blurred vision, sensitivity to light, weeping
Respiratory: hacking cough, laryngitis
Gastrointestinal: burping, dry mouth, metallic taste in mouth, rectal itching, thirst
Urinary: frequent, urgent or painful urination
Muscular: backaches

Emotional/Mental: floating sensations, forgetfulness, mood changes
General: chills, tingling, weakness

APPENDIX

Sources for products and services

Many people with allergies find that they can use the following products with no problems. While listing these products and services does not constitute an endorsement by the author or publisher, we hope that this guide will help you to find household and personal products that you can use safely.

Because anyone can be allergic to anything, highly sensitive people should read labels carefully or write to the manufacturer for ingredient descriptions before using a product for the first time.

Air purifiers

Astec Ltd
31 Lynx Crescent, Weston
Industrial Estate, Weston-Super-Mare, Avon BS24 9DJ

Beta Plus
177 Haydons Road, Wimbledon,
London SW19
Tel. (01) 543 1142

air treatment equipment of all kinds

Coast Air
Unit 2
Chilton Industrial Estate, Mills
Road, Sudbury, Suffolk

Patent Enterprises Ltd
PO Box 426, Chippenfield, Kings
Langley, Herts WD4 9PJ

M. W. Sullivan
3 Station Road, Lidlington,
Bedfordshire
Tel. 0525 403021

cleans central heating filters, reducing the amount of impurities in the air

Allergy Identification

Action Against Allergy
43 The Downs, London
SW20 8HG
Tel. 01–947 5082

provides advice, information and reading list

National Society for Research into Allergy
PO Box 45, Hinkley,
Leicestershire LE10 1JY

provides information on the management of allergies, mainly by the desensitizing methods

Society for Environmental Therapy
521 Foxhall Road, Ipswich,
Suffolk IP3 8LW

a society for scientists and lay people alike, concerned with the role of environmental factors in the causation of disease

Asthma

Asthma Society and Asthma Research Council
300 Upper Street,
London N1 2XX

Miss M. Knowles
46 Fleetwood Close,
Chalfont St Giles,
Buckinghamshire HP8 4DR

information on the Knowles method of breath training for asthmatics

Bedding

Futon Co.
138 Notting Hill Gate,
London W11 3QG
Tel. (01) 221 2032

futon mattresses made from high quality raw cotton

Green Farm Nutrition Centre
Burwash Common, East Sussex
TN19 7LX

cotton bedclothes

Keys of Clacton Ltd
Old Road, Clacton, Essex

cotton mattresses and pillows

Blood testing

Larkhall Laboratories
225 Putney Bridge Road,
London SW15 2PY

for detection of likely food allergies based upon recent advances by a British research laboratory. Cytotoxic testing with rapid results and computerized individualized diet based upon results

Breathing Aids

R. H. Hinchcliffe & Sons
39 High Street, Pershore,
Worcs

hay fever helmet and air cleaner (plastic bubble)

Central heating systems

Church Hill Systems
Frolesworth, Lutterworth,
Leics. LE17 5EE
Tel. 0455 202314

non-gas 'IMSTOR' Economy 7 boiler – very low running costs

Cleaning supplies

Quince Honey Farm
North Road, South Molton,
North Devon EX36 3AZ
Tel. 07695 2401

unperfumed furniture cream supplied by post

Clothing and fabrics

Aldrex Ltd
Dept AAA, Newnham, Glos.
GL14 1AG

cotton nightdresses, underwear, etc

Birkett and Phillips
PO Box 35, 1 Howard Street,
Nottingham NG1 3AR

mainly cotton underwear

Cotton On
29 North Clifton Street, Lytham,
Lancs FY8 5HW

mainly children's wear, but they also supply cotton blankets

Liberty & Co.
Regent Street, London W1

cotton materials, upholstery fabrics, silks, wools

Cosmetics

Almay
225 Bath Road, Slough, Bucks

hypoallergenic cosmetics and skin care products; 100 per cent fragrance-free, dermatologist and clinically tested. (Will provide materials for patch testing if you have an adverse reaction to one of their products. When feasible, individualized formulations omitting ingredients causing allergic reactions are provided at nominal cost, or a substitute product may be recommended)

Clinique Laboratories Ltd
54 Grosvenor Street,
London W1

hypoallergenic cosmetics and skin care products for men and women; 100 per cent fragrance-free, allergy tested

Crimpers Ltd
63–67 Heath Street, Hampstead,
London NW3 6UG

hypoallergenic hair care products

Green Farm Nutrition Centre
Burwash Common, East Sussex
TN19 7LX

range of cosmetics using natural products

Shaklee
Worldwide Postal Service,
43 The Downs,
London SW20
Tel. (01) 947 5082

natural personal care products

Eczema

National Eczema Society
Tavistock House North,
Tavistock Square,
London WC1H 9SR
Tel. (01) 388 4097

small medical charity which aims to provide support and information for people with eczema and their families, to increase public awareness about eczema and to raise money for research and projects. The Society also welcomes professional enquiries from those who have to deal with the problems that the condition can present. There is a national network of contacts/groups/branches. They also publish a wide range of literature, including Information Packs, and a quarterly journal EXCHANGE

Face masks

Allsafe Medway Ltd
11 Peel Street, Maidstone, Kent
ME14 2SA

Astec Ltd
31 Lynx Crescent, Weston
Industrial Estate, Weston-Super-Mare, Avon BS24 9DJ

Charcoal Cloth Ltd
Park Court, 1A Park Street,
Maidenhead, Berks SL6 1SW

Racal Safety
No. 1 Building, Beresford
Avenue, Wembley, Middlesex
HA0 1QJ

Waygood Peerless
Airport House, Purley Way,
Croydon, Surrey CR9 4LS

Foods

British Organic Farmers
Legatto Park, Potters Bar, Herts
EN6 1NZ

list of suppliers and growers

Mr B. Brook
Claypitts Farm, Beer Hackett,
North Sherbourne, Dorset

organic vegetables and fruit. Member of The Soil Association

Mr Hugh Coates
Springhill Farm, Dinton,
Aylesbury, Bucks
Tel. 0296 25333

wheat, flour and bread. Member of The Soil Association

Henry Doubleday Research Association
Ryton-on-Dunsmore,
Coventry CV8 3LG

advice on all aspects of non-chemical agriculture for both amateurs and professionals. They also have a constantly updated list of sources of organic produce

Foodwatch
Butts Pond Industrial Estate,
Sturminster Newton, Dorset
Tel. 0258 73356

supply a wide range of basic foodstuffs especially tailored to the needs of allergics. Margarine (milk-free), wheat flour (no additives), soya products, dried fruit, goats' milk, sweeteners, egg white replacer. Information and recipe leaflets. Also sample products sent on request

Granose Foods
Stanborough Park, Garston,
Watford, Herts WD2 6JR

Vegetable protein foods, no animal ingredients. Also milk substitutes: Granolac-infant soya milk, Soyagen milk powder, Granose Soya Milk-Liquid

Hockeys
Newtown Farm, South Gorley,
Fordingbridge, Hampshire
Tel. 0425 52542

organic farm meats: no chemicals or hormones used at any stage in the production of beef, pork, lamb, chicken and other farm produce. Home-made sausages, pâtés, burgers and faggots without the use of colouring or preservatives. Colour-free free-range eggs, home cured bacon and gammons

F. A. & J. Jones
Red House Farm, North Scarle,
Lincs
Tel. 052277 224

additive-free meat: beef, pork, lamb, chicken. No hormones, drugs, artificial flavouring, colouring or preservatives

Larkhall Laboratories
225 Putney Bridge Road,
London SW15
Tel. (01) 870 0971

special diet food for allergics, including flour substitutes

Living Pseuds Ltd
PO Box 660, Hove,
East Sussex
Tel. 07013 226

gluten-free rice cakes made from 100 per cent whole organic rice, puffed with salt or salt-free. Also gluten-free rice snaps in five flavours, baked not fried, so no added oil. Also instant low-calorie soups, no additives, with or without seaweed

Organic Farmers and Growers Ltd
Abacus House, Station Yard,
Needham Market,
Suffolk IP6 8AT

list of suppliers and growers

The Soil Association
86 Colston Street,
Bristol BS1 5BB

there are over 100 Soil Association Symbol Holders who supply vegetables, fruit, beef, lamb and cereal products, all of which are produced according to the rules laid down by the Association, i.e. crop rotation is encouraged, and use of pesticides and artificial fertilizers are kept to a minimum (actual amounts can be obtained from the Association)

Stewart Bell
Southleaze Farm, Elcombe,
Swindon, Wilts. SN1 4NT
Tel. 0793 523134

natural sheep milk. Supplies retail in Bristol, London and Dorset, as well as at the farm gate and local Wiltshire health food shops. Also natural sheep yoghurt and cheese

Tregaron Foods Ltd
Station Road, Tregaron, Dyfed
SY20 6HX
Tel. 09744 8944

goats' milk: produces the only British goats' milk powder packed in cartons containing five sachets, each making up to a pint of milk. Available from health food shops, Holland & Barrett and selected supermarkets

Welfare Foods Ltd
63 London Road South,
Poynton, Stockport, Cheshire
SK12 1LA

bread substitutes: all the low protein products are gluten-free and most items in the range are wheat-free. Colours used are natural ones, e.g. caramel, annatto, beta carotene. Also supply a range of milk-free and egg-free products. Details, recipes, etc sent on request

Wholefood Butchers
31 Paddington Street,
London W1
Tel. (01) 486 1390

meat and poultry naturally reared and additive-free. Also organically grown fresh fruit and vegetables, dried fruit, fruit juices, cereal grains, rice, maize, buckwheat, millet and whole flour. Additive-free dairy produce includes goats' milk (fresh, frozen and dried), goat and sheep milk cheeses and yoghurts and soya milk

Worldwide Postal Service
43 The Downs, London SW20

coffee substitutes: non-instant chicory and dandelion

Furniture

Futon Co.
138 Notting Hill Gate
London W11 3QG
Tel. (01) 221 2032

furniture made from high quality raw cotton

Keys of Clacton Ltd
Old Road, Clacton, Essex

Ionizers

The Ionizer Centre
65 Endell Street, Covent Garden,
London WC2
Tel. (01) 836 0251

largest selection

Medion Ltd
4 Beadles Lane, Oxted, Surrey
Tel. 088371 2641

Nutritional supplements

Bio-Health Ltd
13 Oakdale Road,
London SW16 2HP
Tel (01) 769 7975

mail order company which manufactures its own vitamin products which are totally free from additives

G&G Food Supplies
175 London Road,
East Grinstead,
West Sussex

vitamins and minerals suitable for allergics

Green Farm Nutrition Centre
Burwash Common,
East Sussex
TN19 7LX

produce a wide range of vitamin, mineral and amino acid supplements which are hypoallergenic. Natural sources are used for all the tablets and natural excipients are used for binding them

Klaire Laboratories
121 Acomb Road,
York YO2 4EY
Tel. 0904 793231

a wide range of gluten-free, milk-free supplements, including Vitamin C, amino acids, B vitamins, and Vital Dophilus for Candida management. Will send a list detailing what each supplement contains on request

Larkhall Laboratories
225 Putney Bridge Road,
London SW15
Tel. (01) 870 0971

suppliers of a wide range of supplements which are hypoallergenic

Nature's Best Health Products Ltd
PO Box 1,
Tunbridge Wells,
Kent TN2 3EQ
Tel. 0892 34143

vitamins and minerals. Most products are hypoallergenic and are used by clinical ecologists in Britain and elsewhere. Catalogue on request

Shaklee
Worldwide Postal Service,
43 The Downs, London SW20

additive-free, yeast-free vitamins and minerals. Ideal for allergics. Multi-Vi-Min, B. Complex, Vitamin C Powder (no corn) and others. Samples on request

Water filters

Brita (UK) Ltd
Yssels House,
Queens Road, Hersham,
Walton-on-Thames, Surrey

Foodwatch
Butts Pond Industrial Estate,
Sturminster Newton, Dorset
DT10 1PS

Living Pseuds
PO Box 660, Hove,
East Sussex
Tel. 0273 571772

the Magrei 2000 fits neatly on to taps and filters water efficiently and cheaply

Wine (Organic)

Infinity Foods Cooperative
25 North Road
Brighton BN1 1YA

Wholefood
24 Paddington Street
London W1M 4DR
Tel (01) 935 3924

as well as wine, organically grown fresh fruit and vegetables, dried fruit, fruit juices, cereal grains, rice, maize, buckwheat, millet and whole flour. Additive-free dairy produce includes goats' milk (fresh, frozen and dried), goat and sheep milk cheeses and yoghurts and soya milk. Also a bookshop with comprehensive stock of relevant publications

The Organic Wine Company Ltd
PO Box 81, High Wycombe,
Bucks HP11 1LJ

Sources for products and services in Australia

Many products are now being manufactured or imported into Australia that can be used by people with allergies. The Associations listed are extremely helpful in providing information on resources available in each State. Suppliers of other products are also listed and, of course, chemists and healthfood stores are good suppliers of products for people with allergies.

While listing these Associations and products does not constitute an endorsement by the author or publisher, we hope that this guide will help you to find household and personal products that you can use safely.

Because anyone can be allergic to anything, highly sensitive people should read labels carefully or write to the manufacturer for ingredient descriptions before using a product for the first time.

Associations providing self-help support

Allergy Association Australia

Allergy Association Australia is a self-help group for people suffering from allergies and sensitivities to substances in their environment whether ingested, inhaled or touched. AAA has helped to set up many branches whose various services include regular newsletters, discussion groups, dissemination of information, counselling on allergy problems. Guest speakers are invited to regular meetings. AAA also aim to cooperate with the medical profession and to support research into the causes and treatments of allergies.

Members of the Association have access to the bi-monthly newsletters and/or resources information. There are branches in all states. For more information, the main state Associations are:

Allergy Association Australia – Victoria
PO Box 298, Ringwood,
Vic 3134
Tel. (03) 720 3215

Allergy Association Australia – NSW
PO Box 74, Sylvania, Southgate,
NSW 2224

Allergy Recognition and Management Inc – Allergy Association Australia – Tasmania
PO Box 604F, Hobart
Tas 7001
Tel. (002) 29 6047

Allergy Association Australia – Brisbane North
PO Box 45, Woody Point,
Qld 4019
Tel. (07) 283 4786

Allergy Association – WA
c/o Ms Hilary Lane, 52 Dempster Street, Karrinyup, WA 6018
Tel. (09) 447 5661

Allergy Association Australia – SA
37 Second Avenue, Sefton Park,
SA 5083
Tel. (08) 269 3130

Associations focussing on hyperactivity

There are various self-help groups in each State which focus on the problems of children with hyperactivity and accept that many of the causes are allergies. The Associations are involved in research into the problems and causes and publish bi-monthly newsletters which also list resources. For more information the main State Associations are:

Active
Hyperkinetic Childrens' Association, PO Box, 17,
Doncaster, Vic 3109

Hyperactivity Association of NSW
Room 24, 29 Bertram Street,
Chatswood, NSW 2067

Tasmanian Hyperactivity Association
c/o Mrs H. Bresnaham, Castle Hill,
Kempton, Tas 7409

Allergy & Hyperactivity Organisation
PO Box 107, Yeronga, Qld 4104
Tel. (07) 848 2321

Hyperactive Help
77 Penhurst, Crescent, Balga,
WA 6061

Hyperactivity Association of SA Inc
18 King William Road, North
Adelaide, SA 5006

Hyperactivity Association of ACT and Southern NSW
PO Box 64, Garran, ACT 2605

Other associations providing services

Allergies and Intolerant Reaction Association
PO Box 1780, Canberra City, ACT 2610

Has links with AAA

Nursing Mothers Association of Australia National Headquarters
PO Box 231, Nunawading, Vic 3131
Tel. (03) 878 3304 (for counselling) or (03) 877 5011

A voluntary organization with local groups throughout Australia which supports and encourages mothers who wish to breastfeed, through support groups, discussions, counselling, newsletters, resources etc. Will be able to provide information and support to mothers of allergic babies.

Australian Society for Environmental Medicine
Executive Secretary: Sister Margaret Macgregor, c/o Suite 4, 20 Collins Street, Melbourne, Vic 3000

A society for doctors and medical practitioners. If you think you have a problem which may be ecological, the society can provide you with information on doctors living nearby who can test for allergy to environmental substances and advise on treatment.

Sensitivity Awareness Organisation
PO Box 66, Kenthurst, NSW 2154

A Sydney-based self-help group for people with allergies.

Suppliers and/or manufacturers of allergy free products

Many products can be bought from chemists and healthfood stores. The following provide items directly or items not easily available elsewhere.

ALLERSEARCH

Allersearch supply through pharmacies and direct to the public by mail order. They will provide mail lists and samples on request. Their range includes:

- Bedding for dust and mould allergies – duvet covers, mattress covers, pillow covers etc.
- Sprays for containing dust, dustmites and mould
- Face masks – dust masks and charcostatic masks for chemical allergies
- Air cleaners – to eliminate pollen, dust, mould spores, pollutants, cigarette smoke, chemical fumes
- Allergo range of soaps, shampoo, laundry and dishwashing detergents for chemically sensitive people
- Ionizers
- Water purifiers
- Products for asthma sufferers – nebulizer pumps, peak flow meters.

Head Office:
Allersearch Asthma and Allergy Aids
8 Marco Avenue, Revesby, NSW 2212
Tel. (02) 771 6944

Agencies of Allersearch:
VIC: Allersearch, 82 Lewis St, Wantirna, Vic 3152. Tel (03) 221 6011
QLD: Allersearch, Medical and Surgical Requisites, 50 Vulture St, West End, Qld 4101 Tel. (07) 844 2966
WA: Allersearch, c/o Thomas Surgical, 12 Ellen Street, Subiaco, WA 6008 Tel. (09) 381 5344

ALLERGY AID CENTRE

Mail order service direct to the public. Catalogue supplied on request. Wide range of stock and will also search out items on request. Stock includes:

- Bedding – sheets, pillowcases, duvet covers, blankets, mattress covers etc.
- Beds and mattresses

Face masks including activator charcoal masks
Herbonics range of soaps, laundry and dishwashing detergents for chemically sensitive people
Ionisers
Water purifiers and distilled water
Products for asthma sufferers – nebulizer pumps
Cosmetics – including Nutri-metic and Biochemical ranges
Foods
Furniture – made without glue etc.
Nutritional supplements
Toiletries – deodorants, shaving brushes, toothpaste etc, including Herbonics range
Carpets
Books

Address:
Allergy Aid Centre, 325 Chapel Street, Prahran, Vic 3181
Tel. (03) 529 7348

NUTRICOLOGY

Mail order service direct to the public. Stock includes:
Books
Vitamins, including the Nutricology range from USA that are for especially allergically sensitive people
Water filters
Candida education information

Address:
Nutricology, PO Box 191, Coria, Vic 3214
Tel. (052) 75 7045

GF DIETARY SUPPLIES

Mail order service direct to the public. Mailing list available which is updated every three months and sent to members of coeliac and allergy societies through newsletters. Stock about 200 non-fridge foods including macaroni, spaghetti, rice, flour, bread and cake and biscuit mixes and specialize in gluten-free and allergy-free foods.

Address:
GF Dietary Supplies, PO Box 146, Balaclava, Vic 3183
Tel. (03) 531 9007

NUTRI-METICS INTERNATIONAL (AUST) PTY LTD

A direct-selling company supplying cosmetics, vitamins and detergents, some of which can be safely used by allergic people. Will provide information on ingredients on request, and will replace or refund costs if goods prove to be allergic. Contact head office for details of nearest local direct-sales contact:

Nutri-Metics International (Aust) Pty Ltd
102 Elliott Street, Balmain, NSW 2041
Tel. (02) 818 9011

AMWAY OF AUSTRALIA PTY LTD

A direct-selling company supplying full range of household cleaning and laundry products which are low in perfumes and preservatives and can therefore be used by some allergy sufferers. Will provide information on suitability of use for allergic people on request. Also supply nutritional supplements – Amway grow their own sources for vitamin products. Contact head office for details of nearest local direct-sales contact:

Amway of Australia Pty Ltd
Home Shopping Service, 46 Carrington Road, Castle Hill, NSW 2154
Tel. (02) 680 2222

SHAKLEE PRODUCTS

A direct-selling company supplying a natural range of skin care products and naturally derived nutritional supplements.
Contact head office for details of nearest local direct-sales contact:

Shaklee Products
Lifetime Marketing Pty Ltd
Unit 7, Castle Corporate Park, 15 Carrington Road, Castle Hill, NSW 2154
Tel. (02) 634 7600

WATER FILTERS

Water filters are available through many outlets nowadays – both those that are attached to taps and those that fit onto mains pressure. However, Mr Rod Neilson also manufactures and supplies direct to the public. He is also happy to modify filtration equipment to suit. He also supplies purified water.

Address:
Mr Rod Neilson
10 Kingswood Drive, Chernside Park, Vic 3116

INDEX

Peter G. Hanson MD
The Joy of Stress £7.95 (hardback)

The mismanagement of stress can be fatal. Under stress, people don't feel at their peak, they don't perform at work to the best of their abilities, they are more likely to be sick, and ultimately they are most likely to die before their time.

The key to surviving and thriving on stress is control. The Hanson Method teaches you how to ignore what you can't control, and to control what you can. It's a *practical* plan that you can put to work immediately and continue to use forever. So don't hide from stresses; go out and challenge new ones. Take the *thrill* from stress, but leave the *threat* behind. Thrive under pressure and learn the true Joy of Stress!

Dr Richard Mackarness

Not All In The Mind £2.50

In this new vitally important book, Dr Richard Mackarness, doctor and psychiatrist, shows how millions may be made ill, physically and mentally, by common foods such as milk, eggs, coffee and white flour.

He relates case after case from his clinical practice where patients with chronic ailments resistant to other methods of treatment were cured by identifying and eliminating foods to which they had developed unsuspected allergy.

Gordon Bourne FRCS FRCOG

Pregnancy £5.95

Having a child can be one of the most exciting and fulfilling experiences in a woman's life, provided she has the confidence that comes from knowing exactly what pregnancy involves.

This comprehensive guide is written by Dr Gordon Bourne, Consultant Obstetrician and Gynaecologist at one of London's leading teaching hospitals. It provides full information, guidance and reassurance on all aspects of pregnancy and childbirth. An indispensible aid to the expectant mother, it will also be of great interest to her husband and family.

'Sets out in a clear, factual and reassuring way every possible aspect of pregnancy . . . I would recommend this book to anyone who can buy or borrow a copy' MARRIAGE GUIDANCE

All these books are available at your local bookshop or newsagent, or can be ordered direct from the publisher. Indicate the number of copies required and fill in the form below.

Send to: **CS Department, Pan Books Ltd., P.O. Box 40, Basingstoke, Hants. RG21 2YT.**

or phone: 0256 469551 (Ansaphone), quoting title, author and Credit Card number.

Please enclose a remittance* to the value of the cover price plus: 60p for the first book plus 30p per copy for each additional book ordered to a maximum charge of £2.40 to cover postage and packing.

*Payment may be made in sterling by UK personal cheque, postal order, sterling draft or international money order, made payable to Pan Books Ltd.

Alternatively by Barclaycard/Access:

Card No. | | | | | | | | | | | | | | | | |

____

Signature:

Applicable only in the UK and Republic of Ireland.

While every effort is made to keep prices low, it is sometimes necessary to increase prices at short notice. Pan Books reserve the right to show on covers and charge new retail prices which may differ from those advertised in the text or elsewhere.

NAME AND ADDRESS IN BLOCK LETTERS PLEASE:

....

Name______________________________________

Address_____________________________________

____

____

____

3/87

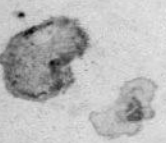